Company Share Options

Dedicated to the memory of
Albert Edward Casson

Company Share Options

Peter Casson

JOHN WILEY & SONS, LTD
Chichester · New York · Weinheim · Brisbane · Singapore · Toronto

Other Wiley Editorial Offices

John Wiley & Sons, Inc., 605 Third Avenue,
New York, NY 10158-0012, USA

WILEY-VCH Verlag GmbH, Pappelallee 3,
D-69469 Weinheim, Germany

Jacaranda Wiley, Ltd., 33 Park Road, Milton,
Queensland 4064, Australia

John Wiley & Sons (Asia) Pte, Ltd., 2 Clementi Loop #02-01,
Jin Xing Distripark, Singapore 129809

John Wiley & Sons (Canada), Ltd., 22 Worcester Road,
Rexdale, Ontario M9W 1L1, Canada

Library of Congress Cataloging-in-Publication Data

Casson, Peter.
    Company share options / Peter Casson.
        p.   cm.
    Includes bibliographical references and index.
    ISBN 0-471-96659-2 (cased)
    1. Employee stock options.   2. Employee ownership.   3. Pensions.   I. Title.

    HD4928.S74 C37 2000
    658.3'225—dc21   99–059515

British Library Cataloguing in Publication Data

A catalogue record for this book is available from the British Library

ISBN 0-471-96659-2

Typeset in 11/13pt Palatino from the author's disks by Vision Typesetting, Manchester
Printed and bound in Great Britain by Biddles Ltd, Guildford and King's Lynn
This book is printed on acid-free paper responsibly manufactured from sustainable forestry, in which
at least two trees are planted for each one used for paper production.

Contents

Preface

My aim in this book is to examine share option schemes for a company's senior managers and its employees against the background of political debate in the US and UK on policies to contain the payment of excessive compensation to senior managers on the one hand, and to promote employee share ownership on the other. In the early 1990s there was debate in the US Congress about the excessive amounts of compensation being paid to the senior executives, and especially to the chief executive officers (CEOs), of US corporations. Share option compensation was a particular focus of interest. A number of major changes followed this debate. Tax law changes prevented public companies from deducting non-performance-related compensation paid to certain executives in excess of $1m. The Securities Exchange Commission (SEC) introduced new disclosure rules on executive compensation that significantly increased the disclosures of share option compensation in proxy statements. The SEC also modified its rules to facilitate shareholder voting on compensation issues. Finally, the Financial Accounting Standards Board (FASB) issued an exposure draft of a proposed accounting standard that would have required companies to account for the *fair* value of share option compensation in their income statements. The focus of debate, following the publication of the FASB exposure draft, shifted from concern about excessive compensation to the important role share option compensation played in the growth of the US economy, and the developing technology sector in particular.

In the UK too there was concern in the early 1990s about "fat cat" compensation packages, especially of the directors of privatized utility companies. As in the US, interest focused on share option compensation. The Greenbury Committee was established to identify good practice in determining directors' compensation and to prepare a Code of such practice. One of the committee's conclusions was that there is not a good reason why executive share option schemes should receive favourable tax treatment. On the day after the Greenbury Report was published, the then Chancellor of the Exchequer, Kenneth Clarke, announced that he proposed to introduce new tax rules on share option compensation.

Share option compensation could well become the subject of debate in the UK in the early years of a new millennium. One element of such debate is likely to be about taxation. In his 1999 Budget Statement, the chancellor, Gordon Brown, announced proposals for an *All-employee Share Plan* and an *Enterprise Management Incentives* (EMI) scheme for selected employees. These proposals formed part of a package of measures which the chancellor said was founded on " . . . the central idea that our future depends on enterprise and fairness together". The proposal for the *All-employee Share Plan* was specifically described as a measure to make Britain ". . . a *democracy of enterprise*, that gives all who create wealth a greater stake in the wealth they create" (italics added). The chancellor did not propose the use of share options for the all-employee scheme, rather he outlined a share-purchase scheme where employees could purchase shares out of pre-tax income, and where employers would be able to match, tax-free, what each employee buys. Full details of the *All-employee Share Plan* were not, however, revealed until shortly after the chancellor's Pre-Budget Report in November 1999.

In introducing the *Enterprise Management Incentives* (EMI) scheme, the chancellor proposed " . . . a tax reform that will reward risk and stimulate new enterprise at the cutting edge of technology" and went on to indicate that he wanted to " . . . recruit, motivate and reward Britain's risk-takers, the innovators capable of creating wealth and jobs in the Britain of tomorrow". He noted that whereas in the past share option schemes had been used to reward " . . . those already at the top whose risks are low and rewards already high," the proposed tax reform would be targeted at "those who are prepared to move from secure jobs and venture their time and

effort to create wealth for our country". The following day the
Inland Revenue issued a technical note setting out a possible
framework for the proposed EMI scheme. Although the basic
framework of the proposed scheme was described in the technical
note, the details were not known until shortly after the chancellor
made his Pre-Budget Report in November 1999 when the Inland
Revenue issued draft legislation and commentary on the scheme.
As the details of the proposed legislation did not appear until after
the main text of this book was finished, they are presented here in
the Preface. The main features of the new scheme are that a qualifying
company, which is basically an independent company, quoted or
unquoted, trading in the UK with gross assets not exceeding £15m,
will be able to grant EMI options to a maximum of 10 key employees
at any one time. Each employee will be able to hold options over
shares worth up to £100,000 at the time of grant. In order to be
eligible, the employee must devote a significant proportion of his or
her working time to the company and must not hold a material
interest in it. Within these restrictions, it will be up to the company
to decide which employees should receive EMI options.There will
normally be no income tax or National Insurance Contributions
(NICs) liabilities on employee and employer when the options are
exercised. Instead there will be a charge to capital gains tax when
any shares acquired on the exercise of the options are sold. The
shares will be counted as *business assets* and so will qualify for
business taper relief, the relief starting from the date the options are
granted. As most employee shares are not *business assets*, and even
where they are taper relief would run from the date the shares are
acquired rather than the date the option is granted, the tax treatment
of EMI options is extremely favourable and could mean that an
employee who is a higher rate taxpayer would be liable to capital
gains tax on any profits from the disposal of shares at a rate of 10%.
Finally, the EMI rules will allow companies flexibility in the design
of share option schemes. In order to qualify for relief the options,
which must be on the company's fully paid up ordinary shares,
must be exercised within 10 years of grant. Employees must not
receive more than £100,000 of EMI options in a three-year period,
and those who exercise options within three years are not able to
top up their EMI options until the three-year period has expired.
Unlike other approved share option schemes, the rules for EMI

options will allow the use of nil cost and discounted options. However, the employee will be charged, at the time of exercise, to income tax and NICs on the difference between the exercise price and the market price of the shares on the date of grant, and the company will have to account for NICs on the amount of the discount where the shares are readily convertible into cash. The Government intends that legislation will be introduced in the Finance Bill 2000 so that companies will be able to use EMIs from the time of Royal Assent, expected to be July 2000. Although the proposed EMI scheme has some of the features of earlier discretionary share option schemes, it is clearly focused on small and medium sized enterprises, and on key employees within these companies. There is also greater flexibility for companies to design share option compensation schemes to suit their particular needs. The Inland Revenue estimates that, over the first three years, more than 2200 companies will take up EMIs.

One relief offered by both the *All-employee Share Plan* and the EMI scheme is in respect of NICs. Although consideration is not given to social security taxes in relation to share option schemes in this book, it may be appropriate to give some attention to NICs here. Until 5 April 1999, the NICs charge relating to share option compensation outside of Inland Revenue approved schemes arose at the time an option was granted. This generally meant that a liability did not arise. Provisions contained in The Social Security Act 1998 to align the National Insurance and income tax treatments of share options, which apply to options granted on or after 6 April 1999, mean that the charge will now arise at the exercise date and is on the difference between the market price of the shares on that date and the exercise price. While the upper ceiling on employee NICs means that a liability does not arise on many employees, there will be liability on the employer for NICs. This may create a disincentive for companies to use share option schemes other than those approved by the Inland Revenue. David Potter, chairman of Psion Plc, and Robin Saxby, chief executive of ARM Holdings Plc, are reported in *the Guardian* (27 October 1999) as leading protesters from the technology sector against this legislation. Martin Turner, finance director of 365 Corporation, a company that provides internet content and telephone services, is reported in the *Financial Times* (22 December 1999) as having criticized the government for the NICs liability on some share options, and is quoted as saying that they " . . . encourage us to provide staff with share options and then force us to pay the price for doing just that". Therefore, while the Government seem to be promoting enterprise and entrepreneurship through income tax reforms targeted at certain types of company, and at key people within those companies, the recent change in NICs rules could act as a restriction on the use of share option schemes elsewhere.

The other possible element of the UK debate has to do with the accounting treatment of share option compensation. The Accounting Standards Board (ASB) is expected to issue a Discussion Paper on its proposals for *Accounting for Equity* sometime in 2000. This Discussion Paper will include consideration of accounting for share option compensation. Although at the time of writing, the ASB had not publicly revealed the nature of its proposals (if any), newspaper reports appearing towards the end of 1999 suggested that the ASB may require companies to account for the fair value of share option compensation. The *Financial Times* (25 October 1999), for example, carried a front page report that "(T)he accounting regulator is planning to *crack down* on the growing use of share options as a way of paying workers" and that the ASB's proposals " . . . are likely to cause an *outcry* from industry, as they may mean profits will have to be scaled down to take more account of share option awards" (italics added). In anticipation of the ASB issuing a standard which would require companies to account for the fair value of share option compensation, David Potter is reported in *the Guardian* (27 October 1999) as suggesting that such a requirement could place UK high-technology companies at a disadvantage to overseas competitors. He is quoted as saying that "(W)e have to be very careful not to dis-incentivize British industry by following some theological accounting practice without examining properly all the possible consequences". *The Guardian* also reports that The Boots Company Plc expects the charge against profit in the first year in respect of share option compensation to be £63m, and £20m in subsequent years. If the ASB does propose to require companies to charge the fair value of share option compensation in calculating profit, we may see a reaction in the UK in the early years of the new millennium similar to that in the US following the publication of the FASB exposure draft.

Share option schemes cannot be looked at in isolation. As already noted, they evoke considerable public interest. They are associated with excessive senior executive compensation packages. In order to explore share option compensation it is necessary to consider it in the context of corporate governance. If corporate governance is viewed as dealing with problems that arise from the separation of the ownership and control of public companies, then share option compensation is often seen as a method for aligning the interests of managers with those of shareholders. However, it is necessary to move further to examine how various governance mechanisms may constrain excessive compensation. Increasingly, non-executive directors and shareholders, especially institutional shareholders, are seen to have an important role to play. Not all share options are awarded to senior executives; companies often grant share options to their employees. It is therefore necessary to consider the case for all-employee share option schemes. However, as share option schemes are probably best viewed as a mechanism of facilitating employee share ownership, it is necessary to look at the more general rationale for employee share ownership. One reason advanced for promoting employee share ownership schemes is that their adoption is associated with improved company performance. However, employee share ownership may be promoted for other reasons. For example, for Gates (1998) employee share ownership is a component of *participatory capitalism* which is seen to " . . . link a nation's people to their workplace, their community, their economy, their environment—and to each other".

As well as examining the role of share option schemes within the context of the literature on corporate governance and considering the case for employee share ownership, this book explores the accounting and taxation treatments of share option compensation. There is, as already shown, public and government interest in the way in which share option compensation is taxed and in how it is accounted for. The approach I have adopted in the book is to compare and contrast the accounting and tax treatments of share option compensation as adopted in both the UK and the US. The book should in no way be viewed as a technical reference on the accounting and taxation of share option compensation in either country. These are complex areas that justify specialist texts that are relevant to each of the two countries.

One of the issues raised when the FASB proposed that companies account for the fair value of share option compensation in their income statements is the problem of measuring its fair value. There have been suggestions that the methods used for pricing exchange-traded options can be adapted to measure the fair value of share option compensation. However, there are a number of crucial differences between exchange-traded options and the options granted to executives and employees that make it difficult to adapt methods for pricing exchanged-traded options to measuring the fair value of share option compensation. These differences, and their implications for the measurement of share option compensation, are explored in the book.

Finally, I generally refer to *share option compensation* in the book. This can, at best, be described as a mid-Atlantic compromise between *stock option compensation*, as used in the US literature, and *share option remuneration* as more commonly used in the UK. Where in the book it is appropriate to refer to share option compensation in general, I have used ESOs to refer to both *executive share options* and *employee share options*.

Winchester
January 2000

1
Introduction

In 1993 the US accounting standard setting body, the Financial Accounting Standards Board (FASB), issued an exposure draft inviting comments of a proposed standard *Accounting for Stock-based Compensation*. Instead of the usual quiet, considered response to an exposure draft, the exposure draft on stock-based compensation prompted a storm of protest that threatened the very existence of the FASB. The problem lay in the treatment of share option compensation. Under the then current accounting standards, share option compensation usually had little impact on reported earnings[1], although it was incorporated into reported earnings per share. This would have changed had the proposed standard been implemented, as companies would have been required to charge the fair value of share option compensation as an expense. The reported earnings of many US companies, especially high-technology businesses, were threatened. Dennis R. Beresford, who was then Chairman of the FASB, reported in an interview that he had seen one "study" which suggested that the total expense that would be recognized under the new rule would be about $15 billion. On the basis that the average price–earnings ratio of public companies at that time was about 10:1, the study predicted that if the expense were to be recognized, the US stock market would fall by about $150 billion.

Political lobbying by the corporations led to a bill, The Equity Expansion Act, containing provisions directing the Securities and

---

[1] The existing accounting standard, Accounting Principles Board *Opinion No. 25 Accounting for stock issued to employees* requires that companies usually charge the difference between the market value of the underlying shares at the time of grant and the exercise price of the option as an expense in the income statement. Share options are generally granted with an exercise price equal to the market price of the shares at the time of grant. There is therefore usually no expense to charge.

Exchange Commission (SEC) not to require companies granting share options to recognize them as an expense. It also led to resolutions being debated in both Houses of Congress for the FASB to withdraw its proposals. Although in 1993 Congress recognized the important role that share option compensation played in the American economy, 2 years earlier the position appears to have been somewhat different. The concern at that time was the large amounts being paid to the executives, and especially the chief executive officers (CEOs) of public companies[2]. Murphy (1995) suggests that ". . . few issues in the history of the modern corporation have generated the fury aroused by escalating chief executive officer (CEO) compensation in United States companies" (p. 713). He goes on to identify two responses to the CEO compensation controversy: one is a response to *populist* concerns which is aimed at reducing absolute levels of executive pay, and other is a response to *legitimate shareholder* concerns intended to create more effective pay structures.

In 1991 Congressman Martin Sabo introduced the Income Disparities Act which would disallow corporate tax deductions for any executive's pay that exceeds 25 times the pay of the lowest employee in the company[3]. Congressman Sabo was troubled by the dramatic shift that had occurred in the distribution of incomes in the US[4]. While recognizing that his measure would not stop excessive salaries of top executives, he saw his proposals as making ". . . a clear statement that public policy of this country does not support extreme

[2] Quinn (1995) expresses the view that high level of concern about CEO pay in the early 1990s can be attributed to the fact that a large number of people, including managers, were laid off during the 1980s as a part of downsizing, and at the same time executives were receiving high levels of compensation. She comments that a ". . . lot of headline-making executive compensation news was based on the reporting of stock-based compensation" (p. 770).

[3] In introducing the bill, he drew attention to the widening differences of income in the US. Congressman Sabo also noted that Plato has suggested that no one should earn more than five times the pay of the ordinary worker and that ". . . the management guru Peter Drucker suggested that CEOs should not earn more than 20 times as much as the company's lowest paid employee". A supporter of the bill was Ben Cohen, then Chairman and CEO of Ben & Jerry's Homemade, Inc. Until 1994, Ben & Jerry's had a policy that the pay of the CEO be limited to no more than seven times that of the lowest paid employee. Congressman Sabo ". . . proposed 25 times because that is approximately the relationship of the President's salary to the minimum wage".

[4] Using the 1991 Green Book issued by the House Ways and Means Committee, Congressman Sabo suggests that in 1977 the combined after-tax income of the bottom 40% of Americans was more than double the total after-tax income of the richest 1%. Eleven years later the richest 1% had the same after-tax income as the combined after-tax income of the bottom 40%.

distortions in the incomes people make". In the same year Senator
Carl Levin introduced the Corporate Pay Responsibility Act. Like
Congressman Sabo, Senator Levin was worried about the disparity
of incomes, suggesting that something ". . . is out of whack when
the average pay for a CEO in our largest corporations is over 100
times the average pay of the average worker". He also proposed
that executive pay is ". . . out of whack with corporate performance
today, and a primary reason is stock options", and that current
accounting rules ". . . keep this growing form of executive pay off
the corporate books as an expense, hiding its true cost and fueling
excessive pay". Senator Levin's concern was not so much with the
amount paid to executives, and particularly CEOs, but with the
apparent lack of relationship between pay and performance. This
he attributes to the "cozy relationship" that exists between the
CEOs of US companies and the companies' directors who have
responsibility for setting pay[5], and to SEC rules which restrict the
ability of shareholders to control the pay of CEOs. The purpose of
Senator Levins's bill was to ". . . remove federal barriers to stockholder efforts to limit executive and director pay in publically-held
corporations". There are three main elements of the proposed
legislation, effected through amendments to the Securities Exchange
Act of 1934 and requirements for the SEC to amend its rules and
regulations. These are: (a) measures to allow a shareholder vote on
recommendations for changes in the way in which the pay of the
CEO and the directors is determined as well as other matters
relating to shareholder voting; (b) improved disclosure of executive
and director compensation packages; and (c) specification of the
method for calculating the present value of share option compensation
and a requirement that this cost be reflected in corporate earnings
statements.

Although the legislative proposals of Congressman Sabo and
Senator Levin were not enacted, they provide the basis of reform
in the early 1990s. President Bill Clinton's 1993 budget contained a
provision limiting the tax deductibility of compensation exceeding

[5] Senator Levin quotes a witness to the Government Affairs Oversight Subcommittee as
saying that ". . . (T)he board members are dependent upon and thus beholden to just one
person, the CEO, for their positions, pay and perks. So it doesn't surprise me a bit that there
is not a lot of argument when it comes to the day where the board approves the CEO's pay.
It is a you-scratch-my-back, I'll-scratch-yours system of corporate governance".

$1 million that is paid to each of the CEO and four other highest paid officers of publicly held companies[6]. This limitation, however, only applied to compensation that is not performance related. Following Congressman Sabo, President Clinton is using the federal tax code to influence executive pay. Present Clinton's proposals are, however, more directed to the relationship between pay and performance than to the amounts paid to executives relative to other employees. In the budget debate he claimed his intention with the proposals was to encourage companies to focus more clearly on their compensation policies, and to shift spending from excess compensation to investment. The details of the budget proposals and of the resulting legislation reflect the influence of the SEC's new disclosure rules on executive compensation that were published in 1992. The content of the resulting tax legislation includes provisions concerning the corporate governance structure within which pay is established and defines performance related compensation.

The SEC preempted parts of Senator Levin's Corporate Pay Responsibility Act by changing its proxy rules and disclosure requirements. In 1992 the SEC reversed its policy that shareholder proposals dealing with executive compensation could be excluded from proxy statements because executive compensation was seen as a day-to-day operating issue and so excludable as *ordinary business*. Later in the year the SEC released its proposals on the disclosure of executive compensation in proxy statements. Linda Quinn, a director of the SEC, has said that underlying the Commission's proposed disclosure rules was the view that the market, and not government, should set compensation (Quinn, 1995). The new rules would require companies to present: (a) a table summarizing the major components of compensation received by named executive officers (NEOs); (b) tables describing in greater detail the grants and exercise of options, together with option holdings; (c) a chart showing the company's share price performance relative to the market and the company's peer group; and (d) a report of the compensation committee describing the company's compensation philosophy. Quinn (1995) reports that the most vociferous reaction to the SECs proposals was opposition over the valuation of stock options.

---

[6] Now section 162(m) of the Internal Revenue Code.

The third element of the Corporate Pay Responsibility Act is the specification of a method for calculating the present value of share option compensation and the requirement that this be treated as a compensation expense in the income statement. The importance of this element is expressed by Senator Levin who said in the Senate that stock options ". . . are particularly controversial because a company can issue them without taking any charge against company earnings". The FASB had added stock-based compensation to its agenda in 1984, although work on the project seems to have been suspended in 1987. Work was resumed on the project early in 1992 and the Board issued its exposure draft in June 1993. While the underlying principle in the exposure is consistent with the provisions of the Corporate Pay Responsibility Act, the issue of this exposure draft unleashed new political concerns about share options. However, instead of being seen as an integral component of the evil of excessive executive compensation, share option compensation is now viewed as an essential factor in the growth of the American economy.

In June 1993, Senator Joseph Lieberman introduced legislation, The Equity Expansion Act of 1993, creating a new class of stock option, the performance stock option (PSO), and directing the SEC to overturn the FASB's proposal to change the accounting treatment of stock options. One of the features of this new class of stock option, which would receive preferred tax treatment, is that at least half must go to "non-highly compensate" employees. In introducing the bill, Senator Lieberman said that: "America's best companies learned long ago that the key to success in the world's toughest markets is a dedicated work force that shares the common goals for their company. Nothing spawns that commitment better than the opportunity for equity ownership through broad-based employee stock options and stock purchase plans". The main thrust of his argument is that the use of share option schemes improves the performance of American companies, and that an increasing number of companies are adopting company-wide share option schemes. The debate is therefore moving from concern over share options as a component of executive compensation to the promotion of more broadly based schemes. This explains the objection to the FASB's proposals. Senator Lieberman, in introducing his proposals, said that: "(I)t is well known that the political pressure on FASB stems in large part from the mistaken belief that stock options only go to top executives. It's painfully ironic that FASB's new accounting rule would translate that premise into a self-fulfilling prophesy. Top executives will always be able to bargain for equity compensation, and boards of directors will want them to have it, even if FASB doubles the cost. What will be lost, however, is the tradition of granting stock options to a company's entire work force".

The other attack in Congress on the FASB's proposals came in the form of a concurrent resolution relative to accounting standards. The resolution itself indicates that ". . . the accounting standards proposed by the Financial Accounting Standards Board will have grave economic consequences, particularly for businesses in new-growth sectors, which rely heavily on entrepreneurship". It is, therefore, not the conceptual issues of accounting for share option compensation that are being addressed. Rather, the problem is the perceived impact that reduced reported profits will have on companies. Here the introduction to the resolution refers to the fact that: (a) ". . . new business in new-growth sectors, such as high-technology industries, often lack financial resources and must rely on stock options to attract qualified employees"; (b) ". . . the Board's proposal will reduce incentives to grant stock options, thereby limiting an important element in the feasible compensation mix of these companies and posing a threat to entrepreneurship in general"; (c) ". . . employee ownership in American companies has greatly expanded through the use of stock compensation plans, and a majority of the emerging growth companies distribute stock options to most or all of their employees"; (d) ". . . stock compensation plans have the potential to stimulate American productivity and enhance American competitiveness; and (e) ". . . discouraging the use of stock options will reduce the ability of new businesses to obtain proper financing and reduce America's ability to compete in the world economy". The resolution reflects the concern from many quarters about the FASB's proposals. For example, Senator Bill Bradley requested that a letter from the American Electronics Association, the National Venture Capital Association, and the Industrial Biotechnology Association be included in the Record[7]. The authors of the letter suggested that: "Stock options are the primary vehicle by which

---

[7] Letter to Senator Bill Bradley dated 6 August 1993.

our companies attract, retain, and motivate employees . . .They encourage management and employees to work together to achieve excellence, and are the lifeblood of our companies . . . In a May, 1993 report, the Wyatt Group Company, an international human resources company, said the proposal would reduce the profitability of high tech companies by close to 50%. Reporting greatly lower profits will limit our ability to raise investment capital and to offer options to our employees".

The debate in the US Congress on share option compensation provides a useful backdrop against which to examine share option compensation. The debate during the early 1990s, and the reforms introduced as a result of this debate, illustrates the complexity of the issues surrounding share option compensation. On the one hand there is the general issue of excessive executive pay, and on the other hand there are the perceived economic advantages that flow from broad-based employee share, and share option, schemes. Somewhere between the two is the problem of accounting for share option compensation. As highlighted in Congressional debates, excessive executive compensation is a symptom of poor corporate governance[8]. A similar conclusion was reached in the UK where executive pay also became a topic of intense political debate in the 1990s[9]. Corporate governance is about the processes and structures used to align the interests of managers with those of a company's shareholders. One way of achieving this is by using incentive compensation contracts, and possibly including share options within the contracts. A second component of corporate governance is monitoring senior executives' performance by shareholders, and by the board of directors acting in the interests of shareholders. Both the incentive and monitoring components of corporate governance are brought together in the debate of share option compen-

---

[8] Shleifer and Vishney (1997) suggest that "(C)orporate governance deals with the ways in which suppliers of finance to corporations assure themselves of getting a return on their investment. How do the suppliers of finance get managers to return some of the profits to them? How do they make sure that managers do not steal the capital they supply or invest it in bad projects? How do suppliers of finance control managers?" (p. 737).

[9] Conoley (1999) writes: "The perceived excesses of company executives pushed corporate governance in general, and executive pay in particular, to the centre of political debate. The result was the establishment of a series of august committees to report on how companies should be run and how people who run them should be paid. The intense political and media interest in executive pay made the chairman of these committees, Messrs Cadbury, Greenbury and Hampel household names". (*Financial Times*, 5 August).

sation. The SEC reforms to shareholder voting and disclosure of executive compensation, together with the provisions of section 162(m) of the Internal Revenue Code, are intended to strengthen corporate governance mechanisms in so far as they relate to executive compensation. The other element of the debate is the perceived importance of share options to economic growth. This aspect of the debate is almost completely absent from discussions in the UK. Share option compensation, unlike cash payments, does not affect the company's cash-flow or its reported earnings[10]. It is also a method of achieving the claimed benefits of employee share ownership which include retaining and motivating employees, and improving industrial relations.

Share option schemes, especially those for senior executives, are viewed by some as exploiting aspects of the regulatory structure. This is apparent in Senator Levin's legislative proposals. Unlike other types of compensation, the cost to the company of share option compensation is not a charge against earnings nor, until the new SEC compensation disclosure rules, has its value been disclosed to shareholders. There was consequently a high degree of opacity about share option compensation. An argument raised against both SEC's proposed disclosure rule and the FASB's proposed accounting standard was that it is not possible to measure the value of share option compensation at the time the options are granted. Share options, especially those granted to senior executives, are also seen as being used to avoid, or reduce, taxation. However, tax incentives have been provided to facilitate the use of share option schemes, both for senior executives and for the workforce as a whole. Although not addressed in the Congressional debates, the preferential tax treatment of share options granted to executives has been a political issue in the UK.

The remainder of the chapter considers the various components of the share option compensation controversy: (a) corporate governance and executive compensation; (b) employee share ownership;

---

[10] The view that share option compensation is valuable is indicated in the following extract from the Lex Column of the *Financial Times*: "Accounting purists can argue all they like about how best to value the options that companies distribute like confetti. But there is no escaping the fact that the software giant (Microsoft) has handed out a stunning $60bn of benefits that have never touched its profit and loss account. That was the value of unexercised employee options at the end of last year. Meanwhile, based on the options outstanding six months ago, Cisco's staff have a $17bn pay-day coming" (16 March 1999).

(c) the valuation of share options; (d) accounting for share option compensation; and (e) taxation of share option compensation.

CORPORATE GOVERNANCE EXECUTIVE COMPENSATION

The controversy over executive pay is basically about *excessive* compensation. That is, the payment to individuals of more than is justified by the services rendered. The problem of excessive pay arises when one party to the pay bargaining process is unable, or unwilling, to bargain effectively so as to maximize self interest. In the context of executive pay, the bargaining is between an executive and the company's board of directors acting, in theory, in the interests of its shareholders. Elson (1995) suggests that "(I)f the board is reluctant to bargain effectively with management because, despite its fiduciary obligations, it finds itself more closely aligned with management than with shareholders, the product of such a 'bargain' may be no bargain at all to the corporation and its owners" (p. 655). Excessive executive compensation may therefore be viewed as part of the wider problem of corporate governance.

The image of the UK and US company that dominates much of the literature owes much to the work of Berle and Means (1932). In their book, *The Modern Corporation and Private Property*, they chart the development of the public company. They document the separation of the ownership of a company and its control. Ownership is in the hands of shareholders while control resides with professional managers. Separation is seen as being almost complete where the largest shareholder only owns a small fraction of the company. This is true of most large public companies. Alongside the growing separation of ownership and control is the development of capital markets in which shareholders can trade their ownership interests. The combination of companies owned by a large number of investors, each owning a small proportion of the companies' shares with developed capital markets naturally leads to the "Wall Street Rule". A rational investor should sell shares if he or she is unhappy about a company because intervention in the company's affairs is costly for the individual, and any benefits would be shared between all shareholders.

The problem of corporate governance is one of aligning the interests of a company's professional managers with those of shareholders. Three main sets of factors operate to achieve an alignment of interests between managers and shareholders. First, there are the markets for labour, products and capital. Managers may be construed as building reputational capital so as to allow them to move, and progress, within the labour market. It is assumed that reputational capital is reduced when managers are seen to act in their own self interest, rather than in the interests of shareholders, or when they are not operating effectively. Signals indicating the effectiveness, or otherwise, of managerial decisions are provided by product markets. Managerial decisions, it is suggested, are reflected in product markets through the price and volume of sales of the company's goods and services. Finally, capital markets both serve to indicate company quality and act as a market for the transfer of corporate control. The indication of the market's view of the quality of management is assumed to be reflected in the share price. Capital markets also facilitate the takeover of one company by another. It is assumed that managerial performance is monitored by potential bidders. The possibility of the company being taken over, with the associated loss of managerial position, is seen to act as a threat that reduces managers' non-value maximizing behaviour. The market for corporate control is therefore seen to align the interests of managers with those of the shareholders by threatening management should their performance be poor. When the threat does not work, the company is taken over and the existing non-value maximizing management is replaced by a more efficient one.

A second set of factors in corporate governance relate to the design of incentive contracts to align the interests of managers with those of the shareholders. Incentives that align managers' interests with those of the shareholders may be provided through cash bonuses or share schemes. The problem with cash bonuses is that it is usually not possible for shareholders to directly observe the way managers perform their duties. As a consequence it is necessary to link management bonuses with a measure of the output associated with its actions. The problem is determining a suitable performance indicator. Generally, performance indicators are based on accounting measures or measures associated with the company's shares. As an alternative to cash bonuses, incentives may be provided through share and share option schemes.

Finally, there are factors relating to the internal governance of companies that monitor managerial performance on the behalf of shareholders. Two of the mechanisms that have been suggested as indicators of *good* governance are the appointment of non-executive directors to the board and the separation of the roles of chairman and chief executive. The management of a company is usually delegated to its full-time executives who may, or may not, sit on the board. Other members of the board, the non-executive directors, do not have an active role in the company's day-to-day management but may be seen as providing the executives with advice and counsel on such matters as corporate policy and strategy, and monitoring the performance of the company's executives on behalf of the shareholders. Included in the monitoring role of non-executive directors is the evaluation of managerial performance and the implementation of appropriate reward schemes. In this context, the role of the board chairman is to chair the board and to hire, fire and compensate the CEO (Jensen 1993). If this is the case, it is difficult for the CEO to separate his or her personal interests from the role of board chairman and so, it is argued, the two roles should be split.

The image of the modern corporation is based on the Berle–Means view that the ownership of public companies is in the hands of investors, none of whom holds a significant proportion of the companies' shares. Rational investors will follow the "Wall Street Rule". The past quarter-century has seen a movement away from the holding of shares directly by individuals towards indirect holdings through institutions. This change has become associated with the notion of *investor activism* by which institutional investors monitor managerial performance and intervene to correct poor performance and managerial self-dealing.

Share options are often viewed as a component of excessive compensation, but they also are part of the solution to the problem. By linking the value of compensation to share price performance, share options are seen as providing incentives that align the interests of managers with those of the shareholders. Incentive compensation packages may therefore include appropriately structured share options. However, as with other forms of senior executive compensation, share option schemes are open to abuse. It is assumed that such abuse can be contained by appropriate governance structures.

These governance structures depend on information. The revised SEC disclosure requirements on executive compensation for US companies, and the increased disclosure requirements for UK companies, ensure more information is available to shareholders. The importance of a compensation committee, with a membership that is restricted to non-executive directors, is recognized both in the UK and US. Finally, there is the role of shareholders in monitoring and controlling executive compensation. SEC reforms to shareholder proxy resolutions are an attempt to strengthen the role of shareholders. Shareholder approval is often required for share and share option schemes in both countries. In the UK, organizations representing institutional shareholder interests have developed scheme guidelines for shareholder approval.

EMPLOYEE SHARE OWNERSHIP

Congressional debate on share options before the publication of the FASB exposure draft was almost exclusively focused on concerns about excessive executive pay. After the publication of the exposure draft the debate seemed to shift to the value of company-wide share option schemes. In particular, concern was expressed about the effect that the proposed accounting rules would have on the profits of high-technology companies. It was suggested that this would lead to companies suspending their company-wide share option schemes. One perceived advantage of share option compensation is that it helps to preserve companies' cash resources. Another was that employee involvement in the financial performance of the company through share options is a way of improving company performance. Although it is clear that a company's cash resources are preserved if employees are willing to forego part of their cash compensation in exchange for share options, the claims about the relationship between employee share option schemes and company performance are not so clear.

It is unlikely that those arguments that have been used to support share ownership by senior executives to improve company performance apply to all-employee share ownership schemes. If employees have the characteristics of "rational economic man" then the incentive effect of employee share ownership is through the possibility of financial gain from the shares. Like all group incentives, however, the rewards of each individual in an all-employee share scheme depend on the efforts of everyone else. In such a situation, each employee is tempted to shirk because the effects of shirking will have a small impact on the rewards of individual employees. Employee share ownership schemes therefore have the problem of encouraging "free-riding". Weitzman and Kruse (1990), however, argue that under certain conditions the free-riding problems can be resolved. These conditions are basically a corporate culture that promotes cooperation and encourages social enforcement mechanisms. The conclusion reached from this literature is that employee share ownership *per se* is unlikely to be effective in improving company performance. In order to improve company performance it is necessary to combine share ownership with methods of industrial democracy ranging from consultation with employees to their full involvement in the company's decision making.

The relationship between employee share ownership and company performance has been viewed in the industrial relations and psychology literatures as being mediated through changes in employee attitudes. Employee share ownership is thought to improve employees' attitudes to the company, to reduce feelings of *them* and *us*, to make employees aware of the competitive pressures on the company, and so on. Such changes in attitudes are assumed to lead to improved effort by employees, increased monitoring of fellow employees, and reduced employee turnover. These changes feed through into improved company performance.

Employee share ownership may, however, be promoted for reasons other than enhancing company performance. Employee share ownership was seen by Brookings (1929) as a method of achieving economic democracy which he saw as ". . . America's answer to socialism and communism". More recently, Gates (1998) has used the idea of participatory capitalism, in which employee share ownership has an important role. Greater economic participation is seen to ". . . link a nation's people to their workplace, their community, their economy, their environment—and to each other". Share ownership by employees has been seen in the UK as part of a movement to achieving wider social and economic goals. It had a position in the new economic order envisaged by the Liberal Party in the 1970s, and in the Conservative Party's concept of a "property-owning" democracy. More recently employee share ownership has been seen to have a role within the concept of "stakeholder capitalism".

VALUATION OF SHARE OPTION COMPENSATION

Share options are granted to employees and executives in return for employment services. These may be past services, or future services, or a combination of the two. One approach that could be taken to valuing stock option compensation would be to estimate the fair value of the services provided in exchange for the options. This, however, is normally not possible. The alternative approach is to calculate either the cost of the options to the company or the value of the benefit to the recipients. The basis for valuing ESOs[11] is to be found in the methods used for pricing traded options. This method of valuation is to be seen in the SEC disclosure requirements on executive compensation as well as in the FASB's standard on stock option compensation. The breakthrough in the pricing of traded options was made by Black and Scholes (1973) in their derivation of a formula for pricing of European call options on the shares of non-dividend paying companies. A European call option represents the right, but not the obligation, for its holder to purchase shares in the company for a set price, the *exercise price*, on the *expiry date*, the date the option expires. Holders will exercise the option if the option is "in-the-money", i.e. the market price of the share on the expiry date is above the exercise price. Otherwise, the option holder will let the option lapse if the option is "out-of-the-money". Modifications are required to the basic option pricing model in order to price a European option on shares of a company that pays dividends and to price American options, that is options that may be exercised on, or before, their expiry date. Traded options are written by persons who are not connected with the company on whose shares the options are written. Options granted by a company on its own shares, usually referred to as *warrants*, are more difficult to price. This is because the exercise of the warrant dilutes the interests of existing shareholders in the company's profits and net assets. It is however possible to further adapt basic option pricing models to value warrants.

---

[11] ESO is used to refer to both an executive share option and an employee share option.

Although it is often assumed that basic option pricing models can be used to value ESOs, ESOs are more complex financial instruments than traded options or warrants. First, the holder of an ESO usually cannot exercise it during the *vesting* period which is in the early part of the option's life. The ESO can then be exercised at any time on, or before, its expiry. ESOs therefore have the characteristics of *Bermuda* options. Second, unlike traded options, ESOs are usually non-transferable. This means that the holder can only realize their intrinsic[12] value by exercising the option and selling the underlying shares. Third, holders of ESOs usually forfeit the options if they leave the company during the vesting period, and may be obliged either to exercise the options or forfeit them if they leave after the options have vested. The possibility of forfeiture and early exercise make it is necessary to incorporate expected termination of employment into the pricing model. Finally, stock options granted to senior managers may incorporate performance criteria. For example, it may be that the options can only be exercised if the company's earnings per share increases at, or above, a set rate over the early years of the options' life. It is necessary to incorporate the probability of performance criteria being met into the pricing model where performance criteria are incorporated into ESOs.

One of the main assumptions underlying the models used to price traded options is that investors and option writers can form riskless hedges with the options and the underlying shares[13]. This is one of the most important contributions of Black and Scholes (1973) as it means that the risk-free rate of interest can be used as the discount rate. A problem in pricing ESOs is that institutional and wealth constraints generally prevent holders of ESOs forming such hedges. Further, because the options are non-transferable, holders of ESOs cannot sell them to someone who can construct a riskless hedge. This means that it is necessary to consider risk preferences in determining the discount rate to be used in valuing ESOs. It also raises the possibility that the value of ESOs to their holders may be

[12] The intrinsic value of an "in-the-money" option is the greater of the difference between the market value of the underlying shares and the exercise price of the option. "Out-of-the-money" options do not have an intrinsic value.

[13] An alternative assumption is that the options' payoffs can be replicated by investing in shares and bonds.

different to the cost of the company, or its shareholders, in granting them.

ESOs, once they have vested, have the characteristics of American options. As with traded American options, it is necessary to consider the conditions under which the options will be exercised. In the case of traded American options it is assumed that the options will be only exercised at expiry or immediately before an ex-dividend date prior to expiry. Investors who require liquidity, or who believe that the market price of the underlying shares will fall, can realize the value of the option by selling it in the market. This is not possible for holders of ESOs who are only able to realize their intrinsic value by exercising the options and selling the shares acquired on exercise. ESOs may therefore be exercised earlier than otherwise equivalent traded options. It may also be rational for risk-averse holders of ESOs to exercise them early. To the extent that the expected exercise date is an important determinant of option value, the value of ESOs is related to the liquidity and risk preferences of their holders.

Unlike investors holding traded options, holders of ESOs are connected with the company as employees or managers. One reason for granting ESOs is to improve company performance and share-holder wealth. In particular, it is frequently suggested that options are granted to self-interested senior managers in order to align their interests with those of the company's shareholders. By granting share options to align the interests of managers and those of the shareholders it is assumed that the actions and decisions of senior managers can affect the market price of the company's shares. Self-interested managers can increase the value of their holding of ESOs through their decisions about the company's investments, its capital structure and the amount of its distributions. In valuing ESOs at the time of grant it is therefore necessary to estimate the effect that the grant will have on the actions and decisions of their holders, and thereby on the value of the company's shares.

Implementation of the SEC's disclosure rules and the FASB's accounting rules on stock option compensation require a method for determining the fair value of ESOs at the time of grant. The approaches to the valuation of ESOs adopted by the two bodies are founded on models developed to price traded options. The FASB, in its accounting standard, indicates how models of traded options can be adapted to value ESOs. In particular, the FASB suggests how the effects of forfeiture, early exercise and performance criteria may be dealt with.

ACCOUNTING FOR SHARE OPTION COMPENSATION

Senator Levin's proposed Corporate Pay Responsibility Act contains two measures affecting the accounting treatment of share option compensation. These are improvements to the SEC disclosure regulations on executive and director compensation packages, and the requirement to charge the present value of the compensation cost of share options in the company's income statement. In conjunction with provisions to facilitate shareholder voting on executive compensation issues, enhanced disclosure of executive compensation is seen as a mechanism for containing excessive compensation. The second of the provisions deals specifically with reflecting the cost of share option compensation in the income statement. Publication of the FASB's proposed standard on share option compensation, which incorporated such a provision, was met with hostility. If implemented, the proposed standard, it was argued, would have threatened the growth of the US economy in general, and high-technology businesses in particular.

Disclosure rules on executive compensation have developed considerably during the 1990s in both the UK and US. The rules identify the individuals about whom disclosure should be made, and what should be disclosed about the compensation itself. Public companies in both the US and UK are obliged to disclose information about *named* individuals. In the case of the US companies the disclosure is restricted to the compensation of the CEO and a group of highest paid directors, whereas in the UK it is the compensation of all the directors that must now be disclosed. In contrast to these requirements to disclose the compensation of named individuals, a recent report by a committee under the chairmanship of Marc Viénot has recommended that French companies only disclose the aggregate compensation of the board, keeping the amounts paid the individual directors confidential. Viénot is quoted[14] as saying that the compensation of individual directors should be withheld

[14] *Financial Times*, 26 July 1999.

on the basis of "the right to protect private life", and that compulsory disclosure would be "discrimination against the socio-economic category [of managers]".

The most controversial aspect of the SEC's proposals to amend its disclosure requirements on executive compensation was the disclosure of information about share options. Specifically, the Commission required public companies to disclose the value of share option compensation. By so doing, the Commission had to specify methods for valuing stock option compensation and, as indicated in the previous section, valuation of stock option compensation is more complex then the valuation of traded options. The UK Urgent Issues Task Force (UITF) reached a different conclusion to that of the SEC on the valuation of share option compensation by indicating that ". . . it is not presently practicable to specify an appropriate valuation method for options as a benefit in kind". It is, however, possible to provide information to shareholders and others about share options without valuing the instruments. First, it is possible to provide details of the share options in terms of exercise price, expiry date, vesting period, performance criteria, and so on. Second, information can be provided about the number of shares over which options are granted during the accounting period, the number of shares over which options have been exercised, or lapsed, over the period, and number of shares that are subject to options at the end of the period. Third, disclosure can be made of the market price of the underlying shares at the time of exercise. Finally, information on specific issues can be disclosed. For example, some companies *re-price* options, effectively reducing the exercise price of the options and transferring wealth to the option holders[15].

Disclosure of information on share options can be placed in the context of the company's compensation policies and the relative performance of the company. Good corporate governance practice is increasingly seen to imply that senior executive compensation, and especially that of the CEO, should be in the hands of a

---

[15] For example, *The Times* (1 January 1999) reported that executives at E*Trade ". . . have given themselves a Christmas present worth $100 million (£60 million) after repricing their share options. According to Securities and Exchange Commission documents, the company rewrote option schemes when Internet shares were at a low in October. Since then, the sector has staged a stunning return to new heights".

compensation committee whose membership is comprised of non-executive directors. Disclosure can be made of the compensation policies adopted by the committee. It is also increasingly recognized that the rewards given to senior executives should be related to the *relative* performance of the company. Information can therefore be provided about the performance of the company as compared with, say, stock market indices, an index of companies in the same sector, and companies regarded as similar to the reporting company.

The grant of share options for less than their fair value represents a wealth transfer from shareholders to option holders. This transfer has been reflected in a company's financial statements in two ways. First it is treated as a *dilution* to earnings per share (EPS). Under current UK, US and international accounting standards, it is assumed that the options are exercised at the beginning of the accounting period and the proceeds used to purchase existing shares of the company. When the option is "in-the-money" the effect of this is to increase the number of shares that is used in the denominator in calculating EPS. Second, share option compensation can be charged as an expense in the computation of a company's income or profits. The problem is one of determining the value of the expense. This can be the *intrinsic* value of the option at the time of grant or when all conditions connected with the options, such as meeting performance criteria, are resolved. As the exercise price of many options is set at, or above, the market price of the shares at the time of grant, the options have no intrinsic value and so there is not charge to income. The alternative to charging the intrinsic value of options against profit is to charge their fair value. This is broadly what Senator Levin recommended and the view taken by the FASB in its proposed standard. A major problem with this approach is one of determining the fair value of the option at the time of grant. It is also difficult to decide whether to charge all the fair value of the options against the income of the period in which the options were granted, or whether to spread the expense over the life of the options, or a part of their life. This depends, at least in theory, on when the employment services are provided in return for the share option compensation.

THE TAXATION OF SHARE OPTION COMPENSATION

In his tax message to Congress in 1963, President John F. Kennedy identified the problem of share option compensation by proposing that the taxation of this form of compensation violates the principle of fairness if it is not taxed in the same way as other forms of compensation. One part of the problem lies in determining when the compensation benefit of share options arises. Another part of the problem is in determining the value of the share option compensation at the time it arises. Finally, there is the differential tax treatment of income and capital gains. Income tax is usually charged in relation to the period in which the income accrues, whereas capital gains are generally taxed when the gain is realized, that is when the taxpayer sells the asset. Further, until 1965, there was no tax of capital gains in the UK and since then rates of capital gains tax have tended to be below those of income taxes.

If share options are to be treated like other forms of compensation then it would seem reasonable to assume that the benefit is received at the time the options are granted. After the grant, the holders of ESOs may be argued to be in a similar to investors holding warrants issued by the company. Following this line of argument, holders of ESOs would be charged to income tax on the difference between the fair value of the options at the time of grant and any amount paid for the options. Any subsequent profits arising on the exercise of the ESOs and the disposal of the underlying shares would be charged to capital gains tax. This is broadly the conclusion reached in the UK courts. There are a number of problems, however, with this conclusion. First, ESOs, unlike traded warrants, are not transferrable so their holders cannot realize their value at the time of grant. Second, there is often a vesting period which means that the options are forfeited if the holder leaves the employment of the grantor company. It may therefore be argued that ESOs are in a sense "earned" over the vesting period. Third, holders of vested ESOs generally must exercise or forfeit them if they leave the company. Again, some of the value of ESOs is "earned" by holders remaining with company. Finally, and perhaps most importantly, it is difficult to value ESOs at the time of grant. Mainly for this reason, both UK and US legislation usually taxes share option granted under non-statutory schemes at the time the options are exercised.

If share option compensation is treated as other types of compensation then the grantor company should be allowed a tax deduction in respect of the compensation. This is provided for under US, but not under UK, legislation.

Holders of ESOs granted under non-statutory schemes are subject to income tax on all the profits on the exercise of the options. This treatment was thought to inhibit the use of share option schemes. Legislation was introduced in both the UK and US to provide tax advantaged share option schemes. The schemes provide income tax relief if all the conditions are met and profits in respect of ESOs are charged to capital gains tax when shares acquired on the exercise of options are sold. In both countries there are basically two types of schemes: a discretionary scheme intended primarily for senior executives, and an all-employee scheme. In order for options to qualify under discretionary schemes, they must have certain defined characteristics. For example, they must be non-transferable, the exercise price must not be less than the market price of the underlying shares on the date of grant, and the expiry date must not be after 10 years from the date of grant. There are also restrictions on the value of shares over which options may be granted. The provisions of the all-employee share schemes are intended to ensure that all eligible employees have the opportunity to participate in the schemes on equal terms. Again there are restrictions on the characteristics of the options granted under the scheme and on the value of shares that may be acquired. One significant feature of all-employee schemes is that the options may be granted at a discount. The UK scheme, unlike the one in the US, combines a share option scheme with a tax-preferred savings scheme to ensure that employees have funds to use in exercising their options.

PLAN OF THE BOOK

There is no doubt that there is controversy over share option compensation. This is illustrated in the debates that took place in the US Congress in the early 1990s. In part, the controversy is about excessive executive compensation. Senior executive compensation has generally been increasing at a higher rate than the compensation paid to employees, thereby increasing the differential between managerial and employee compensation. Excessive compensation can be understood as executives receiving more either than a "fair" multiple of average, or of minimum, income, or than is justified by their, or the company's, performance. Excessive compensation, in this second sense, is generally seen as a problem of poor corporate governance. Recommendations have been, and continue to be made, on strengthening corporate governance, with many of these recommendations relating to share option schemes. Chapter 2 contains a review of corporate governance, looking in particular at those mechanisms used to align the interests of a company's managers with those of the shareholders. Share option compensation emerges in this review both as a solution and as a problem.

The turning point in the series of Congressional debates in the early 1990s followed the publication of the FASB proposals for a standard on accounting for share compensation. Up until this point attention was focused on excessive executive compensation. Many companies have all-employee share option schemes, and it was argued that these were threatened if the FASB's proposal was implemented. All-employee share schemes were seen as an important factor in the growth of the American economy, particularly in the high-technology sector. One reason advanced for share option compensation is that it enables companies to preserve scarce cash resources. Other reasons had to do with productivity. The rationale for employee share ownership is explored in Chapter 3. Here it is shown that it is far from clear why companies adopt, and governments support, share ownership by employees.

Although it is generally accepted that ESOs have a monetary value, there are difficulties in measuring this value. It is frequently assumed that models used to price traded options can be used to value share option compensation. ESOs are, however, more complex than traded options. For example they are generally non-transferable, have vesting provisions and may have to be exercised or forfeited if the holder leaves the grantor company. In addition, the holder of ESOs cannot be assumed to have the same characteristics as investors in traded options. The problems of valuing ESOs are examined in Chapter 4. Some of the approaches to valuing ESOs are also described in this chapter.

The debate in the US Congress highlights the problems of accounting for share option compensation. Two main aspects of accounting for share option compensation can be identified: disclosure of information on directors' compensation and the way in which share option compensation is recognized in computing a company's earnings. Chapter 5 contains a description and comparison of the disclosure and measurement requirements under US and UK disclosure and accounting rules. One important difference between the rules of the two countries is shown to be the requirement under US, but not under UK, rules to measure the fair value of share option compensation.

Taxation may have an important role to play in a company's decisions about whether to adopt share option schemes, and if so, what sort of scheme to adopt. In both the US and UK a distinction can be drawn between non-statutory and statutory schemes, the latter receiving preferential tax treatment. The statutory schemes can be divided into those intended for a limited number of individuals within a company and those aimed at the workforce as a whole. Chapter 6 contains a description and comparison of US and UK tax law in relation to share option schemes. In addition, the chapter contains an outline of the US tax rules to limit the deductibility by the company of excessive executive compensation. The strands of the argument about share option compensation are brought together in the final chapter.

2
Corporate Governance

Berle and Means, in their book *The Modern Corporation and Private Property* published in 1932, document the development of the US quasi-public company. They note that the private, closely held company had given way to the quasi-public company, "... a corporation in which a large measure of separation of ownership and control has taken place through the multiplication of owners" (p. 4). Ownership of a company is with its shareholders while control is in the hands of professional managers. The separation of ownership and control is seen to be almost complete where, in the case of a management control company, the largest shareholder only owns a small fraction of the company's shares. Berle and Means see two characteristics of the modern corporation as growing out of this separation: its size and the develop of markets in which corporate securities can be traded. They write that in "... the overwhelming bulk of cases, corporations fall into the quasi-public class when they represent large aggregations of wealth and their securities are available in the open market; for in such corporations part or most of the owners have almost invariably surrendered control" (p. 6).

The image of the modern corporation as being owned by a large number of shareholders, each holding a small fraction of the company's shares, and being controlled by professional managers has dominated much of the literature. In particular, the image of the Berle–Means company underlies the literature on the principal–agent problem and on corporate governance. The principal–agent problem, as developed within agency theory, basically considers the situation where there is a separation of management and finance. Individuals with available funds are seen to need the specialist skills of managers in order to generate returns on their funds; while managers, whose own wealth is restricted, need the funds of investors. The problem is one of determining the conditions under which investors can be sure that managers will not expropriate their funds or invest them in unattractive projects. This problem has been the subject of the agency theory, and the corporate governance, literatures.

As developed by Jensen and Meckling (1976), agency theory adopts the image of the modern corporation as presented by Berle and Means. The separation of ownership and control creates problems of aligning the interests of managers with those of the shareholders. Managers are assumed to act in order to maximize their own utility. In particular, managers are seen as averse to both risk and effort, and as having a propensity to derive non-pecuniary benefits from the company. Shareholders, on the other hand, would like managers to maximize shareholder wealth. The interests of managers and shareholders are most likely to diverge when managers' ownership interest in a company is either limited to a small fraction of the company's shares, or where managers have no ownership interest whatsoever.

Jensen and Meckling define the agency relationship as ''. . . a contract under which one or more persons (the principal[s]) engage another person (the agent) to perform some service on their behalf which involves delegating some decision-making authority to the agent'' (p. 308). The differing interests of shareholders (principals) and managers (agents) are dealt with first, by principals, who may seek to limit the divergence of interests by offering appropriate incentives and by incurring costs to monitor the activities of managers (*monitoring costs*). Managers may wish to incur costs (*bonding costs*) so as to ensure that they do not take actions that harm shareholders. There may still be divergence, even where shareholders have incurred monitoring costs and bonding costs have been borne by managers, between the actions of managers and the interests of shareholders. This is referred to as a residual loss. Jensen and Meckling define *agency costs* as being the total of the monitoring costs borne by shareholders, the bonding costs borne by managers and the residual loss.

Agency theory provides a backdrop against which to look at corporate governance. Shleifer and Vishny (1997) suggest: ''Corporate governance deals with the ways in which suppliers of finance to corporations assure themselves of getting a return on their investment. How do the suppliers of finance get managers to return some of the profits to them? How do they make sure that managers do not steal the capital they supply or invest it in bad projects? How do suppliers of finance control managers?" (p. 737). Although corporate governance can be viewed from an agency perspective, it is a complex process that involves the interaction between legal and economic factors.

Companies come into existence under the laws of a state and in turn are regulated by law. These laws, which vary from country to country, may define the mechanisms for protecting the interests of shareholders, the duties of managers, and the remedies available when managers fail in their duties to shareholders. Shareholders in UK companies, for example, have rights that can be exercised in general meetings. Included here is the right to appoint board members. Board members have a duty to act in what they believe to be the interests of shareholders. Legal considerations may also impinge on economic factors in corporate governance. For example, shareholders in Anglo-Saxon companies typically have one voting right for each of the shares they hold. This is essential for the effective operation of the market for corporate control.

A complex array of economic factors interact to form the governance system. First, markets for labour, products and capital may act in various ways to ensure managers act to the benefit of shareholders. Managers can be seen as building reputational capital that enables them to move within the labour market. Reputational capital is reduced where managers are seen to act in their own self interest rather than in the interests of shareholders, or when managers are not operating effectively. Product markets provide signals as to the effectiveness of managerial decisions. Where managers are making good decisions, product markets signal quality through the price and volume of the company's goods and services. Then, capital markets serve both to indicate company quality and act as a market for the transfer of corporate control. A second set of factors in corporate governance relates to the design of incentive contracts to align the interests of managers with those of shareholders. These rely on performance indicators such as accounting earnings and share price performance. Finally, there are factors associated with the internal governance of companies that relate to monitoring managerial performance on behalf of shareholders. Two mechanisms that have been suggested as indicators of *good* governance are the separation of the roles of chairman and chief executive, and the appointment of non-executive directors to the board.

A further component of corporate governance is the role of institutional shareholders. The past quarter-century has seen a movement away from the holding of shares directly by individuals towards indirect holdings through institutions. This is a movement away from the image of a Berle–Means company towards one where institutional investors collectively hold a large fraction of a company's shares. Associated with this change is the notion of *investor activism*. By this is meant the idea of institutional investors monitoring managerial performance and intervening to correct poor performance and managerial self-dealing.

INCENTIVE CONTRACTS

The agency problems associated with the separation of ownership and control in the modern corporation can be dealt with, at least partially, through providing managers with incentives designed to align their interests with those of the shareholders. Such incentives are typically incorporated into the method by which managers are compensated. As it is usually impossible for shareholders to observe directly the way in which managers perform their duties, it is necessary to link managerial compensation to some measure of the output associated with their actions rather than with the actions themselves. Output may generally be assumed to a function of managerial effort and random factors that are outside the control of managers. The effect of random factors on the output makes the design of the compensation packages difficult. This is because risk averse managers may be assumed to prefer a compensation system that does not expose them to factors over which they have no control. It is also less costly for risk neutral shareholders to bear all the effects of the random factors[16]. Generally, the more that can be inferred about managerial actions from an output measure, the more sensitive managerial compensation should be to that output.

Incentives that align the interests of managers with those of the shareholders may be provided through appropriately constructed

---

[16] Where both managers and shareholders are risk averse, however, it is necessary to devise some method by which risks are shared.

compensation packages. Such compensation packages may include cash bonuses, in which case it is necessary to identify performance indicators on which the bonus is based. These performance indicators should both provide appropriate incentives to managers so to encourage them to act in the interests of shareholders and be sensitive to managerial decisions and actions. Two main types of performance indicators are candidates for incorporation into cash bonus schemes. One type of performance indicator is based upon accounting measures, such as turnover and earnings; the other relies on information from share prices. Alternatively, share and share option schemes, which are sensitive to share price performance, can be used to link managerial reward to company performance.

The relationship between managerial compensation and company performance has been the subject of a number of empirical studies. These studies have addressed a set of related questions. On the one hand there are studies that attempt to determine whether the amount of managerial compensation is related to company performance. Other studies have addressed the question as to whether company performance is improved by making managerial compensation sensitive to company performance. A third line of enquiry assesses the market reaction to the announcement of compensation schemes.

Accounting Measures and Compensation Contracts

Accounting measures of company performance may be incorporated into the contracts of senior managers to provide an indicator of managerial effectiveness. It is assumed that managerial decisions and actions to maximize accounting earnings are in the interests of shareholders. There are however a number of ways in which managers may manipulate accounting measures such as earnings. Such manipulation may be achieved through the choice of accounting methods used in determining earnings and in the timing of income and expense recognition.

Watts and Zimmerman (1986) review the early literature on earnings management and managerial compensation. The results of this early literature are inconclusive. Many of these studies rely on crude measures of the type of the bonus schemes used to reward managers and so do not take account of the structure of the bonus scheme. The importance of the structure of the bonus scheme in determining whether managers manipulate earnings is demonstrated in a study by Healy (1985). Many schemes place an upper ceiling, and a lower floor, on the level of earnings that determine the amount of the bonuses. Healy found evidence of manipulation to increase earnings when earnings were in the zone between the floor and ceiling used in setting bonuses. A study by McNichols and Wilson (1988) finds evidence of manipulation to reduce earnings when earnings are unusually high or low. More recent studies by Holthausen et al. (1995) and Gaver et al. (1993), however, fail to find evidence of earnings manipulation.

Senior management compensation is usually set by a compensation committee. It would be expected that if compensation committees are operating effectively, they would adjust bonuses to take account of any earnings manipulation. The evidence is inconclusive on whether compensation committees actually act in this way. While Defeo et al. (1989) report evidence which indicates that unadjusted earnings are used in setting compensation, the results of studies by Abdel-Khalik et al. (1987) and by Clinch and Magliolo (1993) provide evidence that compensation may be based upon adjusted earnings.

Share Price Returns and Managerial Compensation

The managerial incentive problem arises where managers own a small fraction of companies' equity. One way of aligning the interests of managers with those of shareholders in such circumstances would seem to be by linking managerial compensation to share prices. This can be done either by basing cash bonuses on such measures as *total shareholder return* (dividends plus capital gains on shares over the measurement period), or through share and share option schemes. In reviewing the research literature, Paul (1992) notes the major role that accounting earnings play in determining managerial compensation as earnings are relatively insensitive to share price performance. The wealth of senior executives is, nevertheless, strongly linked to share prices. Hall (1998) indicates that when the pay of chief executives is defined to include share and share option revaluations, pay to performance from such revaluations is of far greater significance than changes in salary and bonuses. Hall and Liebman (1998) report that where company performance is measured by changes in shareholder value, share and share option revaluations account for approximately 98% of the relationship between chief executive compensation and company performance.

While the sensitivity to share price performance of equity-linked managerial compensation may create appropriate incentives for managers, there are also costs associated with such compensation. Two components of the risk of holding shares are frequently identified: *specific* risk that is associated with factors specific to the company, and *systematic* risk that has to do with the effect of market-wide factors on the movement in share prices. The results of portfolio theory are that an investor can largely eliminate specific risk by holding a diversified portfolio of securities. Diversified investors are therefore only exposed to systematic risk. Managerial wealth, even in the absence of equity-linked compensation, is connected to the company because their investment of human capital in the company. Managers are unlikely to be in a position to diversify their human capital and the extent to which they can diversify the risk associated with equity-linked compensation is likely to be limited. Therefore, unlike rational investors, managers bear both specific and systematic risks. This means that, if they are restricted from selling equity instruments, managers attach less value to any share-related assets they hold in a company than do diversified investors.

The comparative advantages of shares and share options as incentives are discussed by Hall (1998). In both cases he suggests that it is necessary to differentiate between the granting of shares and share options and the changes in the value of these instruments over time. This means, for example, it is necessary to distinguish between the value of share options granted during a period, and the change in the value of share options (those previously granted plus new ones) over the period. Hall argues that when considering changes in value of the instruments the pay-to-performance sensitivity of an option on one share is less than the sensitivity of one share. However, the oppositive is the case when comparing packages with the same value. This is because the gearing inherent in options means that there is a much greater exposure per unit of value of options than there is in the underlying shares.

Although the value of share options is sensitive to changes in share prices, the use of share options in aligning the interests of managers with those of shareholders is complex. First, Hall (1998) found that many managers did not understand how the value or sensitivity of their options changes with change in the value of the underlying shares. Second, share option schemes may also create adverse incentives. The value of share options increases when there is a decrease in the expected dividends that are to be paid on the underlying shares during the life of the options. The value also increases with an increase in volatility of the underlying shares. Share option schemes therefore provide incentives for management to either cut the dividend or not to increase it when an increase is justified. Share price volatility can be changed through companies' investment and financing decisions. Share option schemes therefore may provide incentives for managers to undertake more risky investments and/or increase gearing. This is harmful to shareholder interests if the increased risks are excessive. On the other hand, the incentive to increase volatility may be positive if it acts as a correction to managers' risk aversion[17].

Relative Performance Evaluation

The problem with incentive contracts based upon accounting numbers and share prices is that managerial rewards depend on factors outside the control of the managers themselves. Both accounting earnings and share prices are determined by factors connected specifically with the company, and with industry- and economy-wide factors over which managers have no control. Holmström (1982) demonstrates that where there is a common factor affecting the performance of managers, and where there is a sufficient number of companies to obtain a precise estimate of the common factor, it is more efficient to design performance contracts where the common factor is filtered out. By filtering out the common, or systematic factors, risk-averse managers are only exposed to the risks connected with the company. As a consequence, the overall level of risk is reduced without a reduction in managerial incentives.

If the incorporation of relative performance evaluation (RPE) is more efficient, then it would be expected that companies would use this in setting determining managerial compensation. The empirical literature on the use of relative performance in determining the

---

[17] The effect of share option schemes on dividend, investment and financing decisions is discussed further in Chapter 4.

compensation of senior managers is reviewed by Pavlik et al. (1993). Two forms of the RPE hypothesis are identified: (a) the strong form RPE hypothesis, which predicts that the correlation between compensation and the systematic component is zero; and (b) the weak form RPE hypothesis, which predicts that there is a greater relationship between compensation and the specific component than there is with the systematic component. Pavlik and her associates conclude that, in general, the way in which companies reward their senior managers is not explained by either the strong or the weak form RPE hypothesis. More recently, Aggarwal and Samwick (1999) report no evidence of RPE.

Aggarwal and Samwick (1998) attempt to explain the lack of strong empirical support for the use of RPE by suggesting that relative performance contracts may induce managers to act in such a way as to lower industry returns by pricing too aggressively, so lowering the returns to shareholders. They show that shareholder wealth increases when managers are not rewarded for undercutting their rivals. When contracts are based on the performance of both the company and its rivals, Aggarwal and Samwick demonstrate that these should be *positively* related to the performance of rival companies.

Empirical Studies

Managerial incentive contracts, it is suggested, may be used to align the interests of managers with those of shareholders. It is, however, an empirical question as to whether companies in fact use incentives in compensating their managers. There is a considerable empirical literature examining the relationship between managerial compensation and company performance. This has been reviewed by Pavlik et al. (1993). One of the problems is the measurement of managerial compensation. A restricted definition of compensation may include only cash salaries and bonuses, whereas a broader definition would also include changes in the value of shares and share options held by managers. Pavlik and her associates conclude that the evidence suggests that compensation is linked to accounting and share price performance. Accounting measures are better at explaining compensation when it is defined in terms of cash payments, whereas when compensation is defined to include wealth changes in shares and share options, share price changes are a better indicator of the level of compensation. This conclusion is supported by Hall (1998).

There are questions as to whether pay is sufficiently sensitive to company performance. Jensen and Murphy (1990) examine the relationship between shareholder wealth and chief executive compensation and find that, on average, each $1000 change in shareholder wealth corresponds to a change in salary and bonus in the year, and in following year, of about 2 cents. Using a broader definition that includes incentives from shareholdings and dismissal, they find this increases to $3.25 per $1000 change in shareholder wealth. Jensen and Murphy comment that although the incentives generated by share ownership are relatively large compared with pay and dismissal incentives, most chief executives only hold a small fraction of their company's shares, and that the fraction is declining. Whether or not a relationship of this magnitude is sufficient depends on the perspective adopted. If considered in the context of total shareholder wealth, the incentive looks small. However, the incentive looks different in the context of managerial wealth.

The relationship between compensation and future performance has been examined by looking at the relationship between the sensitivity of pay to performance in one period, and company performance in the following period. Pavlik and her associates suggest that ". . . there is only weak and inconclusive evidence supporting the hypothesis that rewarding managers based on performance improves future performance" (p. 160).

Finally, the effectiveness of compensation schemes in aligning the interests of managers with those of shareholders should be seen through the share price response to changes in such schemes. A number of studies have examined market reaction to the adoption of long-term incentive performance (LTIP) plans. One of the problems with these studies is in identifying the relevant period in which there should be a market reaction. There is, however, some support for the view that the adoption of LTIP plans are viewed positively by the market.

THE MARKET FOR CORPORATE CONTROL

The takeover market is seen as playing a disciplinary role in ensuring that a company's senior management acts to maximize the wealth of shareholders rather than its own utility. It is seen to do so in two ways. First, managerial performance is monitored by potential bidders and the possibility of a takeover, with the associated loss of managerial position, is seen to act as a threat that reduces managers' non-value maximizing behaviour. The market for corporate control is therefore seen to align the interests of managers with those of the shareholders by threatening management with a takeover of the company should their performance be poor. Second, when this threat does not work, the non-value maximizing existing management is replaced by a more efficient one. Not all takeovers, however, are motivated by the need to correct the non-value maximizing behaviour of managers of target companies. In addition to *disciplinary* takeovers there are those motivated by the possibility of gaining benefits by combining the existing companies. The gains in these *synergistic* takeovers may come from a variety of sources. These include gains arising from an increase market power, elimination of functions common to the combining companies, and amalgamation of research and development activities.

There is an intuitive appeal to the argument that the market for corporate control serves a disciplinary function. It is, however, necessary to consider what empirical evidence there is that takeovers are in fact serving this function. One source of evidence comes from share price movements associated with the announcement of a takeover bid. Typically, there is a large increase in the price of shares in the target company and either a small increase or decrease in the price of the bidding company's shares. There is generally an increase in the value of the combined target and bidding companies' shares during the period between the bid being announced and either successful completion, or failure, of the takeover. This overall gain, however, could reflect the market's expectations of gains arising from the replacement of existing management, or from synergistic gains resulting from the merger of the companies. It is therefore necessary to incorporate a distinction between disciplinary and synergistic takeovers into empirical studies. Having made this distinction, evidence that the market for corporate control is effectively disciplining managers comes from examining the pre-takeover performance of target companies, management changes after the takeover, and the post-acquisition performance of successful takeovers. The remainder of this section will examine the reasons for takeovers, the share price performance of companies between the announcement of a takeover and its completion, or failure, before looking at the evidence that the market for corporate control has a disciplinary role.

Disciplinary and Synergistic Takeovers

The role of the takeover market in disciplining managers is identified by Manne (1965). He suggests that the market for corporate control, as a disciplining device, depends on managerial efficiency, or inefficiency, being reflected in the price of the company's shares. A relatively low price, reflecting managerial inefficiency, is important for two reasons. First, it makes it cheaper to acquire the compensation currently being paid to existing managers. Manne, however, points out that it is doubtful whether the compensation recoverable from existing managers explains more than a fraction of takeovers. The second reason is more important. This is that the extent to which the current share price reflects managerial inefficiency indicates the potential gain to be make by replacing existing management with a more efficient one.

The motivation for takeovers may also be to achieve synergistic gains. This means that the value of the combined companies is expected to be greater than the value of the two companies separately. Such gains may come from real operating efficiencies and/or from financial synergies. Real operating synergies may come from economies of scale and economies of scope, such as where one company has the ability to produce a unique product and the other company has the sales organization to market it. Romano (1992) identifies three distinct theories that explain financial synergies: (a) reduced risk of bankruptcy when the cash flows of the combining companies are not perfectly positively correlated; (b) better use of tax shields in the combined company; and (c) the cost differential between internal and external funds. Although it is frequently suggested that there may also be accounting advantages resulting from the combination, these should not usually affect the value of the companies.

Both disciplinary and synergistic takeovers are seen to be motivated by the desire to obtain gains for shareholders in the target and bidding companies. The problem is distinguishing between the two types of takeover. Two approaches are to be found in the literature. One is a distinction found in the US is between *mergers* and *tender* offers; the other is a distinction between *hostile* and *friendly*, or *contested* and *non-contested*, takeovers.

A merger, in the US context, usually involves the issue of shares by the acquiring company, rather than the payment of cash, as consideration for the shares in the target company. It also generally requires approval by the existing management of the target company and its shareholders. A tender offer, on the other hand, is an offer made by the management of the bidding company to the shareholders of the target company. The consideration may be cash and/or shares of the bidding company. The offer does not require the approval of the board of the target company. Jensen and Ruback (1983) also refer to the tone of the bid: the tone being friendly in the case of a merger, and aggressive in the case of a tender offer.

The other distinction is between hostile and friendly, or contested and non-contested, takeovers. As mergers are, by definition, friendly takeovers, it is necessary to distinguish between hostile and friendly tender offers. This is usually based on the initial response of the target company's management to the takeover offer. A hostile takeover is therefore one in which the takeover bid is rejected by the target company's management. Schwert (1997), however, argues that initial rejection of a takeover bid is a part of a negotiating strategy with the bidding company's management, and an announcement may be made because it has been necessary to make the bid public. The use of the target board's initial response to the takeover bid in distinguishing between hostile and friendly takeovers therefore presents problems because the rejection of an offer may be part of a negotiating strategy that will be in the interest of shareholders. In the case of a genuinely hostile takeover, however, rejection of the bid is interpreted as an attempt by the incumbent management of the target company to protect its interests.

Abnormal Returns in the Period Between Announcement and Takeover

There has been a considerable amount of work on the share prices of both target and bidding companies between a takeover announcement and completion or rejection of the takeover. This work mainly attempts to estimate the size of abnormal price changes, i.e. the difference between the changes expected from general movement in the market, or a particular segment of the market, compared with actual changes. Gains to shareholders would be expected in both disciplinary and synergistic takeovers as there would be value added by either more efficient management or the benefits of synergy. The distribution of any gains between the shareholders of the target and bidding companies is largely an empirical question. Reviews of this literature are provided by Jensen and Ruback (1983) and Dodd (1986).

The price of shares of the target company typically rises on the announcement of a takeover bid. This is to be expected because the acquisition is always at an offer price above the current market price of the shares. Jensen and Ruback (1983) report that the evidence indicates that the shareholders of target companies earn significant positive abnormal returns on the announcement of the offer. For successful takeovers, this continues throughout the period from announcement to completion. In the case of unsuccessful takeovers, the positive abnormal returns continue through to the realization of failure. The announcement gains are, however, lost if the takeover target does not receive an additional offer in the next 2 years.

Shareholders of bidding companies tend, in the case of successful tenders, to earn positive abnormal returns. Although the level of these returns may be statistically significant, the size of the returns is considerably smaller than for the shareholders of target companies. Shareholders of successful bidding companies in a merger, on the other hand, have abnormal returns of approximately zero. The returns to the shareholders of bidding companies that are unsuccessful, both tender and merger offers, are generally negative.

The total gains to the shareholders of both target and bidding companies in successful takeovers are significant. Shareholders of target companies receive significant abnormal returns, and shareholders of bidding companies experience either smaller, but significant, positive gains or zero gains. A study by Servaes (1991) indicates that the highest returns are to be found where the Tobin's Q[18] for

[18] Tobin's Q, which is the ratio of the market value of the company to the replacement costs of its net assets, is thought to reflect the management capability of a company. A high Tobin's Q is thought to reflect superior management that adds value to the company.

the target company is low and for the bidding company is high, and the lowest returns are found when the target company has a high Tobin's Q and the bidding company a low Q.

Evidence that Takeovers are Disciplinary

A number of approaches have been adopted to understanding the disciplinary role of takeovers. First, if takeovers serve a disciplinary role then the performance of the target company prior to the takeover bid should be inferior to other companies. As no predictions are made about the pre-acquisition performance of companies that are acquired for reasons of synergy, it is necessary to distinguish between disciplinary and synergistic takeovers in order to test this proposition. Second, if managers of the target company are failing to maximize the value of shareholders' wealth then it would be expected that there will be management changes after the takeover. Here, it is possible to either look at management changes in disciplinary takeovers, however defined, or ask whether companies with high post-acquisition management turnover have poor pre-acquisition performance. Finally, there should be superior post-acquisition performance of the combined companies under both disciplinary and synergistic reasons for takeovers.

If takeovers serve a disciplinary role then it would be expected that poorly performing companies would be subject to takeover bids. Studies distinguish between disciplinary and synergistic takeovers on the basis of whether the bid is hostile or accepted by the target company's management. Mørck et al. (1988) find that companies subject to hostile takeovers are smaller, older, slower growing, and have a lower Tobin's Q than companies where the takeover bid is friendly. A study by Martin and McConnell (1991) did not find differences between the pre-acquisition performance of companies subject to hostile takeovers and those where the takeover bid is accepted by management. Finally, a study by Franks and Mayer (1996) only found differences in Tobin's Q. Although there is some evidence that companies subject to hostile takeovers are poorly performing, the evidence is far from conclusive. The problem may, however, be that the division of takeovers into hostile and friendly is not a good indicator as to whether the takeover is disciplinary and synergistic.

The second approach to determining whether takeovers serve a disciplinary role is to look at management changes in the target company after a successful takeover. If the takeover has a disciplinary purpose then it would be expected that inefficient management would be replaced after the takeover. Franks and Mayer (1990) found that management changes were more frequent with contested than with non-contested bids. However, Martin and McConnell (1991) found no difference in management turnover between hostile and non-hostile takeovers. An alternative research strategy is to examine the pre-acquisition performance of companies where there have been management changes following a successful takeover. It would be expected that significant post-acquisition management changes are associated with poor pre-acquisition performance. Martin and McConnell (1991) divided target companies on the basis of post-acquisition management changes. They found that all takeovers were in industry sectors that were performing well in comparison to the market. However, companies where there were significant management changes were performing poorly relative to the industry sector whereas non-disciplinary were performing in line with the industry sector. Franks and Mayer (1996), on the other hand, found little evidence that post-acquisition management changes are associated with poor pre-bid performance.

The third approach is to examine the post-acquisition performance of successful takeovers. If, as a result of a takeover, inefficient management is replaced with a more efficient one, or if there are synergistic gains, then the post-acquisition performance of the combined companies should be superior. Higson and Elliott (1996) found positive excess return of 12.8% over 2 years after acquisition in the case of hostile takeovers, but a negative excess return of 3.74% for the total sample. This result is consistent with Loughran and Vigh (1997) who found positive excess returns of 61.7% in a 5-year period after acquisition in the case of cash tenders, but negative excess returns of 25% in the case of stock mergers over the 5-year period. Loughran and Vigh suggest their results consistent with two hypotheses. First, tender offers are usually hostile to target company management and the gains are due to the replacement of managers with more efficient managers. Second, following Myers and Majluf (1984), company managers are more likely to issue shares when they believe the company is over-valued by the market.

The results therefore represent a correction to the market price of the shares.

BOARD STRUCTURE

A company's articles of association invariably provide that the company's business shall be managed by directors who act collectively as a board. The management of a company is usually delegated to its full-time executives who may, or may not, sit on the board. Other members of the board, the non-executive directors, do not have an active role in the company's day-to-day management. In this context the board, and especially its non-executive directors, is seen to have two functions. The first is to provide executives with advice and counsel on such matters as corporate policy and strategy. Many non-executive directors are, or have been, senior executives of other companies and so are in a position to give advice and offer an alternative perspective on issues. The second function of the board is to monitor the performance of the company's executives. This includes evaluating managerial performance, implementing appropriate reward schemes, replacing executives when necessary, and checking that executives are not acting in a way that could be construed as self serving.

The monitoring role of the board of directors, and especially the non-executive directors, is seen as necessary where the share ownership of a company is widely dispersed. Such a view underlies, for example, the recommendation of the Cadbury Committee that boards of public companies should have a minimum proportion of non-executive directors. If non-executive directors are to perform a monitoring role, it is necessary that they do not have conflicts of interest and loyalty between their duties to the company and their relationships with the executives who they are monitoring. A distinction is therefore drawn between independent non-executive directors and other non-executives, sometimes referred to as *grey* directors.

Another issue is that of the roles of board chairman and chief executive. Jensen (1993) argues that: "The function of the chairman is to run the board meetings and oversee the process of hiring, firing, evaluating and compensating the CEO. Clearly the CEO cannot perform this function apart from his or her personal interest.

Without the direction of an independent leader, it is more difficult for the board to perform its critical function. Therefore, for the board to be effective, it is important to separate the CEO and chairman positions" (p. 36). The Cadbury Committee also came to the view that the roles of chairman and chief executive should be split. The Committee sees the chairman as being primarily responsible for the workings of the board, its balance of membership, ensuring that all relevant issues are on the board's agenda, and ensuring that directors are encouraged to play a full part in the board's activities. Although there are arguments favouring the separation of the roles of chairman and chief executive, there are opposing views. For example, Brickley et al. (1997) suggest that the agency costs of unitary leadership can be reduced through the adoption of other mechanisms to align the interests of chief executives with those of shareholders. They suggest such mechanisms include ". . . large CEO stockholding and options, a well functioning takeover market, effective monitoring by an independent board, or effective oversight by large blockholders and institutional shareholders" (p. 196).

Can Non-executive Directors be Effective Monitors?

The monitoring role of non-executive directors has been emphasized in a number of reports, and is reflected in most codes of "good" corporate governance. Opinions differ, however, about whether non-executive directors can act as effective monitors. One view is that non-executives are powerless to control management, basically because the boards are themselves controlled by management. The alternative view is that non-executives have incentives to act in the interest of shareholders.

The view that non-executive directors are ineffective in monitoring management is supported first by the assertion that managers, and in particular the chief executive, have significant influence in selection procedures and on the appointment of new directors. Such influence may arise because the chief executive is also chairman of the board. A chief executive, however, may exert influence on the determination of new appointments even where a board has a nominating committee consisting of independent non-executive directors. Second, even in the absence of biases in the nomination and selection process, there are seen to be constraints on the ability of non-executives to effectively monitor the activities of management. These have to do with agenda setting and information flows, the abilities of non-executive directors, and board culture. The chief executive, especially where he or she is also board chairman, may have control over setting the agenda for board meetings and in determining the information that is made available to directors. Non-executive directors may lack the necessary expertise to monitor the decisions of managers. For example, they may not have the necessary knowledge of the industry in order to determine the appropriateness of the decisions made by full-time executives. Finally, it has been suggested that non-executive directors do not have the incentive to effectively monitor management. It has been usual for non-executives to receive a flat fee that, in relation to their other income, is often small. In addition, they usually do not have significant holdings in the company's shares.

The alternative view is that non-executive directors do have incentives to effectively monitor the activities of management. This view is founded mainly on legal rules and upon the reputational capital of non-executive directors. Directors have a duty to act in the interests of the company and in exercising this duty of care, directors may feel they have incentives to effectively monitor management[19]. Perhaps more importantly, non-executive directors have an interest in their own reputations. For reasons of self-esteem, obtaining positions on the boards of other companies, and in obtaining consultancy work, non-executive directors are concerned about their track record. They may therefore monitor management in order to ensure that they are not shown to be deficient in performing their duties where there is a company failure and/or involvement in a scandal.

Empirical Studies

The effectiveness of non-executive directors in monitoring management can only be addressed empirically. There is a growing body of research, mainly in the United States, looking at the effectiveness of non-executive, especially of independent non-executive, directors. This research examines the relationship between company performance and the composition of the board of directors, and also

---

[19] The duty that directors owe to the company is, however, different from the rights of shareholders to protect the value of their interests in the company.

looks at specific situations where there may be a conflict between the interests of senior executives and those of the company's shareholders.

One problem that researchers in this area face is the definition of an *independent* director. The Cadbury Committee, for example, defines an independent director as ". . . independent of management and free from any business or other relationship which could materially interfere with the exercise of their independent judgement". The US Council of Institutional Investors (CII) offer a set of criteria that must be met in order for a director to be considered independent. An independent director is a director who: (a) has not been employed by the company in an executive capacity; (b) is not employed by, or owner of, a company that is the company's paid adviser or consultant; (c) is not employed by a company that is a significant customer or supplier; (d) does not have a personal services contract with the company; (e) is not employed by a foundation or university that receives significant endowments or grants from the company; (f) is not a relative of an executive of the company; and (g) is not part of an interlocking directorate, in which the chief executive or other executive director of the company serves on the board of another company that employs the director. Differing criteria for independent directors makes it difficult to interpret the findings of empirical studies as non-executive directors who do not meet all the above criteria may be identified as independent in some studies. For example, in the study by Cotter et al. (1997), independent directors are defined as non-executive directors who: ". . . are not current or past employees of the corporation, do not have substantial business or family ties with management . . ., nor have business ties with the firm" (p. 199).

Independent Directors and Company Performance

The relationship between independent directors and company performance has been studied in various ways. One way is to examine the reaction of market participants to the appointment of an independent director. Related to this is an examination of the conditions under which independent directors are appointed.

Share price reaction to the appointment of non-executive directors provides an indication as to how market participants view their effectiveness. Rosenstein and Wyatt (1990) found a significantly positive share price reaction to the appointment of independent directors to the boards of US listed companies. Shivdasani and Yermack (1999) distinguish between companies where the chief executives are involved in the appointment of independent directors and companies where they are not. They find a significantly negative share price reaction where there is involvement of the chief executive, and a positive reaction where there is no such involvement. Finally, Klein (1998) finds little evidence of market reaction to the appointment of independent, executive and grey directors. However, when she looks at appointments in relation to specific committees of the board she finds that the market responds positively to the appointment of *inside* directors to investment and to finance committees. This result is interpreted as indicating that ". . . boards need specialized, expert-provided information about the firm's activities to evaluate and ratify the firm's long-term strategies" (p. 278). This finding is consistent with Baysinger and Butler (1985) who find that companies with boards where independent directors represent less than one half of the board have superior performance. They also indicate that there is a diminishing return on the appointment of additional independent directors.

A study by Hermalin and Weisbach (1988) examines the relationship between company performance and the appointment of new directors. They find that poor company performance leads to the appointment of non-executives and to the departure of executive directors. The appointment of non-executive directors may therefore be triggered by the perceived need for greater monitoring of management where a company is performing poorly.

Despite the view that non-executive, and especially independent, directors have an important role in the governance of companies, the empirical evidence is far from conclusive. The evidence, however, points to the need to consider the effectiveness of independent directors within the context of their appointments and in terms of their function within the board structure. In particular there is some evidence that the board structure must balance the need for expertise to enhance the quality of decision making, and the need for independent monitoring.

Conflicts of Interest

The effectiveness of the board of directors in monitoring management and in guarding against executive self dealing has been empirically investigated by looking at situations in which there is a potential conflict of interest between shareholders and senior executives. These situations include the dismissal of the chief executive, executive compensation, takeovers and, in the US, the adoption of "poison pills".

Executive directors may have different incentives to non-executives in considering the dismissal of a chief executive. In many cases, the careers of executive directors are linked to the chief executive. Dismissal of the chief executive may threaten their careers. Non-executive directors, on the other hand, are presumed to have reputational incentives to remove a self-dealing or poorly performing chief executive. Weisbach (1988) has tested the hypothesis that boards dominated by non-executives act differently in the removal of chief executives than do boards dominated by executive directors. Weisbach found that boards dominated by non-executives were more likely to make decisions to remove the chief executive based on performance than were boards dominated by executives. Here company performance was measured by share price returns and earnings.

There is an obvious conflict of interest between shareholders and executives in the determination of executive compensation. Not only do executives want a high level of pay, they also have a preference for a fixed level of pay rather than one that is performance related. However, it is frequently assumed that one method to align the interests of executives with those of the shareholders is to link compensation with company performance. It may therefore be expected that companies whose boards are dominated by non-executives are more likely than boards dominated by executives to ensure that a significant part of executive compensation is related to performance. This proposition is examined by Mehran (1995) who compared the proportion of equity-based compensation in the pay of executives of companies whose boards are dominated by non-executive dominated boards with those employed by companies whose boards were dominated by executives. Pay of executives employed by companies dominated by non-executives was found to contain a greater proportion of equity-based compensation. This is interpreted as suggesting that boards dominated by non-executives are more likely to adopt pay systems that are sensitive to company performance. A study by Core et al. (1999), however, reports that although the compensation of chief executives depends on the proportion of independent directors on the board, the correlation between that part of the compensation related to board composition and the future performance of the company is negative. This may indicate that independent directors are not very good at establishing pay schemes that provide appropriate incentives for senior management.

A third area in which there is a potential conflict of interest is in takeovers. The management of a *bidding* company have incentives to acquire other companies in order to build larger empires and/or to reduce company specific risk through diversification. A study by Byrd and Hickman (1992) suggests that the while the share price return on the announcement of a bid by a company without a majority of independent directors is negative, the returns for company's whose boards are dominated by independent directors is zero. This result is consistent with the view that independent directors constrain management, and particularly CEO, behaviour. On the other side of the takeover, Cotter et al. (1997) find that tender offers to *target* companies with majority independent boards result in higher target company share price returns than for targets without majority-independent boards. The market therefore seems to view the takeover differently according to the composition of the board of the bidding and target companies.

Managers are frequently concerned about the consequences to them personally in the event that their company is taken over by another. They therefore have an incentive to make the company a less attractive takeover target, either through making it more costly for a bidder or by making the post-takeover company less appealing. This may be achieved through the adoption of *poison pills*[20]. The effect of adopting poison pills can, however, be viewed in two ways. One is that they are implemented in order to protect the interests of existing management. The other is that, because they may force bidding companies to pay a high premium in order to

---

[20] Although poison pills are a feature of companies in a number of countries, including the United States, they are rarely found in UK listed companies.

take over the company, the adoption of poison pills is in the interests of shareholders. Brickley et al. (1994) found that the stock market reacted favourably to the adoption of poison-pill provisions by a company whose board is dominated by independent directors, but negatively where independent directors were in a minority on the board. However, Sundaramurthy et al. (1997) found that the stock market reaction was more negative the greater the number of outside directors there were on the board. The decision to adopt poison-pill defences also does not seem to be related to board composition (Mallette and Fowler, 1992; Wahal et al., 1995).

Roles of Chairman and Chief Executive

The case for splitting the roles of chairman and chief executive is supported by Rechner and Dalton (1991) who find that US companies where the roles are split consistently outperform those companies where the roles are combined. However, Baliga et al. (1996) and Brickley et al. (1997) conclude that there is little evidence to support the view that separating the roles leads to improved company performance. All three studies find that only a small proportion of companies split the roles of chairman and chief executive.

Brickley and his colleagues examine the leadership structures of large US companies. They find that, in 1988, the chairman was either the current or former CEO, or a person with special ties to the company. In no case was the chairman an individual who was an independent director. In many companies the roles of chairman and CEO are found to be split during a period of transition, but then revert to a unitary structure.

Explaining Board Structure

An understanding of company boards may be obtained by attempting to identify the factors associated with their composition and structure. Hermalin and Weisbach (1998) do this by asking how boards become the way they are, and what determines who is appointed to, or who leaves, the board. They construct a model in which the chief executive and board negotiate over his or her compensation and choice of new directors. These negotiations, they suggest, determine the level of independence of the board. They suggest their model is consistent with the results of empirical studies: (a) chief executive turnover is negatively related to company performance, and this relationship is stronger where the board is more independent; (b) the probability of an independent director being appointed increases after poor company performance; and (c) the board tends to become less independent over the course of the chief executive's career.

One implication of the work of Hermalin and Weisbach is that no single board structure is appropriate for all companies. This is taken further by Bhagat and Black (1998) who point to two possible types of explanation. The first is that board structure may be linked to the characteristics of the company. For example, they suggest that companies with slow growth may need a high proportion of independent directors to ensure that these companies pay out surplus cash as dividends when they lack profitable reinvestment opportunities. The other possible explanation is that the mechanisms for controlling agency costs in large companies may act as substitutes or complements. It is therefore necessary to consider possible interactions between, say, independent directors, interest of institutional investors, takeovers, and compensation structure. This is also consistent with the view of Brickley et al. (1997) on splitting the roles of chair and chief executive.

INSTITUTIONAL INVESTORS

The Berle and Means (1932) image of the modern public company is of one owned by diverse shareholders, each with a small percentage claim on the company, and controlled by professional managers. A rational investor with a small shareholding has no incentive to monitor the performance of the company's management as to do so is costly. Although the costs would be borne by the investor, any benefits of monitoring, and any intervention in the company's activities, would be shared by all investors. As a consequence there is an incentive to "free-ride".

The pattern of shareholding in US and UK companies has changed over the post-war period. This period has seen a decline in the proportion of shares owned directly by individuals and an increase in investment by institutions. These include pension funds, insurance companies, unit trusts, investment trusts and, in the US, mutual funds. In the UK, institutional investors owned 22% of shares in

listed companies in 1963, this reaching 43% in 1975, 59% in 1985 and
61% in 1990. A similar pattern of change is evident in the US. Black
(1990) notes that ". . . the model of public companies owned by
thousands of anonymous shareholders simply isn't true. There are
a limited number of large shareholders, and they know each other"
(p. 576).

Change in the ownership structures of public companies has
been associated with *shareholder activism*. This is defined by Smith
(1996) as including ". . . monitoring and attempting to bring about
changes in the organizational control structure of firms not perceived
to be pursuing shareholder-wealth-maximizing goals" (p. 227).
Smith suggests that the rise of institutional holdings, and corresponding decline in the market for corporate control, has focused
attention on the role of institutions as monitors of corporate performance. A similar line is taken by Maug (1998) who indicates that,
with a decline in the number of takeovers, institutional investors
have attempted to achieve higher returns through governance-related
activities. In addition there may also be pressures on institutional
investors to adopt a social agenda. For example, institutional investors
may be lobbied to encourage companies to adopt ethical and
environmental policies.

Institutional investors are perceived as having an important role
to play in the governance of companies. For example, the Hampel
Report recommends that: (1) institutional shareholders have a
responsibility to make considered use of their votes; (2) companies
and institutional investors should each be ready, where practicable,
to enter a dialogue based on the mutual understanding of objectives;
and (3) when evaluating companies' governance arrangements,
particularly those relating to broad structure and composition,
institutional investors should give due weight to all relevant factors
drawn to their attention (Committee on Corporate Governance
(Hampel) 1998). However, individually institutional investors have
weak incentives, and limited capacity, to monitor, and intervene in
the affairs of, companies.

Intervention by Institutional Investors

Institutional investors have significant investments in many companies. However, these investments may only represent a relatively

small fraction of each company's share capital[21]. It is therefore necessary to attempt to understand why institutional investors may wish to intervene in a company's affairs. One explanation is the growth of index funds which has meant that investors must hold shares in companies in the index. Del Guercio and Hawkins (1997) suggest that an index fund may wish to change the behaviour of companies in general by targeting companies with inappropriate corporate governance or poor financial performance. The publicity associated with an institution's activism may then lead other companies to make changes in order to avoid publicity. A second explanation for intervention has to do with the effect on share prices of selling a large holding. Share prices may fall if an investor attempts to liquidate a large block of shares in an underperforming company. Institutional investors may, therefore, be unable to follow the "Wall Street Rule", i.e. if an investor is unhappy about a company then he or she should sell the shares. Intervention in a company's affair may be the only rational alternative.

Institutional investors, as large shareholders, may therefore have incentives to monitor the activities of these companies and, when appropriate, intervene in the affairs of those companies. The issues on which institutional investors have focused on are:

- Shareholders' rights which includes opposition, in the UK, to issuing of non-voting ordinary shares and reducing pre-emption rights.
- Board structure and composition. Many institutional investors hold beliefs about "good" corporate governance. These may include the view that there should be: separation of the roles of the chairman and chief executive, outside and/or independent directors on the board, and separate audit and/or compensation and/or appointment committees.
- Anti-takeover provisions. Institutional investors in the US have opposed the adoption of anti-takeover provisions. Such provisions are rarely found in listed companies in the UK.
- Executive compensation. Although the public is concerned mainly with the large amounts paid to senior executives of some

---

[21] Georgen and Renneboog (1999) suggest that the average of the largest shareholdings owned by institutions in UK listed companies is 5.5%.

companies, institutional investors have mainly been concerned with the structure of compensation schemes.
- Financial results. Institutional investors may intervene in the management of a company with poor results and share price performance. In such cases intervention may be to change the company's management and/or its strategy.

The main focus of intervention by institutional investors has been on corporate governance issues—shareholder rights, board structure and composition and anti-takeover provisions—and on executive compensation, rather than on direct intervention in the management of companies.

As shareholders, institutional investors have voting rights that they can use in a meeting of the company's shareholders. They can use their votes to block resolutions proposed by the company's directors. In this case institutional investors are exerting *negative* control over the company. Alternatively, they can propose a resolution to be considered at the meeting. As holders of a significant number of shares, institutional investors may have an important role in determining the outcome of any resolution. Institutions are large buyers and sellers of shares, and so their investment decisions may have an impact on a company's share price. They may also express their views through the media. Institutional investors, unlike individual investors holding a small number of shares, may therefore have access to a company's management, and may be able to use informal "jawboning" (influencing or pressurizing through strong persuasion) to effect changes in company management and strategy. Finally, institutional investors may form coalitions with other investors to effect change in a company.

Disincentives to Monitor and Intervene

Although institutional investors may have both the incentives and means to monitor and intervene in the companies' affairs, there are a number of factors that mitigate against both monitoring and intervention. The rationale for the absence of investor involvement in the affairs of the type of company characterized by Berle and Means may be seen to apply to institutional investors. Despite the fact that many institutional investors hold a significant investment in companies, they rarely hold more than a small fraction of the shares in any one company. If an institution incurs substantial costs in monitoring companies, and intervening where necessary, any benefits that arise from the institution's actions will accrue to all shareholders and not just the institution. The existence of institutional investors therefore only modifies the free-rider problem, it does not eliminate it. There is competition among institutions, and their fund managers, to demonstrate superior performance and so there is little incentive to increase the performance of a company that is also held by rival institutions. The only possible exception is where an institutional fund is overweighted in a particular company, i.e. the company's share represent a higher proportion of the fund's portfolio than it represents in the portfolios of other institutions. In this case, the institution has a higher proportional gain from any benefits of intervention.

Even in the absence of a free-rider problem, there is doubt about the capacity and ability of institutional investors to monitor the companies in which they invest. Institutional investors often receive a fee for managing funds that is related to the value of funds under management. The amount of their spending on monitoring is therefore constrained by the fee income. It has been suggested that even the most active institutions spend less than half a basis point on governance activities. Not only are the amounts spent on monitoring small, but institutional investors do not normally have the ability to intervene in the management of companies.

If institutional investors have little incentive to monitor those companies in which they invest, they have less incentive to intervene in their affairs. First, any benefits of intervention by one institution would be shared with other investors in the company. There is consequently a free-rider problem with intervention. Second, the institution is an agent for the beneficial owners of the assets in the fund. If fund management fees are fixed, the institution will bear the costs of intervention but any benefit will be attributable to the fund's beneficial owners. Third, fund managers depend on companies to supply *soft* information about their affairs. Intervention may lead to a loss of this source of information. Fourth, the act of intervention may be perceived by market participants as indicating that there are problems in the company, so depressing the company's share price. Finally, the performance of fund managers is monitored continually by their clients. There is consequently an incentive for fund managers to attempt to focus on short-term performance measures. Any benefits of intervention are likely to be obtained in the long term.

Institutional investors not only lack incentives to intervene in a company's affairs, but intervention itself may lead to a number of problems. In order to intervene effectively, an institution may need to increase its holding of shares. This may reduce the liquidity of the fund. Liquidity may also be reduced if the institution places one of its employees on the board of a company. In this case, insider trading rules may make it difficult for the institution to trade in the company's shares. Placing an employee on a company's board may also result in conflicts of interest. As a director of the company, the employee will have a fiduciary duty to the company that may conflict with his or her duty to the institution.

There may also be pressures on institutional investors not to intervene in a company's affairs. Institutional investors often provide other services such as banking and insurance to companies, and so any intervention may result in a loss of other business. Institutions may be managing funds, especially pension funds, on the behalf of companies that do not support intervention for fear of retaliation by the managers of the target company's pension funds. Finally, there may be political consequences of intervention if there is public concern about financial institutions intervening in the affairs of industrial companies.

Investor Services, Industry Groups and Coordinated Action

Institutions generally do not have incentives to monitor the companies in which they invest. They also have disincentives, and face practical problems, in intervening in the affairs of companies with poor corporate governance practices or which are performing poorly. Black and Coffee (1994) comment that large shareholders may not intervene because of ". . . imperfect information, limited institutional capabilities, substantial coordination costs, misaligned incentives of money managers, a preference for liquidity, and the uncertain benefits of intervention" (p. 2086). Some of these difficulties can be resolved through institutions acquiring services through an informational intermediary, or by acting together either through industry groups and through coordinated action.

The problem of disincentives, and lack of capability, of institutions to monitor the companies in which they invest is resolved by use of the services of specialized informational intermediaries. Such intermediaries may monitor the corporate governance practices and performance of companies and provide guidance on voting. Such services may be provided by independent companies or through industry groups. The use of intermediaries allows monitoring costs to be shared by institutions and, by so doing, largely eliminate the problem of free-riders.

Institutional investors can also act through industry groups. Coffee (1991) notes that institutional investors in the UK tend to act collectively through *umbrella* institutions in their dealings with corporate managements. He suggests that such umbrella institutions, or industry groups, ". . . have developed, in part, to share the expenses and political burden of confronting and opposing individual corporate management" (p. 1310). Industry groups have tended to focus on corporate governance practice rather than intervention in poorly performing companies. In the UK this has meant: (a) protection of pre-emption rights; (b) board structure and membership—separating the roles of chairman and chief executive, non-executive directors and audit committees; and (c) executive compensation, especially the use of share, and share option, schemes. The attitude of UK institutional investors to intervention may be seen through the views of the Institutional Shareholders Committee (ISC), a committee of a number of UK industry groups. The ISC indicates that: "There will be occasions when an institutional investor will feel it appropriate to vote against a proposal which it considers undesirable. In such circumstances it is important that, wherever possible, representations are made in time for the problem to be considered and for consultation to take place with a view to achieving a satisfactory solution. Where a satisfactory outcome cannot be achieved on an important issue, it may be desirable for a spokesperson to attend the relevant meeting of the company and explain why the particular proposal is being opposed. In such cases a poll should be demanded to ensure that the vote is duly recorded" (para. 3.3, ISC *The Responsibilities of Institutional Shareholders in the UK*, December 1991). The position is therefore that institutional investors should support company boards by a positive use of their voting rights unless they have good reasons for doing otherwise.

Finally, institutional investors may intervene through coordinated action. This is uncommon in the US because a group of shareholders who collectively own 5% or more of a company's shares and who act together on a voting issue have to file with the SEC. Further, they risk legal action by the company and other shareholders who may claim incomplete disclosure of their plans. Although UK shareholders are not subject to similar regulations, coordinated action by institutions is rare.

Empirical Evidence

The empirical evidence on investor activism has been reviewed by Black (1998). First, he reports that if institutional investors have an important role to play in the governance of companies, it may be expected that those companies with a shareholder base that includes a large number of institutional investors will perform better than companies which have fewer shares held by such investors. However, there is an absence of evidence that there is a correlation between the company performance and the percentage of the company's shares held by institutional investors. Second, Black notes that there is generally an absence of a relationship between shareholder activism and company performance. The exception to this are studies by Nesbitt (1994) who reports positive long-term returns of companies targeted by CalPERS, the Californian pension fund, and by Opler and Sokobin (1997) who report above market performance of companies in the year they were targeted by the US Council of Institutional Investors (CII). Finally, he suggests that the results of the effect of institutional activism on such events as change of chief executive and asset disposals is inconclusive. The empirical evidence is therefore consistent with the analysis of the incentives and problems of institutional investors monitoring and intervening in companies.

SUMMARY AND CONCLUSION

The image of the Anglo-Saxon company that dominates much of the literature on corporate governance owes much to the work of Berle and Means (1932). They document the separation of the control of a company and its ownership. This separation is seen as being almost complete where the largest shareholder only owns a small fraction of the company. This is true of most large public companies. Capital markets have developed alongside this increasing separation of ownership and control to enable shareholders to trade their ownership interests in companies. The problem of corporate governance is one of aligning the interests of a company's professional managers with those of shareholders.

Three main sets of factors are often identified as operating so as to align the interests of companies' managers with those of their shareholders. These are the design of managerial incentive contracts, the operation of the markets for labour, products and capital, and internal governance mechanisms to monitor managerial performance on the behalf of shareholders. Cash bonuses and share schemes may be used as incentives. A problem with cash bonuses is that it is usually not possible for shareholders to directly observe the way managers perform their duties and so it is necessary to link management compensation with a measure of the output associated with its actions. Such performance indicators are generally based on accounting measures or measures associated with the company's shares. One of the main problems with accounting measures as a performance indicator is that they are open to manipulation by managers. This leaves share price as a suitable performance indicator. Share price changes may be incorporated into compensation contracts through cash bonuses based on measures such as *total shareholder return* or through share and share option schemes. Movement in the price of shares is usually assumed to be linked to industry-wide and economy-wide factors as well as to specific factors associated with the company. If it is accepted that managers only have control over specific factors then it would seem appropriate to design compensation contracts in which factors not specific to the company are filtered out. The empirical evidence is, however, that relative performance evaluation does not explain managerial compensation.

Although both the labour and product markets play a role in aligning the interests of managers with those of shareholders, it is usually assumed that capital markets have the major role to play. First, the quality of managerial performance is signalled in companies' share prices. Second, and most importantly, capital markets facilitate the takeover of one company by another. The market for corporate control operates in two ways. First, it aligns the interests of managers with shareholders by threatening management should their performance be poor. Second, when this threat does not work, non-value maximizing management is replaced by more efficient management. Management performance is therefore seen as being monitored by the management of acquisitive companies. Takeovers also take place for synergistic reasons. In studying the effectiveness of the market for corporate control as a mechanism of corporate governance it is therefore necessary to be able to distinguish between the two types of takeovers. It is generally assumed that cash tenders, hostile and contested takeovers are intended to replace existing management. On the other hand mergers, friendly and non-contested takeovers are assumed to be motivated by synergistic factors. There is some evidence that target companies in hostile takeovers have lower Tobin's Q ratios than other target companies. If Tobin's Q is assumed to reflect the value of the existing management then this result indicates the inefficiency of hostile targets. The evidence of replacement of existing management in disciplinary takeovers is not strong. Perhaps the best evidence is that where management is changed; the company prior to takeover was performing less well, relative to the industry sector, than where there is little management change. The post-acquisition performance is best where the takeover was a tender offer and the amount paid was in cash.

Finally, two mechanisms that have been suggested as indicators of *good* governance are the appointment of non-executive directors to the board and the separation of the roles of chairman and chief executive. The board of directors is responsible to shareholders for the management of the company. However, the management of a company is usually delegated to its full-time executives who may, or may not, sit on the board. Other members of the board, the non-executive directors, do not have an active role in the company's day-to-day management but may be seen as providing the executives with advice and counsel on such matters as corporate policy and strategy, and monitoring the performance of the company's executives on behalf of the shareholders. A distinction has to be made between non-executive and independent non-executive directors. Some non-executive directors may have links with the company, and its management, other than as a director. Such non-executive directors may not necessarily be independent non-executive directors. More recent interest has been in the role of independent non-executive directors. However, the effectiveness of independent directors in dealing with potential conflicts of interest between managers and shareholders is unclear as contradictory findings are found amongst the studies. To some extent this relates to some studies examining the effectiveness of *independent* non-executives while others look simply at non-executive directors. The other mechanism of *good* governance is the separation of the roles of board chairman and CEO. If a function the board is to monitor management, there would appear to be a conflict of interest if the CEO also serves as board chairman. Although separation of the roles of chairman and CEO is often seen as good corporate practice, there is little evidence to support the notion that this improves company performance.

There has been a significant change in the pattern of shareholdings in companies over the past quarter-century, with a movement away from the holding of shares directly by individuals towards indirect holdings through institutions. This change has become associated with the notion of *investor activism*, by which institutional investors monitor managerial performance and intervene to correct poor performance and managerial self-dealing. Institutional investors are increasingly seen as having an important role in the governance of companies. However, individually institutional investors have weak incentives, and limited capacity, to monitor, and intervene in the affairs of, companies. The empirical evidence is consistent with this view.

It is generally accepted that the market for corporate control is the most effective method in ensuring that managers act in the interests of a company's shareholders. However, this is an expensive mechanism and there are times when takeover activity is low. This makes it all the more important to ensure that other mechanisms are in place. Appropriately designed incentive contracts based on shareholder return, either through cash bonuses or share schemes, may be one solution. Such contracts may be improved by filtering out industry- and market-wide effects so as to base the incentive on company-specific factors that can be controlled by management. Incentive schemes have the potential for abuse by management. It is generally assumed that such abuse can be constrained by non-executive directors and by institutional shareholders. However, this view is not confirmed by the empirical evidence.

3
Employee Share Ownership

Employee share option schemes may be viewed as a component of a broader concern to allow employees to participate in the company in which they work. In order to gain insight into employee share option schemes it is therefore necessary to examine employee participation more generally. Employee participation may be achieved in two broad ways. First it may be achieved by involving employees through a variety of processes that range from disclosure of information to, and for consultation with, employees, to full participation of employees in the company's decision-making. In contrast to this *industrial democracy* approach to employee participation is one that involves employees in the financial performance of the company. As with industrial democracy, there a variety of ways of achieving *economic democracy*. Although often considered separately, the effectiveness of schemes designed to encourage economic democracy may depend on the existence of some form of industrial democracy. This may explain why many companies adopt both industrial and economic democracy approaches to employee participation.

A company may involve its employees in its financial results in one, or both, of two main ways. First, profit-sharing schemes provide employees with a fixed wage together with a variable amount linked to a company's profits, its revenues, value added or some other performance measure. The benefits to employees may be made available immediately or deferred to some future period, and the payment itself may be in cash, shares in the company, or invested in funds for the benefit of employees. Second, employee share ownership schemes allow employees to participate in company performance through an ownership interest in the company. Employees are consequently exposed to changes in the value of the company's shares and may benefit from its dividends. Employee share ownership can come about through the availability of shares at a preferential price, through employee share ownership plans (ESOPs)[22], and the use of share option schemes. Profit-sharing schemes that provide employees with shares may be seen to have the character of both profit-sharing and share schemes.

While the rationale for involving employees in the financial performance of companies can be understood generally as a component of, or a way of achieving, employee participation, the specific case for economic democracy is complex. As it is important to understand the rationale for economic democracy in order to consider employee share schemes, this is considered first. The case for economic democracy is presented in the PEPPER Report[23] (Uvalic, 1991). Although the case for economic democracy, as presented in this report, is to increase company performance by providing appropriate incentives to employees and to increase the stability of employment, the case for employee share ownership is more complex. This can be revealed by examining the arguments used by politicians in supporting, or opposing, legislative proposals that provide fiscal incentives to employee share schemes. These arguments are complex and change over time.

The academic literature related to economic democracy can be divided into two main areas. First, there is an economic literature that is mainly focused on the share ownership as an incentive to improved productivity. Although the effectiveness of incentives where the employee has little impact on overall performance is considered theoretically in this literature, much of the literature consists of empirical studies to determine whether, and under what conditions, employee share schemes affect company performance. Second, there is a behavioural literature derived from industrial relations and psychology that considers the effect of employee share schemes on employee behaviour more specifically, and also examines the subsequent effect on company performance. There are few attempts made in both literatures to distinguish between the effects of alternative types of employee share scheme.

---

[22] An ESOP is a trust is established to acquire a company's shares for the benefit of employees using funds borrowed from the company, a bank, or other lender.

[23] The PEPPER Report: *Promotion of Employee Participation in Profits and Enterprise Results in the Member States of the European Community.*

RATIONALE FOR ECONOMIC DEMOCRACY

There is a long history of economic democracy in the UK, US and France. Despite this, the reasons for involving employees in a company's financial performance are far from clear. Some indication as to what may be the rationale may be obtained from the PEPPER Report (Uvalic, 1991). This identifies three main sets of arguments in support of the use of employee participation in a company's financial performance. These are the incentive effects of employee participation, the effect of flexible pay on employment, and macro-economic effects.

Participation in the company's financial performance is first seen to enhance company performance by providing appropriate incentives to employees that align their interests with those of the company. Company performance may be enhanced because employees are more motivated and/or more productive and/or less likely to be absent or leave employment with the company. The effectiveness of measures that involve employees in the financial performance of the company have been questioned. One argument is that individual employees have little impact on the overall results of a company and, as it is difficult to assess an individual's contribution to company performance, employees may have an incentive to free-ride. This argument is re-examined later in this chapter. Second, profit-sharing and employee share schemes expose employees to excessive risks. Not only do employees bear the risk of unemployment, their income and wealth are also related to profits and/or share price performance. Unlike shareholders, they are unable to reduce these risks through diversification. They are consequently exposed to both systematic and specific risks. Finally there is the view that employee participation in financial performance may provide an incentive for employees to participate in decision making. Such participation is seen by some as weakening managerial control and thereby reducing company performance.

A second set of arguments relate to the association between greater flexibility in total pay, due to its link with company performance, and unemployment. The underlying theory, *stability theory*, holds that profit-sharing arrangements change the incentives of companies to hire and retain employees. The profit element, it is argued, is viewed by companies as a "tax" on profits rather than as a cost. Employees will be retained in the event of a decline in companies' profits provided that their contribution exceeds the cost of their basic wage. For a profit-sharing scheme to be effective in reducing the risk of unemployment it is necessary that the basic rate be reduced on the introduction of the scheme. However, many companies introducing such schemes treat the profit-sharing element as an addition to existing basic pay. In such cases the introduction of profit sharing will have little effect on the incentives of employers to hire or retain employees. Where profit related pay substitutes for a part of the basic wage, the risk of unemployment is seen to be reduced by downward pay adjustments that follow a downturn in company profitability. Such an adjustment is effected directly with the operation of profit-related pay schemes. Kruse (1993) both examines the stability argument and reviews the evidence from other empirical studies. Two basic components of the stability argument are identified. First, there is assumed to be an association between profit sharing and employment stability. Most of the studies reviewed by Kruse found some relationship between profit sharing and employment stability. Second, it is proposed that employers treat profit-sharing payments differently from fixed wages in their decisions to hire or retain employees. Again Kruse concludes that the evidence is generally consistent with this idea. The stability argument for economic democracy is most appropriate for cash profit-sharing schemes, i.e. where employees receive a cash bonus. It works less well in the case of employee share schemes. However, it has been suggested that share ownership may induce moderation in wage negotiations as employees will not wish to cause a fall in share prices by industrial action in support of their pay demands.

Finally it has been suggested that employee participation in financial performance, particularly through cash profit-related pay schemes, will either lead to lower unemployment rates or, according to Weitzman (1987), to full employment. Whilst Weitzman's conclusions have attracted the interests of politicians[24], his work has been subject to criticism. In a follow-up report, referred to as PEPPER II (European Commission 1996), its authors conclude that, as the econometric evidence is inconclusive, the effects of profit sharing on employment through greater wage flexibility are debatable.

[24] Weitzman's work, for example, was used in the justification of the introduction of profit-related pay schemes in the UK (HM Treasury 1986).

THE RATIONALE FOR EMPLOYEE SHARE OWNERSHIP

The reasons why companies adopt employee share schemes are probably complex and change through time. It is, however, difficult to identify the reasons why companies adopt such schemes. Governments have, at various times, introduced measures to encourage companies to adopt employee share schemes. Government support for employee share ownership relates to both economic and social goals. The economic rationale for employee share ownership is mainly that it is associated with improved company performance. Employee share ownership may, on the other hand, be justified as a way of achieving wider social change. An understanding of the rationale for employee share schemes can therefore be gained through an examination of the arguments advanced on both sides of the Atlantic for the adoption of such schemes. The arguments advanced in the US relate mainly to the introduction and promotion of ESOPs. Such schemes have only recently appeared in the UK, and the debate has been more generally about share ownership schemes.

US Employee Share Ownership Plans

Rosen (1991) relates the development of employee share ownership in the US to the "New Capitalism" movement. In 1929 Robert Brookings published a book *Economic Democracy: America's Answer to Socialism and Communism*, in which he noted that a number of large US companies had assisted employees to invest their savings in the companies' shares ". . . thus creating a real 'economic democracy', which is America's answer to socialism and communism with their inherent weakness". The "New Capitalism" was seen as an alternative to socialism and communism, adopted in other countries, with employee share ownership being seen as a way of reducing the friction between capital and labour, thereby promoting the development of a "good" society.

Brookings made the case for wider employee share ownership but it was the work of Louis Kelso that underlies the development of legislation to facilitate the use of ESOPs as a mechanism for achieving the goal of wider employee participation. Kelso and Adler (1958) developed a "two-factor" theory which proposed that there were only two factors of production: capital and labour. With increasing industrialization, capital contributed more to production than labour, and as a consequence there is a wider division between the rich and poor in society. Kelso and Adler suggested that a mechanism is required to allow the economically disenfranchised to acquire capital. One such mechanism is the ESOP. An ESOP is basically a trust established to acquire a company's shares for the benefits of employees. Shares may either be issued by the company or purchased using funds borrowed from the company, a bank or another lender. The company makes payments to the trust to pay off the loan where the trust borrows money. There were technical problems with establishing ESOPs which were resolved as a result of Kelso's association with Senator Russell Long. Long's support of the ESOP concept resulted in the enactment of 25 pieces of legislation favourable to ESOPs.

Employee share schemes, and ESOPs in particular, are therefore being advocated as a mechanism of transforming society by encouraging wider share ownership. This theme has recently been taken up by Gates (1998) in his book *The Ownership Solution*. Gates states as his hypothesis that: ". . . people are likely to become better stewards of all those systems of which they are a part—social, political, fiscal, cultural and natural—as they gain a personal stake in the economic system" (p. xxi). Participatory capitalism is seen as an alternative to an "exclusive, detached and socially erosive" pattern of ownership. A more participatory capitalism would, he suggests, ". . . link a nation's people to their workplace, their community, their economy, their environment—and to each other" (p. xxvii).

The rationale for promoting ESOPs is therefore to facilitate wider share ownership. Any improvement in company performance is incidental to this goal. This is expressed by Rosen (1991) who comments that: "The primary purpose of ESOPs is and always has been to widen the ownership base of substantial capital estates. No other goals are mentioned in any of the legislation governing ESOPs. Nonetheless, many advocates of employee ownership predicted that one of its benefits would be to improve corporate performance by linking the financial interests of employees and companies" (p. 29).

UK Tax Incentives

UK Governments have, at various times over the past 30 years, introduced, modified or abolished tax incentives for companies and their employees to adopt employee share schemes. Three types of scheme are intended for the majority of employees[25]. First, tax incentives for Save-as-You-Earn (SAYE) share option schemes were introduced by a Conservative Government in 1973, abolished in the following year by a Labour Government, only to be reintroduced in a slightly modified form by a Conservative Government in 1980. Second, tax incentives for profit sharing schemes were introduced by a Labour Government in 1978, the time of the "Lib–Lab" pact. Although called a profit-sharing scheme, the scheme combines elements of profit sharing with share ownership. Finally, in 1989 a Conservative Government introduced, with the support of both the Labour and Liberal opposition parties, legislation to facilitate the use of employee share option plans (ESOPs). Employee share ownership is again on the political agenda with a Labour Government issuing a consultative paper on employee share ownership[26].

Examination of the arguments used in Parliamentary debates, especially those in Committee, provides a rich picture of the rationale of employee share ownership. Baddon et al. (1989) identify three themes underlying support for schemes that confer fiscal incentives on share schemes. These are human relations, social ownership and market forces. The theme of market forces is specifically related to discretionary schemes that are intended for director and senior executives. Only the other two themes that are therefore relevant to schemes targeted at the whole workforce. However, there are other themes, not identified by Baddon and his colleagues, that run through these debates. These include incentives to higher productivity, fairness and the broader political Conservative objective of a *property-owning democracy*.

The basis of the *human relations* rationale for employee share ownership is captured in the following statement, quoted by Baddon et al., from David Steel (1986): "Profit sharing schemes . . . can encourage greater involvement, better working conditions, greater

---

[25] Discretionary schemes, intended for directors and senior executives, are considered elsewhere.

[26] *Consultation on Employee Share Ownership.* London: HM Treasury, 1998.

job satisfaction, reduce the rift between management and employees, the 'us and them' attitudes, encourage co-operation, stimulate involvement, improve management competence, reduce waste, boost productivity, and provide a more equitable distribution of the wealth created". The commitment of the Liberal Party to human relations is long standing. For example, in the debate on the 1978 Finance Bill, John Pardoe quoted from the *Yellow Book* of 1928 that ". . . (T)he real purpose of profit-sharing . . . is to show that the worker is treated as a partner and that the division of the proceeds of industry is not a mystery concealed from him, but is based upon known and established rules to which he is a party". Other political parties have taken up the theme. For example, in his 1978 Budget Statement, the Labour Chancellor, Denis Healey, indicated that share schemes ". . . encourage the employees of a company to identify themselves more closely with their company . . . (which) . . . can help improve the relationship between employees and employers"[27], and in the Committee Stage of the 1973 Finance Bill, the Conservative Chief Secretary , Patrick Jenkin, said that ". . . (W)hat the schemes can do is establish a community of interest between company and employee and break down the barriers that are part of the trouble that lies behind the difficulties in industrial relations". Politicians from the three main political parties have therefore, at one time or other, used the human relations theme in support of employee share ownership.

The other theme of *social ownership* is reflected by John Pardoe in the Committee Stage of the 1978 Finance Bill. He said:

> We cannot go on thinking that a capitalist system, based on the rigid distinction between those who own the capital and those who do the work can be maintained any longer . . . I suppose the main reason that I wholeheartedly support the concept of industrial democracy, of which profit sharing is only a minor part—is that I do not believe that capitalism is a sufficient base for the future economic organisation of society.
>
> I see these profit-sharing schemes as a tiny step forward in the direction of a new economic order . . . I do not for a moment believe that this profit sharing scheme will transform the economy, or transform society, or even . . . bury both capitalism and Socialism in the same grave.

[27] *Hansard* vol. 947, c. 1201.

Although the traditional policy of the Labour Party was one of public ownership, the Party has subsequently changed its position. Its commitment to nationalization formed the basis of its opposition to the introduction of a SAYE share-option scheme included in the 1973 Finance Bill. However, the Labour Party supported the Conservative Government's legislation, included in the Finance Act 1989, to facilitate ESOPs. In the Committee stage of the Bill, for example, Nicholas Brown said that: "The Labour Party is solidly in favour of employee ownership plans . . . The structure could lead to genuine worker control and positive and constructive participation in management decision making". The ESOP structure, unlike other employee share ownership schemes, allows employees to acquire a significant stake in a company and so the rationale of social ownership may be restricted to this type of arrangement.

Other themes emerge from political debate on employee share ownership schemes. The Conservative Party has seen employee share ownership as a component of a *property-owning democracy*. In the Committee Stage of the Finance Bill 1978, for example, John MacGregor indicated that employee share ownership ". . . will encourage wider capital ownership among people for whom this form of saving has either not been available or has not been considered in the past. I see this as the next logical extension of a property-owning democracy"[28]. He also reiterates the content of a Green Paper by the Conservative Party which indicates employee share ownership reinforces the objective of "a steady move towards a more deeply-rooted form of individual capital ownership on a wide scale, with a chance to unwind excessive collective ownership".

In his Consultation Document, Gordon Brown has suggested the Government supports employee share ownership schemes for two reasons: fairness and productivity. By fairness he means that tax-preferred share schemes should be available to the whole workforce, and not only to senior managers. The extension of the tax advantages of share option schemes to all employees on the grounds of fairness was seen to be one of the main reasons underlying the introduction of SAYE share option schemes in 1973. The 1972 Finance Act had provided fiscal advantages for executive share option schemes.

[28] Standing Committee A c. 1220.

The productivity argument has been expressed by Patricia Hewitt, when Economic Secretary, in a statement launching the Consultative Document[29]: "Britain's productivity lags behind that of our main competitors, as does the participation in employee share ownership schemes. These schemes have an important role to play in increasing that productivity by harnessing the ambition of employees to see the company in which they work succeed." Although productivity has been considered in the past, it has not been previously used as a major justification for the introduction of employee share schemes. The main reason for this is expressed by Nicholas Brown in the Committee Stage of the Finance Bill 1989. He says: "The link between the worker having a minority share-holding and any consequent incentive is so remote that the idea that an employee will work harder does not stand up to close examination. The benefit to the employee is too small to provide a real incentive. . ."[30]. He then goes on to indicate that the effects on company performance of ESOPs is, on the basis of the evidence from US studies, at best ambiguous.

Government Support for Employee Share Ownership

The political rationale for employee share ownership is complex and changing over time. Employee share ownership, especially in the form of ESOPs, can be seen as a component of social and economic reform. This is seen in the US in the writings of Brooking, Kelso and Adler, and Gates, and well as in the legislation promoted by Long to facilitate the adoption of ESOPs. Themes of social reform also emerge in the UK with John Pardoe's vision of a new economic order, and the Conservative Party's concept of a property-owning democracy. More recently, employee share ownership forms a component of stakeholder capitalism. As expressed by Hutton (1997), stakeholding is based on the idea social and economic inclusion, and inclusion implies the membership. He writes that ". . . a stakeholder society and a stakeholder economy exist where there is a mutuality of rights and obligations constructed around the notion of economic, social and political inclusion" (p. 3).

[29] Treasury New Release 213/98.
[30] House of Commons Standing Committee Debates for the 1988–89 Session, Standing Committee G on the Finance Bill.

Stakeholder capitalism applies these principles to the workings of free market capitalism. Among the proposals made by Hutton are those concerning the work organization. For example, he suggests that ". . . a corporation director is not someone who aims to maximise profits within a given trading period; rather he or she is a trustee who must ensure the responsible use of the firm's assets on behalf of the different stakeholders who constitute the social organisation" (p. 6). The role of employee share ownership in stakeholder capitalism is expressed by Kelly et al. (1997) who write that ". . . (I)n theory the widespread use of employee ownership arrangements seems the ideal vehicle for realising the aspirations of stakeholding in the workplace. It can combine rights with obligations, it gives rise to increased participation and will arguably improve economic efficiency" (p. 252). In the context of social and economic reform, any improvement in company productivity resulting from the adoption of employee share ownership schemes is purely incidental.

The other main political justifications for employee share ownership are improvement in human relations and productivity. While it is possible to see improved human relations separately from enhanced company performance, the two are often viewed as being linked. Improved job satisfaction, greater commitment and cooperation, elimination of "them and us" attitudes, and other human relations improvements lead to increased productivity and company profitability. Evaluation of employee share ownership has concentrated mainly on human relations and company productivity and profitability.

Although nearly absent in parliamentary debate on employee share ownership, Pendleton (1998) has suggested that one of the attractions of employee share ownership is as a mechanism for moving companies away from *short-termism*. The market for corporate control is seen to focus company management on maintaining high levels of dividends and *current* profitability. As a result, there is reluctance to make longer-term investments. It is suggested that employee share holders have a longer time horizon than outside shareholders, particularly financial institutions, as they are interested in their long-time employment security.

EMPLOYEE SHARE OWNERSHIP, ATTITUDES AND COMPANY PERFORMANCE

Although there are many reasons why a company may implement an employee share scheme, and why a government may promote such schemes, only the effectiveness of share schemes in achieving two objectives, enhanced company performance and improved employee attitudes to the company, has been subjected to extensive systematic investigation. Employee share schemes are seen by some as providing incentives that align the interests of employees with those of the company and its shareholders. Although this argument is similar to the one used in justifying the use of executive share and share option schemes, it cannot be assumed that all-employee share schemes have the same effect as those for senior managers. Employee share schemes are also seen as leading to change in employees' attitudes to the company. From this it may be argued that attitude change is associated with behavioural change that results in improved company performance.

Employee Share Ownership as an Incentive

It is often suggested that share ownership provides employees with incentives that result in improved company performance. Agency theory offers one framework through which this proposition may be examined. The starting point of agency theory in this context is an assumption that most employees have some discretion over the way in which they perform their work. This includes discretion over the degree of effort they put into their work, the amount of initiative they use, how they cooperate with others, and so on. The company faces the problem of ensuring that employees work in a way that is congruent with the company's interests, usually viewed as being the interests of shareholders. Close monitoring of employees' performance and disciplining those identified as shirking is one approach that can be adopted to ensuring employees act in the interests of the company. However, such an approach is costly as, not only is it necessary to pay managers to monitor the employees' performance, it may also have an adverse effect on the employees themselves. The lack of trust implicit in close monitoring may both antagonize employees and encourage them to behave opportunistically.

Incentive schemes provide an alternative to monitoring. Some incentive schemes are based on individual performance, while others, including employee share schemes, are based upon collective performance. In the case of share schemes it is not only difficult for each employee to see the effect of his or her efforts on the performance of the company's shares, but the schemes may encourage free-riding. This arises where it is difficult for management to monitor each individual's performance and where each individual's reward depends on the efforts of everyone else. If there are n employees who share the reward, then the benefit received by an individual for his or her marginal effort is $1/n$ of the total reward associated with that effort. The larger the value of n, the greater the tendency of each employee to withhold his or her effort while trying to rely on the efforts of others.

The free-rider problem has been used as an argument against incentive schemes based on group performance. Weitzman and Kruse (1990), however, show that group incentives may be effective under certain circumstances. They begin by looking at group incentives as a form of the "prisoner's dilemma"[31]. Although all members of the group are better off if everyone works harder, each employee has the temptation to shirk because the effects of shirking will have a small impact on the rewards of individual employees. While accepting that free-riding is a problem in a single period game, Weitzman and Kruse argue that this may not be so in a multi-period setting. They argue that in such a setting, employees may monitor each other's performance and punish shirkers by, for example, ostracizing them. Group incentives therefore may, under certain conditions, defeat the prisoner's dilemma free-rider problem and induce greater productivity. It is, however, necessary to look at the conditions under which such an outcome is likely to occur.

Weizman and Kruse reach the conclusion that the outcome of a group incentive scheme depends on whether the employer can

---

[31] The "prisoner's dilemma" is a classic game. Two criminals are arrested and detained by the police. The evidence is such that neither can be convicted on the evidence alone. A confession would, however, provide evidence for conviction. By confessing a prisoner shows signs of remorse and can expect to receive a lighter sentence. Each prisoner is questioned separately. The dilemma each prisoner faces is whether to confess and receive a lighter sentence or not confess and either go free or receive a heavier sentence. In deciding what to do, each prisoner has to assess how likely it is that the other will confess.

convince its workforce to cooperate with each other. This is described by Levine and Tyson (1990) as follows: "The game-theoretic approach seems to suggest that whether the cooperative outcome is realized depends on whether an organization can convince its members that everyone pulling together is essentially a better idea than everyone pulling separately" (pp. 186–7). Weizman and Kruse propose that to "... get the productivity-enhancing effects, something more may be needed—something akin to developing a corporate culture that emphasizes company spirit, promotes group cooperation, encourages social enforcement mechanisms, and so forth" (p. 100).

From the perspective of agency theory it is likely to be more problematic to use share schemes as an incentive for employees than it is for senior managers. It is unlikely that employee share ownership will provide appropriate incentives unless the free-rider problem can be solved. Following Weizman and Kruse, and Levine and Tyson, such a solution depends on a company changing its corporate culture alongside the adoption of an employee share ownership scheme.

Employee Share Ownership, Attitudes and Behaviour

The incentive argument for employee share schemes assumes a link between the financial incentive, individual productivity and company performance. An alternative approach to linking employee share ownership to company performance is to examine the effect that ownership has on the attitudes of employees, particularly their attitudes towards the company. The general model that is being applied has three components: change in the attitudes of employees, followed by modified behaviour that is ultimately reflected in improved company performance. Employee share ownership is seen to encourage employees to identify more closely with the company, to be aware of the competitive pressures on the company, to reduce the feeling of *them and us*, and so on. The more favourable attitudes of employees are then thought to be reflected in work behaviour. This includes greater personal effort by employees, increased monitoring of colleagues' work performance, and a reduced likelihood of quitting the company. Finally, changes in individual behaviour are then thought to feed through to improvements in company performance.

The research evidence suggests that share ownership without employee participation in decision making is unlikely to improve employee attitudes and/or company performance. It is therefore necessary to consider the relationship between employee share ownership and participation. In this context, there is some evidence of an interaction between forms of share ownership and the type of employee participation used by the company. The literature would suggest that share ownership may mean more than simply possessing shares in a company. Here it is useful to explore the distinction made by Pierce et al. (1991) between *formal* and *psychological* ownership.

Employee Share Ownership and Employee Attitudes

In her review of the literature on employee share ownership and attitudes, Klein (1987) identifies three models of the psychological effects of employee ownership: an *intrinsic satisfaction* model, an *instrumental satisfaction* model, and an *extrinsic satisfaction* model. She suggests that underlying all three models is the assumption that employees satisfied with the share ownership scheme will be more motivated and committed to the company. The models differ in the assumption made about the relationship between share ownership and employees' attitudes.

The intrinsic satisfaction model, associated with Long (1978a,b), proposes that the fact of share ownership itself is sufficient to increase employees' commitment to, and satisfaction with, the company. Keef (1998) extends Long's model by suggesting that it is possible to identify three facets of organizational commitment: these are identification, involvement and loyalty. The act of becoming a shareholder is assumed to lead to an improvement in all three facets of organizational commitment. As job satisfaction is seen as being positively related to identification and involvement, the act of becoming a shareholder increases employees' job satisfaction, which in turn leads to improved company performance. This model has been tested by: (a) comparing the attitudes of employee owners with those of non-owners; (b) examining the relationship between the number of shares owned by employees and their attitudes to the organization; and (c) comparing employee owned with matched conventionally owned organizations. In their review of the literature, Pendleton et al. (1998) suggest that there is little empirical support for the intrinsic satisfaction model. Share ownership *per se*, therefore, does not appear to influence employee attitudes.

The extrinsic satisfaction model sees share ownership as increasing organizational commitment if such ownership is financially beneficial to employees. This model is therefore consistent with the economic literature on principal–agent relations in that financial incentives are viewed as being constructed so as align the interests of employees with those of the company's shareholders. As expressed by French (1987), this type of model sees share ownership as if it is an investment held by employees that heightens their perceptions of common interests with others in the company, and which results in greater organizational identification. In this tone, Buchko (1993) writes that "(T)he view of ownership as an investment suggests that employee attitudes, actions, organizational identification and commitment are due not simply to the fact of ownership or perception of control but to the financial value of the employee's position within the company" (p. 636). Klein (1987) tests this model by looking at the relationship between employee attitudes and: (a) employers' contributions to ESOPs and (b) share price returns. Although she finds that employee attitudes are positively related to the size of the contribution, no relationship is found between share price returns and employee measures.

Finally, the instrumental satisfaction model proposes that increases in employee commitment are brought about through the influence share ownership has on employee participation in company decision making. Involvement in decision making therefore has a crucial role in determining the effect of share ownership on employee attitudes. Ownership of company shares without employee participation is unlikely to affect the attitudes of employees. The instrumental satisfaction model has been tested by: (a) examining the relationship between worker ownership and worker influence; and (b) comparing employee-owned companies with conventionally owned companies. The research evidence, mainly from the US, provides strong support for the model.

The research evidence suggests that share ownership without participation in decision making is unlikely to have any significant effect on employee attitudes and on company performance. Further, the evidence in relation to the extrinsic satisfaction model would suggest that it is the size of the award that is important and not the financial gains resulting from ownership of the shares themselves. The instrumental satisfaction model receives the most support from the research literature. It is therefore appropriate to consider the relationship between employee share ownership and participation further.

Employee Share Ownership and Participation

Any effect of share ownership on company performance, and on the attitudes of employees, is shown to depend on the participation of employees in company decision making. The relationship between share ownership is emphasized by Jones and Pliskin (1991) in the conclusion to their review of the literature when they comment that the ". . . available evidence is strongly suggestive that for employee ownership schemes to have a strong positive impact they need to be accompanied by provision for worker participation in decision-making" (pp. 59–60). Although the distinction drawn earlier between industrial democracy and economic democracy is analytically useful, if the purpose of employee share ownership is to change employees' attitudes and behaviour and/or improve company, it is necessary to consider the interaction between the methods of economic and industrial democracies.

While it is reasonably clear that employee share ownership is only associated with increased company performance in the presence of some form of employee participation in company decision making, it is not clear what methods of participation are most effective. MacDuffie (1995) has drawn attention to the general notion of *human resource bundles*. By this he means that the various elements of human resources management practices must have a consistent organizational logic. In addition, the human resource management practices must be consistent with a company's strategy and with the production systems it employs. Ben-Ner and Jones (1995) develop a typology of employee ownership based upon the proportion of shares owned by employees and on the extent of the control rights they hold. Four levels of control rights are identified: none, participation in control, sharing in control and dominant control. They conclude that it is not meaningful to talk about schemes as being either good or bad; rather, it is necessary to consider the package of the claims of employees to the company's profits together with the extent of employee control within the company.

More recently McNabb and Whitfield (1998) use a fourfold classification of employee participation: (a) *direct/downward communications*, which includes practices such as team briefings; (b) *upward problem solving*, which includes quality circles and suggestion schemes; (c) *joint consultative committees/representative participation*, which are joint committees of management and employees; and (d) *financial participation* including share, share option and profit-sharing schemes. Consistent with the results of other studies, they find that there are strong interaction effects between financial participation and other types of employee participation. This means that the influence of financial participation on company performance cannot be understood in isolation. For example, they find that employee share ownership is only positively associated with company performance in companies with downward communication. They also find that there are negative interaction effects between employee share ownership and profit-sharing schemes. Profit-sharing schemes therefore may be substitutes for employee share option schemes, but the two do not complement each other.

The Concept of Ownership

The literature on employee share ownership would suggest that the influence of share ownership on the attitudes and behaviour of employees, and on company performance, is complex. Share ownership on its own is unlikely to result in change in the company or its employees. Employee share ownership can be understood further by examining the concept of *ownership* itself. Pierce et al. (1991) distinguish between *formal* and *psychological* ownership. Formal ownership is the set of rights attached to the shares, whereas psychological ownership is the perception of having an ownership stake in the company. Three components of formal ownership are identified: (a) equity possession—the claim on the net assets and profits of the company; (b) influence/control—the right to exercise some influence or control over the company; and (c) information sharing—the right to be informed about the company. These rights are possessed by all shareholders in a company.

Psychological ownership is suggested by Pierce and his colleagues to depend on high levels of equity possession, influence/control and information sharing. It also depends on a range of other factors, including the form of ownership, the commitment of management to employee share ownership, the perception of the legitimacy of ownership, and the expectations and orientation of employees. The psychological experience of ownership therefore not only depends on formal ownership, but on the attitudes and expectations of the employees themselves, and on the philosophy and actions of their employers.

The literature on employee share ownership does not usually distinguish between different forms of share ownership. There is, for example, an implicit assumption that results from studies on ESOPs can be generalized to other forms of ownership such as share and share option schemes. However, different types of ownership structures may differentially affect the individual experience of share ownership. The experience of ownership may also depend on the philosophical commitment of management to employee ownership. For example, Rosen et al. (1986) propose that managers need constantly to renew the feelings of ownership as experienced by employees. Individual expectations about the rights and responsibilities of ownership may also influence the experience of ownership. Such expectations are shaped by social and cultural factors. In both the US and UK the expected rights and responsibilities of share ownership include equity possession, influence or control, and information sharing. A problem is perceived to occur when there is incongruity between expectations and actual experiences. Any employee share scheme that does not incorporate all three components of ownership will therefore be incomplete. Linked to this is the perceived legitimacy of ownership. Employees have a notion as to what is right and proper in respect to the rights of share ownership. Blasi (1987) comments that employees have expectations as to what are appropriate rights in respect of their share ownership and are frustrated when these rights have been withheld. Finally there is the financial orientation of the employee shareholder. Where employees view share ownership simply as an investor, being concerned solely with the returns on their investment, they are unlikely to experience psychological ownership.

The Relationship Between Employee Share Ownership and Company Performance

Most of the research linking employee share ownership with company performance has been conducted in the US on ESOPs. However, improvement in company performance is only one reason why a company may wish to establish an ESOP. In addition to the general rationale for promoting employee share ownership, discussed above, two additional reasons can be identified for implementing ESOPs, both of which relate to regulatory factors. First, ESOPs may be used in order to obtain a tax benefit. Scholes and Wolfson (1992), however, report that the tax advantages that are favourable to ESOPs either are not unique to them or are not sufficiently valuable to cover the additional costs associated with the plans. Second, ESOPs may play a role in the market for corporate control by acting as an anti-takeover device, or "poison pill". It is therefore possible that the performance effects of ESOPs are masked by other factors.

Dhillon and Ramírez (1994) attempt to distinguish empirically between alternative motivations for the adoption of ESOPs by examining the stock market response to an announcement that a company has adopted an ESOP. Their analysis supports the view of Scholes and Wolfson that ESOPs are not implemented in order to obtain tax advantages. The analysis also indicates that the market responded positively to the adoption of an ESOP in the period before the Polaroid decision[32], and negatively afterwards. This result implies that the market viewed the adoption of an ESOP as a method of increasing company performance in the period prior to the Polaroid decision, but viewed it as an anti-takeover device afterwards. The role of ESOPs as an anti-takeover defense is examined further by Park and Song (1995). They argue that the effect of the adoption of an ESOP as an anti-takeover device so as to entrench management's position within the company will be corrected by the existence of a large outside shareholder who will monitor management's actions. Their findings are consistent with this view. The adoption of ESOPs is followed by improved performance in

---

[32] Polaroid issued a significant amount of its stock to an ESOP prior to a hostile tender offer by Shamrock Holdings which had the effect of blocking the takeover. The action of Polaroid was upheld in the Delaware Court in 1989.

companies with large external shareholders, but not in companies that do not have such shareholders.

Where the motivation for the adoption of an ESOP is to improve company performance, Hanford and Grasso (1991) suggest that any improvement may come about in two ways. First, a leveraged ESOP may be used by a company to finance expansion that in turn leads to improved productivity. However, Hanford and Grasso note that only a small proportion of ESOPs are leveraged and that an even smaller proportion of the funds that are raised are used to purchase or modernize plant and equipment. Second, the fact of employee share ownership in itself may lead to improved company performance. Hanford and Grasso suggest that any effects of ESOPs on company performance are more likely to be due to this second factor. If this is the case, the research on ESOPs may provide some indication as to the possible impact of employee share ownership on company performance.

A study by the US General Accounting Office (GAO), reported on by Hanford and Grasso (1991), compares the performance of ESOP companies with matched non-ESOP companies. Using data from the US Internal Revenue Service (IRS), the GAO study finds that, on average, ESOP companies did not consistently perform better than if they had not adopted ESOPs. Hanford and Grasso advance three possible explanations for this result. First, the statistical techniques used in the study may not be sufficiently sensitive to detect performance effects of ESOPs. Second, the ESOP structure itself may be a poor indicator of economic participation as the average size of the accounts is small and the benefit remote[33]. Finally, economic participation may only lead to improved company performance when other factors are present. In particular, they note the view that economic participation without participation in decision making is not sufficient to create a better motivated workforce.

A review of the literature by Thompson (1993) supports the findings of the GAO study. She concludes that although some of the earlier studies report a positive relationship between employee share ownership and company productivity, later research, ". . . which has sought to improve upon the previous work by using more rigorous analytical methods and larger sample sizes, has

---

[33] In the US ESOPs are regularly used as a retirement plan for employees. The situation is different in the UK where shares are distributed the employees prior to retirement.

found that employee ownership *per se* may have no positive effect on corporate profitability and productivity . . . However, these studies have consistently found that when employee ownership and a program of employee participation are combined, marked increases in profitability and productivity can be attained" (p. 828).

SUMMARY AND CONCLUSION

Employees are often provided with ways of acquiring shares in the company in which they are employed. Among the methods used to allow employees to acquire shares on advantageous terms are ESOPs, profit-sharing schemes and employee share options. The different ways of facilitating share ownership by employees are usually treated as substitutes for one another. Apart from the occasional reference to ESOPs as being different from other types of schemes, there is little to indicate why share option schemes may be set up in preference to other types of schemes. It is therefore necessary to consider employee share ownership generally rather than to examine a specific type of share or share option scheme.

A number of authors and organizations, including governments, have advocated that employees should become involved in the companies in which they work. Two types of method can be identified for achieving this goal. One is through techniques of *industrial* democracy; the other is through methods of involving employees in the financial performance of the company. Employee share ownership is one of these methods of *economic* democracy. The PEPPER Reports identify three reasons why government should encourage companies to adopt methods of economic democracy: to enhance company performance, to stabilize employment within companies and to reduce unemployment. The evidence is against the notion that methods of economic democracy can achieve the macro-economic goal of reduced unemployment. In addition, the effect of share ownership, as opposed to cash-based profit sharing, on employment stability is likely to be very limited. This leaves the possibility that employee share ownership may, like other methods of economic democracy, have a positive effect on company performance.

Employee share ownership may, however, be promoted for reasons other than enhancing company performance. In the US, employee share ownership has been viewed as a component of the "New

Capitalism", as a method of allowing the economically disenfranchised to acquire capital, and as a part of a movement towards a participatory capitalism. Share ownership by employees is also seen as part of a movement to achieving wider social and economic goals. Historically, these include the new economic order envisaged by John Pardoe of the Liberal Party, and the Conservative Party's concept of a "property-owning" democracy. Employee share ownership also has a role within the concept of "stakeholder capitalism". Located somewhere between these goals of social and economic reform and the goal of improving company performance, is the notion that employee share ownership is a mechanism for improving industrial relations; in particular it is seen as a mechanism for changing the attitudes of employees. This may be a goal in its own right, or a way of enhancing company performance. Other reasons for advocating employee share ownership include market forces within the labour market, fairness and as a correction to "short-termism".

The effectiveness of employee share ownership therefore has to be assessed against a number of criteria. However, analysis of employee share ownership has focused on it as an incentive to employees to improve productivity and hence enhance company performance, and as a mechanism for changing employees' attitudes. Like all group incentives, share ownership schemes possess the problem of encouraging employees to "free-ride". However, situations can be envisaged where it is possible to overcome the "free-rider" problem. Weitzman and Kruse (1990) characterize such a situation as being ". . . a corporate culture that emphasizes company spirit, promotes cooperation, encourages social enforcement mechanisms, and so forth" (p. 100). The evidence on employee share ownership and attitude change also indicates that share ownership *per se* is ineffective in changing the attitudes of employees. Rather it is necessary to combine share ownership with mechanisms that allow employees to participate in company decision making. There is also evidence that there is an optimal mix of type of share scheme and method of participation. Finally, the empirical evidence suggests that ESOPs on their own do not have an impact on company performance, but that performance is enhanced where ESOPs are combined with a programme of employee participation.

4
The Value of Share Option Compensation

Stock options are granted to employees and executives in return for employment services. Unless is it possible to measure the value of the employment services provided in exchange for the options, the value of the benefit to the employee and the cost to the company can only be determined by valuing the options. Usually it is assumed that this should be measured at the time the options are granted. The basis for valuing ESOs is to be found in the methods used for pricing traded options. The breakthrough in pricing such instruments was made by Black and Scholes (1973) in their derivation of a formula for the pricing of European call options on the shares of non-dividend paying companies. A European call option is one that can only be exercised at maturity. Modifications are necessary to the basic model in order to price a European option on shares of a company that pays dividends and to price American options; these are options that may be exercised on, or before, their expiry date. Options granted by a company on its own shares, usually referred to as *warrants*, present a more complex pricing problem. This is because the exercise of the warrant dilutes the interests of existing shareholders in the company's profits and net assets. Models to price traded options have been adapted to value warrants.

Although ESOs are often likened to options and warrants, they are usually more complex financial instruments. ESOs usually cannot be exercised in the early part of their lives, the *vesting* period, and then can be exercised at any time on, or before, their expiry[34].

---

[34] There may be institutional constraints that prevent options being exercised at certain times after they have vested. For example, an option holder may be prevented from exercising options in the period before the announcement by the company of its results, or when he or she holds *price-sensitive* information.

They therefore have the characteristic of *Bermuda* options, being like European options in the vesting period, and thereafter like American options. Unlike traded options, ESOs are usually non-transferable. This means that the holder can only realize their intrinsic value by exercising the option and selling the underlying shares. Holders of ESOs will usually forfeit the options if they leave the company during the vesting period, and may be obliged either to exercise the options or forfeit them if they leave after the options have vested. As the possibility of forfeiture and early exercise affect the value of ESOs at the time of grant it is necessary to incorporate expected termination of employment into the pricing model.

Investors holding traded options are generally independent of the company on whose shares the options are written. Holders of ESOs on the other hand are connected with the company as employees or managers. It is frequently proposed that share options are granted to senior managers, who are assumed to be self interested, in order to align their interests with those of the company's shareholders. Here, there is an assumption that the actions and decisions of senior managers can affect the market price of the company's equity shares. Self-interested managers can increase the value of their ESOs through decisions about the company's investments, its capital structure and the amount of its distributions. To the extent that the grant of share options affects the actions and decisions of their holders, this influence must be taken account of in determining the options' value.

Models that are used to price traded options assume that investors can form riskless hedges with the options and the underlying shares[35]. Institutional and wealth constraints, however, generally mean that the holders of ESOs cannot form such hedges and, because the options are not transferrable, they cannot sell them to investors who can. The assumption that it is possible to form riskless hedges is important because it means that it is *not* necessary to take account of investors' risk preferences in pricing the options. As holders of ESOs cannot form riskless hedges, or transfer the options, it is necessary to consider their risk preferences in valuing the options. It also raises the possibility that the value of ESOs to

---

[35] An alternative assumption is that the options' payoffs can be replicated by investing in shares and bonds.

their holders may be different to the cost of the company, or its shareholders, in granting them.

In pricing traded American options it is assumed that investors will only exercise the options at expiry or immediately before an ex-dividend date prior to expiry. Investors who require liquidity can realize the value of the option by selling it in the market. Holders of ESOs, however, are prevented from selling the instruments and so are only able to realize their intrinsic value by exercising the options and selling the shares acquired. ESOs may therefore be exercised earlier than otherwise equivalent traded options. It may also be rational for risk-averse holders of ESOs to exercise them early. To the extent that the expected exercise date is an important determinant of option value, the value of ESOs is related to the liquidity and risk preferences of their holders.

Although it is often assumed that models used to price traded options may be adapted to value ESOs, the problem of determining the value of ESOs is far more complex than the problem of pricing traded options. Not only is the instrument itself more complex but also it is necessary to consider a number of factors that are not included in the pricing of traded options. First, as an ESO is forfeited, or is obliged to be exercised early, if the holder leaves employment with the grantor company, it is necessary to consider the likelihood of the holder leaving the company at each point between grant and expiry of the option. Second, the holders of ESOs may, through their actions and decisions, change the value of the company and its shares, and so this effect must be considered in the ESO valuation. Finally, holders' liquidity and risk preferences may result in early exercise. Some attempts have been made to incorporate some of these factors into pricing models.

PRICING MODELS FOR EUROPEAN OPTIONS

Approaches to determining the value of ESOs are founded on those models used for price traded options. Here the major breakthrough was the work of Black and Scholes (1973) in the derivation of a formula for pricing European options. There have been two main approaches to option pricing in the quarter century since the publication of the paper by Black and Scholes. One is an analytical approach that derives from the work of Black and Scholes; the second approach, based upon numerical models, contains the binomial model developed by Cox et al. (1979) as well as methods based on Monte Carlo simulation and finite difference methodology.

Development of Modern Option Pricing Models

The development of modern option pricing theory dates from the work of Bachelier (1900). He deduced an option-pricing formula based on the assumption that share prices follow a Brownian motion with zero drift. Although there are flaws in the economics and mathematics of Bachelier's approach, his work contains insights and techniques that were to be used in subsequent attempts to price options. Sprenkle (1961), Boness (1964) and Samuelson (1965) developed models that price an option in terms of the expected payoffs, dependent on the movement in the price of the underlying shares, at the expiry of the option. The distribution of the expected payoffs must then be discounted to the present using an appropriate discount rate. Pricing options then became a problem in determining the appropriate risk premium. This depends on investors' risk preferences. One of the main contributions of Black and Scholes (1973) is to show that it is, in fact, not necessary to use any risk premium in pricing traded options.

Black and Scholes made a number of assumptions in deriving their pricing formula: (a) the option is European; (b) the rate of return on the underlying shares follows a log normal distribution; (c) the risk-free rate and the variance on the rate of return on the shares are constant throughout the life of the option; (d) no dividends are paid on the shares; (e) there are no transaction costs in buying and selling the shares or the option; (f) it is possible to borrow at the risk-free rate any fraction of the price of a security in order to buy or hold it; and (g) there are no restrictions or penalties for short selling. At the centre of their work is the notion of a riskless hedge constructed of a long position in the share and a short position in the option[36]. A small change in the share price will lead to a change in the value of the option. If the price of the share moves in a particular direction, the gain on one side will be compensated for by a loss on the other side. For example, consider an European call option that gives it

---

[36] Alternatively it is possible to create a *reverse hedge* with a short position in the share and a long position in the option.

holder the right to buy one share for 500p, and assume that if the price of the share changes by 20p, the value of the option changes by 10p. An investor can purchase one share and write (sell) two options. If the price of the share goes up 20p, the investor has a gain of 20p on the share and a loss of 20p on the options; the reverse will be true if the price of the share goes down. As the share price changes, however, it is necessary to adjust the ratio shares to options in order to maintain the hedged position. If the portfolio of shares and options is continuously adjusted so as to maintain a perfect hedge, then the return on the portfolio should be equivalent to the return on a risk-free security. Any other rate of return would mean that there is a possibility of arbitrage profits. Using assumptions about the way in which the price of the share evolves through time and the costless adjustment of the hedge portfolio, Black and Scholes derive a partial differential equation, the solution to which is the pricing formula.

The Black–Scholes Model

The Black–Scholes pricing formula contains five variables: (a) the current share price (S); (b) the exercise price of the option (E); (c) the risk-free rate (r); (d) the time to expiration of the option (T); and (e) the volatility of the share price (σ^2). The price of the call option, C, is given by:

$$C = SN(d_1) - Ee^{-rT}N(d_2)$$

where

$$d_1 = \frac{\ln(S/E) + (r + \sigma^2/2)T}{\sigma\sqrt{T}}$$

$$d_2 = d_1 - \sigma\sqrt{T}$$

$N(d_1)$ and $N(d_2)$ are cumulative normal probabilities. Three of the variables in the Black–Scholes model are directly observable. These are the exercise price, the current share price, and the time to the expiration of the option. The other two variables, the risk-free rate and the volatility of the share price, have to be estimated. There are problems in estimating both these variables.

The Black–Scholes formula indicates that the value of a European call option is the difference between the expected share price at expiration $(SN(d_1))$ and the expected cost of the option if it is exercised $(Ee^{-rT}N(d_2))$. The formula indicates how the value of a call option varies with changes in each of the variables. A call option is more valuable when: (a) the share price is higher; (b) the volatility of the share price is higher; (c) the time to expiration of the option is longer; (d) the probability of the option being exercised is greater; and (e) the risk-free rate is higher. The formula also suggests that when the probability of exercise is high, the value of a call option is $S - Ee^{-rT}$.

The Binomial Pricing Model

The binomial pricing model, derived by Cox et al. (1979), represents the other widely used approach to determining the value of a call option. The main difference between the binomial and the Black–Scholes models is the assumption made about the movement in the share price over time. Instead of the continuous process assumed in the Black–Scholes model, the binomial model divides the time until the expiry of the option into a finite number of periods, each of the same length. The share price at the end of each period is assumed to be either u times the price at the beginning of the period, or d times the initial price.

The price of an option is determined by creating a portfolio of the underlying share and a risk-free bond that replicates the payoffs from the option. If there are no arbitrage possibilities, the value of the option must be equal to the value of the *replicating portfolio*. In order to illustrate the construction of the replicating portfolio, consider an option with a life of one period. The value of the shares at the end of the period will be:

$$S_0 \diagrams{uS_0 \\ dS_0}$$

and the value of the option:

$$C_0 \diagdown \begin{array}{l} C_u = \text{Max}(uS_0 - E, 0) \\ C_d = \text{Max}(dS_0 - E, 0) \end{array}$$

If the exercise price of the option is 100, the current price of the share is 100p, u is 1.1 and d is 0.9, then at the end of the period the option will be worth 10p if the price of the share increases, otherwise it will be worthless. Now consider a portfolio consisting of a share and borrowing of 85p at the risk-free rate of 6% for the period. At the end of the period it will therefore be necessary to repay 90p. If the share price increases, the share will be worth 110p at the end of the period and, less the loan of 90p, the portfolio will be worth 20p. On the other hand, if the price of the share falls the share will be worth 90p and the portfolio will be worth nothing. As this portfolio exactly replicates the pay-offs from the call option, the value of the option must be the same as the value of the portfolio at the beginning of the period. In this example, the value of option is 15p[37]. If the price of the option were anything other than 15p there would be an opportunity to make riskless profits from arbitrage.

The intuition seen in the single period setting can be applied in a more realistic multi-period one. As the number of periods into which the life of the option is divided increases, the assumption that the share price follows a binomial process becomes more plausible. The value of a call option in a multi-period setting is calculated by considering a *lattice* representing the movement of the share price over the life of the option. By calculating the values of the option at expiration, it is then possible to use this information to construct a replicating portfolio for each of the point in the lattice one period before expiration. This process is then repeated for each period, with the final calculation indicating the option's current value. Cox and his associates show that the binomial formula converges to the Black–Scholes model where the probability distribution of share prices is lognormal and where the time to expiration is divided into increasing numbers of sub-intervals.

---

[37] The formula for a call option is $C = (pC_u + (1 - p)C_d)$ where $p = (r - d)/(u - d)$ and $(1 - p) = (u - r)/(u - d)$ and r is one plus the risk-free rate.

The Risk-free Rate and Volatility

Both the Black–Scholes and the binomial models for pricing a European call option use five variables, three of which, the exercise price, the current share price, and the time to the expiration of the option, are directly observable. However, the other two variables, the risk-free rate and the volatility of the share price, have to be estimated. The risk-free rate is usually derived from a government security with a maturity equal to that of the option[38].

Volatility may be estimated in one of two ways: one is to look at what the variance in the share price returns have been in the past. This raises the issue of what is an appropriate sampling period and what is the appropriate sampling frequency within the chosen period. There are also problems in deciding what price should be observed. For example, if it is decided to use daily prices, should the volatility estimate be based upon opening or closing prices, or on highs or lows, or on daily means or medians. An alternative to the volatility estimate derived from historic data is *implied* volatility. This is the volatility estimate that is calculated using a pricing model and information about the market price of the option and an estimate of the risk-free rate. The assumption underlying this implied volatility is that the pricing model faithfully captures the way in which traded options are priced in the market.

DIVIDENDS, AMERICAN OPTIONS AND WARRANTS

There are many differences between the ESOs granted by companies and traded European options written on the shares of non-dividend paying shares. Before looking at the particular problems of valuing ESOs, it is useful to consider the effects of payment of dividends on the underlying shares, to examine the problems of pricing American options, and to look at the problems of pricing warrants rather than options.

---

[38] The rate given for the government security has to be adjusted for use in the option pricing models. In the case of the Black–Scholes model it is necessary to calculate the continuously compounded rate and it is necessary to determine the rate for the length of each period in the case of the binomial model.

Dividends

The payment of a dividend during an option's life has an effect on the price of the underlying share. It is usual for the price of a company's share to fall when the share goes ex-dividend[39]. If the dividends to be paid during the life of the option are known, and if it is assumed that the price of the share will fall on the ex-dividend date by the amount of the dividend, then it is possible to view a European call option as being made up of two components. The first of these is a *riskless* component that represents the present value of all the dividends that will be paid during the life of the option discounted at the risk-free rate. The other is a *risky* component represented by the current share price less the present value of the dividends to be paid during the life of the option and whose volatility is that of the underlying share adjusted to take account of the present value of the dividend. The Black–Scholes model can be used to calculate the value of the risky component, and the value of the option is equal to that of the risky component plus the present value of the dividends[40].

It is also possible to adjust the binomial model to take account of dividends paid on the underlying stock. This is relatively straightforward where dividends are assumed to be paid continuously or where a dividend with a known yield, i.e. a proportion of the share price, is paid. It may be more complex where a known fixed dividend is to be paid.

American Options

An American option, one which can be exercised on or before the expiry date, is more complex to value than a European option. This is basically because in valuing the instrument it is necessary to consider the point in the option's life when the option will be exercised. In considering the exercise of American options it is necessary to examine call options on non-dividend paying shares separately from those on dividend paying shares.

American options on non-dividend paying shares should never

---

[39] The fall in the price of the share is, for tax and other reasons, usually less than the amount of the dividend.

[40] An alternative way of incorporating dividends into the Black–Scholes model is to assume that the dividend is paid continuously at a known yield.

be exercised early. This is because in exercising the option early the holder is sacrificing the time value of the option, i.e the difference between the options value and its intrinsic value. This may be illustrated by considering two situations. The first is where the option holder wishes to exercise the option early and keep the shares until a time after the option would have expired. In this case, if the option holder exercises an in-the-money option early, he or she will lose the amount of interest that could have been earned on the exercise price between the date of exercise and the expiry of the option. The investor will also lose the advantage of not acquiring the share if the option is out-of-the-money on the exercise date. The second is where the option holder wishes to exercise the option early because he or she believes the price of the share will fall before the expiry date. If the option is exercised early the option holder will gain the intrinsic value of the option at that time. However, the current share price represents the market's current expectations of the future price of the share and so, for the reasons described above, there must be an investor who is willing to pay a price for the option that is greater than the intrinsic value of the option. Therefore the option should be sold rather than exercised. Because an American option on the shares of a non-dividend paying company will not be exercised until the expiry date, such an option can be valued *as if* it were European.

The position is more complex in the case of an American call option on the shares of a dividend paying company. In this case it may be optimal to exercise an American option immediately before an ex-dividend date. If the option holder exercises the option before the ex-dividend date he or she acquires shares that hold the right to the dividend. The price of the share is expected to fall immediately the shares go ex-dividend because shares acquired after the ex-dividend date do not have the right to the dividend. The fall in the share price on the ex-dividend date in turn leads to a reduction in the value of the option. It is optimal to exercise an American option immediately before an ex-dividend date if the dividend is greater than the expected time value of the option immediately after the shares go ex-dividend.

A number of models have been developed to price American options on the shares of dividend paying companies. The binomial model has been adapted to incorporate the conditions under which an American option will be exercised early, and there have been a number of analytical models have been proposed.

Warrants

Unlike options which are written by third parties, warrants are written by a company and give investors the right to acquire that company's own shares. If the option is exercised then the company issues new shares to the warrant holder. Therefore, unlike options, the exercise of a warrant results in a change to the capital structure of the issuing firm. An investor will only exercise a warrant if the share price is at least as high as the warrant's exercise price. When a warrant is exercised, therefore, the company will usually issue shares for an amount less than their current market price. This will have the effect of *diluting* the interests in the company of pre-existing shareholders.

In order to determine the value of warrants it is therefore necessary to incorporate the effects of dilution into the pricing model. It is not only the dilution that occurs on the exercise of the option that needs to be incorporated into the pricing model, it is also the potential dilution that is reflected in share prices throughout the life of the warrant. The usual approach taken is to view warrants as options on a company's total equity, shares plus warrants, rather than just shares. This means that it is not only necessary to adjust the payoff on exercise of the warrant for the effects of dilution. It is also necessary to incorporate the volatility of the company's total equity rather than just of its shares.

DIFFERENCES BETWEEN ESOS AND TRADED OPTIONS

The basic option pricing models are developed to value European options written by a third party. Modifications have been made to pricing models in order that they can be applied to American style options and to warrants. ESOs are granted by the company and therefore are warrants rather than options. They are, however, more complex as financial instruments than the warrants that are traded in secondary markets. In order to explore the issues in valuing ESOs it is necessary to identify the ways in which they differ from traded options before exploring the ways in which these differences affect the pricing of the instrument. Some of the differences between ESOs and traded options have to do with the structure of the instrument itself; other differences have to do with their holders and the constraints which may be placed upon them.

Structure of ESOs

Although there are variations in the structure of ESOs, there are basic structural features that underlie most ESOs. Those features that have an impact on valuation are: (a) non-transferability—unlike options and warrants that are traded in secondary markets, there are usually restrictions placed on managers and employees which prevent the sale ESOs to third parties; (b) vesting—ESOs cannot generally be exercised during a period, usually 3 years, after grant; and (c) forfeiture—ESOs are usually forfeited if the holder leaves the grantor company. If the holders leave the company during the vesting period then the options are lost, whereas holders of ESOs that have vested may exercise them before leaving their employment or, under many schemes, within a short period afterwards. These three features of ESOs have a profound impact on their valuation.

In addition to the greater complexity of ESOs, it is usually not possible for their holders to form the type of riskless hedge that is assumed if the riskless rate of interest is to be used in determining the options' price. If option holders cannot construct a riskless hedge then, if the option can be traded in a secondary market, it would be appropriate for the holder to sell the option to someone who can construct such a hedge[41]. The inability to transfer ESOs means that their holders must bear risk. Since holders of ESOs are likely to have a considerable part of their wealth, including their human capital, invested in the company, they bear the specific risk of the company as well as market risk.

Vesting provisions give ESOs the characteristic of *Bermuda* options since they have the character of a European option during the vesting period and an American option for the period after vesting until maturity. It is relatively straightforward to price Bermudan options using, for example, a modified binomial model. The problem

---

[41] Schizer (1999) argues that although it may be possible for executives to enter a transaction in the derivatives market that "simulates" the sale of ESOs, there are tax and other barriers that mean that executives rarely adopt such strategies.

in pricing ESOs is the interaction between vesting and forfeiture provisions. If the holder of an ESO leaves the company during the vesting period then the option is lost. However, early exercise may be forced by the holder leaving the company after the ESO has vested. In order to determine the value of ESOs, therefore, it is necessary to consider the probability of the holder leaving the employing company at each point in the option's life.

Traded options usually have a maturity of less than 1 year. On the other hand, ESOs frequently have an expiration date of up to 10 years from the date of grant. Because the grantor company will issue new issue shares if the option is exercised, ESOs are warrants and not options. Although option pricing models can be modified to price warrants, the long maturity of ESOs presents problems. In particular, the long maturity date highlights problems in determining 3 of the variables in option pricing models: the volatility of the underlying share, the risk-free rate of interest, and the expected dividends to be paid during the life of the option.

Some Characteristics of Holders of ESOs

The possibility of constructing a riskless hedge with options and the underlying shares means that it is not necessary to consider the characteristics of holders and writers in valuing traded options. In particular, it is not necessary to consider their risk preferences. This is not, however, the case with ESOs. Holders of ESOs face both practical and legal restrictions in short selling the underlying shares and so cannot construct the riskless hedge. Further, the non-transferability of ESOs means that the options cannot be transferred to those who can construct such a hedge.

The combination of short-selling restrictions and non-transferability makes it is necessary to consider the risk preferences of the holders of ESOs in valuing the instrument. Risk preferences enter into ESO valuation in two ways. First, if ESOs are to be valued from the perspective of those who hold them, it is necessary to identify the discount rate that reflects the holders' risk preferences. Because of the wealth of holders is undiversified, the discount rate will incorporate *both* the specific risks of the company granting the options and market risk. Second, it may be optimal for the holder of ESOs to exercise them on an earlier date than would normally be expected for an American option. Early exercise of ESOs may also be determined by the liquidity preferences of their holders as, because of non-transferability, holders can only realize any gain by exercising the option and selling the shares acquired.

SHARE OPTION SCHEMES AND CORPORATE POLICY

The rationale for the grant of share options to senior managers is often stated as being one of aligning the interests of managers with those of the shareholders. Managerial actions and decision making are therefore expected to change following the grant of ESOs. However, the impact of ESOs on managerial decision making may not necessarily be in the interests of shareholders. The rationale for granting options to managers is that managers, being self interested, will make decisions that increase the value of both the options they hold and the underlying shares. It is, however, possible to increase the value of options by other means: specifically, by changing the volatility of the shares through investment and capital structure decisions, and by reducing dividends paid to the shareholders.

Volatility, Investment Decisions and Gearing

Holders of ESOs have incentives both to increase, and to reduce, the volatility of the market price of the underlying share. The value of ESOs depends on the volatility of the company's share price. *Ceteris paribus*, the value of ESOs increases with an increase in the volatility of the price of the underlying share. It may therefore be expected that the adoption of share option schemes is linked to an increase in the riskiness of the company's projects and an increase in its gearing[42]. On the other hand, managers cannot usually hedge option risk and they invest a significant part of their wealth, including their human capital, in the company. As a consequence their personal wealth is under-diversified. Managers therefore have incentives to reduce the riskiness of the company's earnings by selecting investment projects that reduce the volatility of the company's earnings stream

---

[42] Merton (1974) has shown that if a company has riskless debt, the variance in the returns of the company's shares are equal to the variance of the returns on the company's assets multiplied by the square of the value of the firm to the value of its ordinary shares.

and/or reducing the company's gearing. The effect of ESOs on decision making is therefore an empirical question.

DeFusco et al. (1990) have investigated whether the adoption of ESOs leads to an increase in managerial risk taking. They looked at events surrounding the adoption of share option schemes by a sample of US companies. In particular, they looked at changes in the volatility of the companies' share prices following the announcement of the adoption of a scheme. They did this in two ways: by calculating the volatility implied in traded options on the companies' shares[43], and by estimating the change in the volatility of the share price directly. The volatility of the share price implied by the price of the companies' traded options is found to be higher in the 6 months following the announcement of the adoption of the plan than it was in the 6 months prior to the announcement. This suggests that market participants expect future volatility to be higher. The actual volatilities of companies' share prices are also found to increase after the adoption of the scheme.

As well as examining the effect of the adoption of share option schemes on the volatility of the companies' shares, DeFusco and his colleagues analysed the effect that the announcement had on the price of the companies' shares and their bonds. The shares of a company partly financed by debt can be viewed as call options on the company's assets that can be exercised by paying the face value of the debt. Therefore, like an option, the value of shares in geared companies is increased by increasing the volatility of the companies' net assets. The value of the debt decreases as the volatility of the net assets increases. If managers make more risky investments or increase gearing as a consequence of the adoption of a share option scheme then there should be an increase in companies' share prices with the announcement of adoption of the scheme and a fall in their bond prices. This is what DeFusco and his colleagues found.

Agrawal and Mandelker (1987) adopted a different approach to examining the effect of ESOs on investment and financing decisions. Their study focused on companies that were either acquiring other companies or selling off part of their activities, and they examined changes in the volatility of the companies' share prices and gearing

---

[43] The price of the traded options is assumed to be determined by the Black–Scholes model and an algorithm is used to obtain the value of the volatility of the company's share prices.

in relation to managers' holding of shares and ESOs. They found that the values of shares and share options held by senior managers of companies was greater in the case of companies where the volatility of the share price increased following the acquisition or disinvestment than for companies where the volatility fell after the event. A similar picture emerged in relation to changes in gearing, with senior managers of companies whose gearing increased having larger holdings of shares and share options.

The results of the study by DeFusco and his colleagues would suggest that market participants at least expect senior managers of companies adopting share option schemes to modify their investment and capital structure decisions so as to increase the volatility of the companies' share prices. This is supported more directly by Agrawal and Mandelker who point to the effect of managerial holdings of shares and share options on company investment and capital structure decisions. It has been suggested that managers are more risk averse than shareholders. If this is the case, ESOs may serve to align more the risk preferences of managers with those of the shareholders.

Dividend policy

Most ESOs do not incorporate mechanisms to compensate holders for the effects of dividends paid by the company. *Ceteris paribus*, the payment of a dividend will result in a decrease in the price of the company's shares. The impact of dividends on the price of the company's shares feeds through to the value of the options granted on those shares. Managers therefore have an incentive to reduce the dividend in order to increase the value of the options they hold. Following this argument, Lambert et al. (1989) hypothesized that managers *decrease* the level of dividends, relative to what it would otherwise have been, following the initial adoption of a share option scheme.

Lambert and his colleagues investigated the hypothesis that there is a relative decrease in the level of dividends following the adoption of share option schemes by looking at the dividends paid by a sample of large US companies following the initial adoption of share option schemes. They used a model developed by Marsh and Merton (1987) to forecast what the dividends would have been had the companies not adopted a share option scheme[44], and compared the forecasts with the actual dividends paid by the companies. The results of the study suggest that the initial adoption of executive share option schemes is associated with a reduction in the level of the companies' dividends. Further, there is a downward drift in the level of dividends, compared with the forecasted level, following the initial adoption of the scheme. Finally, the authors found some evidence of an inverse relationship between the change in the level of a company's dividend and the size of the options granted to senior management.

NON-TRANSFERABILITY, SHORT-SELLING RESTRICTIONS AND THE VALUE OF ESOS

Models for pricing traded options assume that the option holder can construct a riskless hedge with the option and the underlying share. This is not possible for the holders of ESOs who face short-selling constraints and who, by the conditions of the options, cannot transfer them. As a consequence it may be optimal for risk averse holders of ESOs to exercise their options early. The expected life of an ESO may therefore be less than the time to its expiry. This will have an impact on the value of the option. The inability of holders of ESOs to construct a riskless hedge also means that it is not possible to use the riskless rate to value the option. The risk aversion of holders of ESOs has an impact on the value the options have to them.

Once vested, ESOs have the character of American options. It is assumed in pricing American options that the holder will follow an exercise strategy that maximizes the value of the option. Where the company does not pay a dividend, it is assumed that the option will be exercised at maturity. Earlier exercise may, as discussed earlier, be optimal where the option is on the shares of a dividend paying company. In the case of ESOs, however, the risk aversion and/or liquidity preferences of holders may make earlier exercise optimal. The effect of non-transferability and short-selling restrictions is therefore twofold. First, early exercise of ESOs affects both their value to holders and their cost to shareholders. Second, it raises the

---

[44] The Marsh–Merton model assumes that dividends are a function of permanent earnings and some long-run dividend pay-out.

possibility that the value of ESOs to their holders may be different to their cost to shareholders.

Risk Aversion and the Early Exercise of ESOs

The optimal exercise strategy for an American style warrant is to exercise the option at maturity or, where dividends are paid on the underlying share, immediately before an ex-dividend date prior to maturity. The features of ESOs, together with the characteristics of their holders, may make earlier exercise optimal. In particular, the risk aversion and liquidity preferences of holders make it optimal to exercise the option early under certain conditions. These relationships have been explored by Kulatilaka and Marcus (1994), Huddart (1994), and Carpenter (1998). There are common features to the models developed in all these papers.

In the model developed by Kulatilaka and Marcus, the holder of an ESO has the choice of continuing to hold the option or exercising it, selling the shares and acquiring a riskless asset. The authors use a simple binomial model in which the option, with a maturity of two periods, is granted with an exercise price at-the-money at the beginning of the first period. The choice about exercising the option is made at the end of the first period. If the option is in-the-money at the end of the first period, the holder has the choice of exercising the option, or keeping the option and receiving an uncertain amount at the end of the second period. If the option is exercised, the profit is invested in a risk-free asset that will provide a certain return at the end of the second period. The holder's choice will depend on his or her level of risk aversion. Above a particular level of risk aversion, the value to the holder of the higher *uncertain* amount will be less than the value of the risk-free asset acquired from the profits of exercising the option at the end of the first period. It is optimal under these circumstances to exercise the option at the end of the first period.

The authors develop an extended model that incorporates a larger number of periods, with the option holder having the choice of exercising the option at the end of each period. Using this model, the authors examine the relationship between early exercise and a number of factors. They show that in general ESOs are exercised earlier the more risk averse the holder, the less non-option wealth of the employee, and the greater the volatility of the underlying shares. Huddart and Carpenter use a similar argument in determining the point at which holders exercise their ESOs.

The inability of managers and employees holding ESOs to construct a riskless hedge, or to sell their options to someone who can construct such a hedge, therefore affects the decisions to exercise their options. As the holder's level of risk aversion, together with the amount of his or her non-option wealth, affects the expected timing of exercise, holders of ESOs with identical characteristics are likely to exercise their options at different times.

Value of ESOs to Holders and Cost to Shareholders

Option pricing models are based on the assumption that the riskiness of the option's payoffs can be perfectly hedged by continuous and costless adjustment of a portfolio containing the option, the underlying share and a bond. The inability of holders of ESOs to do this, together with the non-transferability of the options, means that they do not value ESOs as highly as would be implied by models used to price exchange-traded options. The risk preferences and non-option wealth of holders of ESOs may not only affect the timing of exercise, but also the value of the options given the timing of exercise. ESOs may be worth less to their holders than the cost to shareholders in granting them.

Holders of ESOs, a company's managers and its employees, have a significant proportion of their wealth, including human capital, invested in the company. They are unable to eliminate specific risk through diversification and so bear both company-specific, as well as market, risk. Lambert et al. (1991) examine the effect of degree of risk aversion and amount of wealth linked to the value of the company on the value of ESOs . They show that the value of an ESO to a highly risk averse individual whose wealth is mainly tied to the value of the company is, under given conditions, small compared with the value implied by the Black–Scholes model.

The cost of a company granting ESOs may be assumed to be borne by the company's shareholders. It is therefore necessary to consider the cost of granting ESOs from the perspective of share-holders. Not only may shareholders be assumed to hold diversified portfolios, so eliminating any company-specific risk, but they may also be expected to construct riskless hedges. Therefore, risk-neutral measures of the ESOs are appropriate from the point of view of shareholders.

EARLY EXERCISE OF ESOS

One of the main factors in determining the value of an option is its maturity. Share options granted to managers and employees have the character of both European and American options. They cannot, like a European option, be exercised during the vesting period. After vesting they usually have the character of an American option. In pricing American options it is necessary to estimate when the option will be exercised. For an American option issued by a company that does not pay a dividend, it is optimal to exercise the option at maturity. The situation is somewhat different when the company does pay dividends for, in these cases, it may be optimal to exercise the option immediately prior to an ex-dividend date before the option matures. Modifications can be made to the basic binomial pricing model to provide for the pricing of American options.

Two sets of factors make it likely that holders of ESOs do not follow the same exercise strategy as holders of traded American options. First, as previously discussed, the general inability to construct a riskless hedge combined with the non-transferability of most ESOs means that it is necessary to consider the risk preferences of ESO holders. Risk aversion may, as already seen, may make it optimal for holders of ESOs to exercise them early. The non-transferability of ESOs also means that it is necessary to consider the liquidity preferences of holders. Second, vesting and forfeiture features make it necessary to consider the likelihood of holders leaving employment with the company. The option is forfeited if the holder ceases to be employed by the company during the vesting period. Leaving the company's employment after vesting usually leads to exercise of in-the-money options and forfeiture of ESOs that are out-of-the-money.

Estimating the life of ESOs therefore requires consideration of the risk and liquidity preferences of holders, and of their future patterns of employment. Where ESOs are held widely within a company it may be possible to consider the general characteristics of holders rather than the preferences and likely future pattern of employment of each of them. In these circumstances it is useful to identify *observable* conditions that are associated with early exercise. This is helpful in valuing ESOs from the perspective of a company's shareholders, although not in valuing them from the holders' perspective. It is necessary to consider how the possibility of early exercise is incorporated into pricing models.

Empirical Studies of Early Exercise

The most extensive study of exercise patterns is the one by Huddart and Lang (1996) who examined exercise behaviour of over 50 000 holders of ESOs employed by eight companies. They specifically sought to answer four questions: (a) to what extent are ESOs exercised early?; (b) does early exercise cluster around specific, predictable points during the life of the options?; (c) how well can exercise be predicted on the basis of past history or comparison across companies?; and (d) are there factors other than time that appear to determine early exercise?

The results of the study suggest early exercise is common. Early exercise may mean a significant loss of value to the holders. Huddart and Lang demonstrate that this is so by comparing the intrinsic value of the option[45] with the value calculated using the Black–Scholes model and showed that, in many cases, this difference was large. The study shows that for seven of the eight companies in the study, the median of the amount of the ESOs' lives that had elapsed at the time of exercise ranged from 21 to 38%. In the other company the median is 92%. There is also evidence of different exercise patterns in different grants by the same company. Finally, Huddart and Lang also found that exercise patterns vary according to the level of the employee within the company.

Given that there are differences in exercise patterns between companies, and between grants by the same company, Huddart and Land attempted to identify factors that influence exercise behaviour. These include: (a) returns on the companies' shares in the period prior to exercise; (b) the ratio of the market value of the

---

[45] The *intrinsic* value of an option is the difference between the market price of the underlying shares and the exercise price.

companies' shares to the exercise prices of the options; (c) the volatility of the companies' share prices in the period prior to exercise; and (d) a measure of vesting. The results show exercise is positively associated with returns on companies' shares, the ratio of the market value of the companies' shares to exercise prices, and the volatility of the companies' shares. There is also evidence of a high level of exercise in the 3 months after ESOs vest.

Other studies of exercise behaviour are by Hemmer et al. (1996) and Carpenter (1998). Hemmer and his associates examined the exercise behaviour of 74 senior executives. They looked at the relationship between *investment risk* of the options and the number of years remaining in the life of the option at the time of exercise. Investment risk is measured by the variance of the returns on the ESO. There is evidence from the study that the ESOs with higher volatility are more likely to be exercised early. This result is seen as consistent with the view that managers exercise ESOs early in order to diversify their risks. Carpenter studied exercise from 40 companies, mainly large manufacturers. She looked at the correlations between a number of variables and found, amongst other things, that options with longer vesting periods tend to be exercised later and deeper in the money.

The Implication of Early Exercise for the Valuation of ESOs

The results of the empirical studies indicate that holders of ESOs do not follow an exercise policy similar to the one assumed to be adopted by holders of traded American options and warrants. The value of ESOs is therefore likely to be determined by a larger set of variables than the one incorporated into models to price traded options. These additional variables relate to the characteristics of the ESOs themselves, the underlying shares and the relationship between the two. In particular: (a) the proximity to the vesting date; (b) the volatility of the underlying shares; and (c) the relationship between the market price of the shares and the ESO's exercise price. There is also some evidence that exercise behaviour varies according to the level of the holder within the company. In addition to the above variables, it would seem important to include labour market variables.

VALUATION MODELS

The non-transferability of ESOs affects the pricing of the options in several ways. First, employee risk aversion, due to the inability to construct a riskless hedge with the option or to sell it to someone who can, may result in it being optimal for holders to exercise their ESOs earlier than if they were traded American options. These conditions also mean that risk-neutral valuation is inappropriate in determining the value of ESOs to their holders, although risk-neutral valuation is possible in calculating their cost to shareholders. Therefore, it is necessary to determine the perspective from which the valuation is being made. Non-transferability, combined with forfeiture of the option when holders leave the company, means that the option is actually forfeited if the holder leaves the company during the vesting period or may be exercised early if the option has vested. The pricing model therefore needs to incorporate rates of departure from the company. In incorporating rates of departure it is necessary to consider the relationship between this variable and others in the model.

The effect of risk aversion on early exercise has been considered elsewhere in this chapter, and the works of Kulatilaka and Marcus (1994), Huddart (1994) and Carpenter (1998) could form the basis of pricing models. A basic problem is that the risk preferences of option holders are not observable. Mozes (1995) has taken the basic intuition in these models to develop a method for determining the upper bound of the value of ESOs. Departure rates have also been incorporated into pricing models by Jennergren and Näslund (1993) and by Cuny and Jorion (1995). The need for a practical approach to valuing ESOs is recognized by the FASB.

The Upper Bound of the Value of ESOs

Mozes (1995) has developed a model to determine the upper bound of the cost of ESOs to shareholders. The model is based upon the idea that the inability of holders to construct a riskless hedge with their options and the undiversified nature of their investments leads them to exercise their ESOs early. In this way Mozes is following the line of argument developed by Huddart (1994) and Kulatilaka and Marcus (1994).

Holders of ESOs are seen as bearing both specific and market risk in their options. Following the argument that investors can eliminate specific risk through holding a diversified portfolio, Mozes assumes that the price of securities only reflects market risk. Holders of ESOs are therefore compensated for market risk but not specific risk. At any time that ESOs are in-the-money, their holders can exercise them and realise the intrinsic value of the options by selling the shares. The amount can then be invested in a well diversified portfolio that has the same level of risk as the total, specific and market, risk of the company's shares. However, since all the risk of the diversified portfolio is market risk, all the risk of the portfolio is incorporated into its value. Following this line of reasoning, Mozes suggests that when the price of the company's shares reaches a certain point, the *switching price*, it is optimal for the holder to exercise the option and invest its intrinsic value is a perfectly diversified portfolio.

The upper bound of the cost of ESOs is determined by first identifying the probability distribution of the time that the company's share price first exceeds the switching price. Therefore, the probability of the share price first exceeding the switching price is calculated for each point in time after vesting. This is calculated using a binomial process to model the path of the company's share price. The value of an option with a maturity equal to each point in time after the option vests is calculated using the Black–Scholes model and weighted by the probability of the option being exercised at that time. From this the upper bound of the value of the ESO is determined by summing the weighted Black–Scholes' prices.

Models that Incorporate Departure from the Firm

ESOs are not transferable and typically cannot be exercised after their holders leave the company. Holders must therefore either exercise their ESOs when they leave the company, or else the options are forfeited. Departure from the company means either ESOs are forfeited or exercised early. The expected departure rate of ESO holders therefore becomes important in the valuation of the options. This means a further variable must be incorporated into the pricing model. The problem of doing this is discussed by Noreen and Wolfson (1981). They see identification of the probability distribution of departures from a company as being basically an actuarial problem. However, Noreen and Wolfson suggest that the problem is complicated by the probability of ESO holders leaving the company being dependent on the path of the share price.

Jennergren and Näslund (1993) incorporate the rate at which holders of ESOs may leave their jobs, λ, into a valuation model. In the model, the option is cancelled if the holder leaves during the vesting period, or may lead to early exercise if the holder departs after the option has vested. Although the rate of departure, λ, used in the model is held constant, Jennergren and Näslund acknowledge that it could depend on the share price and time to expiration. Foster et al. (1993) suggest that the magnitude of λ depends on a number of factors, including the mobility and promotion potential of the employee as well as his or her propensity to change employment. These conditions, in turn, are seen to depend on a number of factors including the employee's skills and the transferability of these skills, the employee's utility function, wealth, and probability beliefs, the employee's position within the company, the employee's age, the industry in which the company operates, employment alternatives, and the general economy. The authors note that many of these conditions are likely to change through time.

Cuny and Jorion (1995) reason that, for executives, ESOs give executives an incentive to stay when the price of the underlying share, and so the option value, is high. On the other hand, poor executive performance is reflected in the share price and may lead to dismissals. They consequently expect a negative correlation between share price and departure from the company[46] and incorporate this relationship into a valuation model. Comparing the values of ESOs computed using their model with that of Jennergren and Näslund (1993), they find that ignoring the relationship between share price and departure rates leads to a substantial undervaluation of ESOs.

The FASB Approach

The FASB has developed an approach to valuing ESOs for financial reporting purposes. Basically the Board, in SFAS No. 123 *Accounting*

---

[46] Empirical support for this assumption comes from Coughlan and Schmidt (1985) and Warner et al. (1988).

for stock-based compensation, is allowing companies to choose a pricing model, such as the Black-Scholes or binomial models, and providing guidance as to how these models can be adapted for use in valuing ESOs. The purpose of the valuation is to calculate the *cost* of the ESOs that companies should report. Valuation is therefore from the perspective of shareholders and not the recipients of the options. The adoption of the shareholders' perspective is not only appropriate for the purposes of financial reporting, it also makes it possible to assume risk neutrality in the valuation.

Two main features of ESOs are identified which have an impact on valuation: forfeiture of options during the vesting period and the inability to transfer vested options to third parties. Option values at the time of grant are reduced by the expected forfeiture rate during the vesting period. The FASB indicates the expected forfeiture rate should be based upon historical turnover rates and expectations about the future rate. The non-transferability of vested options is viewed solely in terms of its impact on the expected life of options. ESOs are therefore valued as if they had a maturity equal to their expected life. The Board provides the following guidance in determining the expected lives of ESOs: (a) the average length of time similar grants of ESOs have remained outstanding in the past; (b) the length of the vesting period as, other things being equal, the amount of time employees hold options after the end of the vesting period is inversely related to the length of the vesting period; and (c) the expected volatility of the underlying shares as employees tend to exercise options on highly volatile shares earlier than on shares with low volatility[47]. Determination of the expected life of ESOs is therefore based on past experience, expectations of the future, and the characteristics of the underlying shares and the ESOs themselves.

The value of an option is not a linear function of its expected life. Rather, the value increases at a decreasing rate as the expected life of the option increases. This means that the combined value of options with lives, of say 4 and 6 years, is not the same as two options with lives of 5 years. The cost of ESOs is calculated on the basis of the expected lives of options held by a group, or groups, of employees. Because the value of ESOs is not a linear function of

---

[47] This is consistent with the results of Huddart and Lang (1996) and of Hemmer et al. (1996).

their expected lives, it is important that groups of employees with relatively homogeneous expected exercise behaviour are identified.

Instead of calculating the value of ESOs based directly upon their expected lives, the FASB offers companies the alternative of calculating the value based upon the market price of the share at which the option is likely to be exercised. It may, for example, be expected that ESOs will be exercised when the market price of the company's shares is 150% of the exercise price. The rationale for this alternative approach is that holders seem to be more likely to exercise deep in-the-money options than they are to exercise options near-to-the-money.

As well as providing an adaptation to option pricing models to take account of forfeiture during the vesting period and early exercise, the FASB offers guidance on the choice of the risk-free rate and the estimation of expected volatility and dividends. The risk free rate to be used is the one implied by a zero-coupon US Government issue with a remaining term equal to the option being valued. Although it is recommended that the volatility estimate should be based on the historical volatility of the underlying shares, the Board recognize that adjustments may be necessary for recently quoted companies and to take account of the mean-reversion tendency of volatilities. Dividends are usually incorporated into option pricing models through the expected dividend yield, rather than expected dividend payments. Models can, however, be adapted to incorporate dividend payments. The FASB recommends that companies take account of expected dividend growth where payments are used.

SUMMARY AND CONCLUSION

Among the measures intended to restrain excessive executive compensation in the Corporate Pay Responsibility Act, introduced in the US Senate by Senator Carl Levin, is the specification of the method for calculating the present value of share option compensation and the requirement that this cost be reflected in corporate income statements. It is often assumed that the value of share option compensation can be measured using one or other of the models developed to price traded options. These models can be broadly divided into *analytic* and *numerical* models. The analytic models are mainly based upon the insights provided by Black and Scholes, and the binomial model is probably the most widely used of numerical models. As initially developed, the Black–Scholes and the binomial models focused on the pricing of European options on the shares of non-dividend paying companies. The models have been adapted to price options on the shares of dividend paying companies, American style options and warrants.

Although it is suggested that share option compensation can be valued using option pricing models developed to price traded options, there are a number of features of ESOs which make them considerably more complex to value. First, ESOs are warrants, rather than options, and usually have the character of an American-style warrant for much of their life. They are also usually granted by companies that pay dividends on their equity shares. Second, the long maturity of ESOs forces reconsideration of some of the variables that are used in the pricing models themselves. Third, short-selling restrictions and the non-transferability of ESOs mean that the holders of these instruments cannot use the type of hedging strategy that underlies the models to price traded options. These restrictions make it necessary to consider both the risk and the liquidity preferences of holders. Finally, vesting and forfeiture mean that the valuation model must include the probabilities of holders leaving the company, through their choice or otherwise, during the life of the ESO. Other institutional factors may also affect option values. For example, insider trading laws may restrict the times when the options may be exercised. Finally, at least some holders of ESOs may, through their investment and policy decision, be able to affect the variables in the model.

ESOs differ from traded options in that they are held by individuals who may have the power to make decisions that affect the option's value. Managerial decisions may affect both the level of dividends paid to shareholders and the volatility of the granting companies' share prices. The results of the study by DeFusco et al. (1990) would suggest that market participants at least expect senior managers of companies adopting share option schemes to modify their investment and capital structure decisions so as to increase the volatility of the companies' share prices. This is supported more directly by Agrawal and Mandelker (1987) who point to the effect of managerial holdings of shares and share options on company investment and capital structure decisions. If, as is often suggested, managers are more risk averse than shareholders, ESOs may serve to align more the risk preferences of managers with those of the shareholders. Finally, there is evidence from the study by Lambert et al. (1989) that the adoption of share option schemes has an effect on dividend policy. These results would suggest that in determining the value of ESOs, particularly at the time of grant, it is necessary to assess the impact of the share option scheme on the volatility of companies' share prices and on the size of their dividends.

Models for pricing traded options assume that the option holder can construct a riskless hedge with the option and the underlying share. This may be difficult, or impossible, for the holders of ESOs who may face short-selling constraints and who, by the conditions of the options, cannot transfer them. It may therefore be optimal for risk-averse holders of ESOs to exercise their options early. The risk aversion of holders of ESOs has an impact on the value the options have to them. On the other hand, the cost of a company granting ESOs is assumed to be borne by its shareholders who are not faced with the same constraints as holders of ESOs. Models that assume risk-neutrality may therefore be appropriate used to determine the value of ESOs from the point of view of the grantor company. The non-transferability of ESOs, and the risk and liquidity preferences of holders of ESOs, however, affects their cost to shareholders through the effect these characteristics have on the early exercise of the options. As the timing of exercise is a function of the risk preferences and wealth distribution of ESO holders, the cost of ESOs to shareholders depends on these characteristics of the holders. Where a company grants ESOs to a wide range of employees who hold an equal number of options, shareholders may be viewed as holding a position on a diversified portfolio of options and so the effect of the characteristics of individual holders on exercise policy is trivial. However, where ESOs are concentrated in the hands of a few senior managers, the effect of their individual characteristics on the value of ESOs may be significant.

Option pricing models, incorporating one or more of the features of ESOs and/or the characteristics of their holders, have been developed. Of these, the FASB model probably has the greatest regulatory significance. The margin of error associated with these models is probably large and, given the extensive use of share option compensation by some companies and in the economy as a whole, any error may translate into a large monetary amount. It is not therefore surprising that, at the time of the controversy over the FASB's proposals, some companies and industry groups lobbied on the basis that the models were unreliable.

5
Accounting for Share Option Compensation

The US debate in the early part of the 1990s over share option compensation began with expressions of concern about excessive executive compensation and then proceeded to cover issues of income measurement. One element of reform that followed from Congressional interest in excessive compensation is the SEC disclosure rules on executive compensation. Concern over excessive executive compensation in the UK has also led to improved disclosure requirements on the compensation received by directors. The other element of reform relates to income measurement. Share option compensation reduces the value of existing shareholders' claims on a company's profits and its net assets. It may therefore be expected that share option compensation would be treated as an expense in computing a company's income. However, companies are not usually obliged to treat the fair value of share option compensation as an expense. Warren Buffett, in his "Letter to the Shareholders of Berkshire Hathaway Inc" of 1 March 1999 comments: "If options aren't a form of compensation, what are they? If compensation isn't an expense, what is it? And, if expenses shouldn't go into the calculation of earnings, where in the world should they go?". Answers to these questions emerge in the debate about accounting for share option compensation.

The way in which executive compensation is determined, and its amount and structure, are fundamental aspects of corporate governance. One approach to improving the quality of corporate governance is seen as being through improved disclosure in an attempt to achieve greater transparency about executive compensation. The issues therefore become ones of determining what information should be disclosed, and where and how it should be disclosed. In both the US and UK, the quality of disclosure on executive compensation has improved considerably during the 1990s. The main reform in the US has been through changes in SEC regulations; in the UK the changes have come about through a mixture of accounting regulation, Stock Exchange listing requirements and company law. Underlying the changes in UK disclosure requirements are the reports of the Cadbury and Greenbury committees. Both the regulatory regimes of the US and UK now require information to be disclosed on: (a) who sets executive compensation; (b) the rationale underlying executive compensation, especially incentives and performance criteria; and (c) the value of most, or all, of the elements of the compensation. The UK rules, unlike those in the US, do not require disclosure of the value placed on executive share options.

The grant of a share option may be viewed as a transaction between the employee and shareholders; the grant of the option potentially diluting the interests of current shareholders in the company. Any dilution to the interests of current shareholders may be reflected, under US and UK accounting rules, in *earning per share* (EPS). There is another view that the grant of share options should be recognized as a compensation expense, just like any other type of compensation. The grant of share options has been recognized as an expense under US accounting rules for some time, although the method of calculating the quantum of the expense frequently results in it not being recognized. The US accounting standard setting body, the Financial Accounting Standards Board (FASB) issued an exposure draft of a proposed standard *Accounting for Stock-based Compensation* in 1993. There was intense political response to the proposed standard that eventually resulted in a modified standard being issued. The political debate that followed the publication of the FASB's proposals, unlike that on executive compensation, emphasized the importance of share option schemes to the US economy.

DISCLOSURE

The financial statements of a company may contain disclosures about items that are not directly to do with its financial performance and position. Disclosures of information about directors, their compensation and other relationships with the company fall into this category. In this case the disclosures are associated with issues to do with corporate governance; basically the relationship between directors and shareholders. The disclosures make the directors' interests in, and compensation from, the company more transparent. Greater transparency, in turn, may be seen to enable shareholders to exert pressures to curb any excesses of managers.

The demand for greater disclosure of information on directors' compensation in general, and share options in particular, has come from public concern over the size of executive compensation. There have been political pressures on both sides of the Atlantic which have resulted in the requirement of companies to provide more information about directors' compensation. This section considers the disclosure rules that have developed in the US and the UK. The US rules, those contained in Item 402 of SEC Regulation S-K, are presented before considering the development of regulations in the UK.

SEC Regulations on Disclosure

In 1991 Senator Carl Levin introduced his proposed Corporate Pay Responsibility Act into the US Senate as a response to concerns over excessive executive compensation. Within the proposed Act are provisions requiring the SEC to amend its rules and regulations so as to improve disclosure by public companies of executive and director compensation packages. Three factors are identified by Quinn (1995) as coming together in the early 1990s that made reform of disclosures on executive compensation necessary. First, there had been a decade of downsizing at the same time that many executives were receiving substantial levels of compensation. Second, the company disclosures were opaque and difficult to interpret. Finally, there was growing investor activism which began to focus on corporate governance issues.

In 1992 the SEC announced its initiative on executive compensation. This was to have two interconnected components: one on the shareholder proposal process, the other on disclosure requirements. As executive compensation was seen as a day-to-day operating issue that did not require shareholder approval, shareholder proposals on executive compensation had been traditionally excluded from proxy statements. This position changed so that companies can no longer exclude proposals on executive compensation on the grounds that such compensation is a part of the companies' ordinary business.

The initiative on disclosure was designed to provide full and clear information on executive compensation, on the policies underlying the amount of compensation paid, on the relationship between compensation and company performance, and on the relationship of members of the compensation committee to the company and its executives. Full and clear disclosure on executive compensation is believed by the SEC to provide both shareholders and the market with the information necessary for them to control executive pay. The new rules, contained in Item 402 of Regulations S-K, require clear, concise and understandable disclosure of compensation awarded to named executive officers (NEOs). These are: (a) all individuals serving as chief executive officer (CEO) during the accounting period; (b) the four most highly compensated executive officers other than the CEO who were serving as executive officers at the end of the accounting period; and (c) up to two additional individuals for whom disclosure would have been required under (b) but for the fact that there were not in post at the end of the accounting period. No disclosure is required for any executive, other than the CEO, whose total annual salary and bonus does not exceed $100 000.

A Summary Compensation Table is required to provide shareholders with an overall picture of the compensation of NEOs for the current year and for the 3 preceding years. The disclosure for each NEO is divided into annual, long-term and other compensation. Grants of share options, included under long-term compensation, are disclosed as the number of underlying shares. No amount is given for total compensation as the SEC recognizes that it is inappropriate to aggregate different types of compensation. The Summary Compensation Table is followed by a series of tables that provide more detail about the components of the compensation package. Two tables relate to share options: (a) information about options and share appreciation rights (SARs) granted during the accounting period should be disclosed in a *Option/SAR Grants Table*; and (b) information about options and SARs that were either exercised during the accounting period, or were held at the end of the accounting period should be disclosed in an *Aggregated Option/ SAR Exercises and Fiscal Year-End Options/SAR Value Table*.

The Option/SAR Grants Table, which contains information concerning individual grants of share options (and free-standing SARs) to each NEO during the financial year, contains information on: (a) the number of securities underlying options and SARs granted; (b) the percentage the grant represents of total options and SARs granted to employees during the year; (c) the per-share exercise or base price of the options or SARs granted and if the exercise or base price is less than the market price of the underlying security on the date of grant, then additional disclosure is required of market price on the date of grant; (d) the expiration date of the options or SARs; and (e) either the potential realizable value of each grant of options or freestanding SARs, or the present value of each grant. The Table therefore gives basic information on options (number of shares, exercise price and maturity) together with an indication of their value at the time of grant. In addition, information on the options granted to each NEO as a proportion of the total options granted during the year is included to show whether grants of options are confined mainly to top executives, or whether they are granted to employees more generally.

Companies are able to choose between two approaches to indicating the value of share options at the time of grant. One, the potential realizable value of each grant of options or freestanding SARs, assumes that the market price of the underlying security appreciates in value from the date of grant to the end of the option or SAR term, at annualized rates of 5 and 10%. Alternatively, companies can disclose the present value of the options at the date of grant as determined using any option pricing model. Where a company chooses to disclose the present value of share options granted in the period, it is necessary for it to describe the valuation method used. In the case of a company using a variation of the Black–Scholes or the binomial option pricing model, it is necessary to identify the model it is using and to describe the assumptions made in respect to expected volatility, risk-free rate of interest, dividend yield, time of exercise, and any adjustments for non-transferability or risk of forfeiture. Where another valuation model is used, it is necessary to describe the methodology and any material assumptions that are made.

The Aggregated Option/SAR Exercises and Fiscal Year-End Options/SAR Value Table contains information about share options (and SARs) exercised by the NEOs during the accounting period and about those held by them at the year end. In relation to options, the table shows for each NEO: (a) the number of shares received upon exercise of the options; (b) the aggregate monetary amount realized upon exercise, defined as the difference between the fair market value of the shares at the time of exercise and the exercise price; (c) the number of shares underlying unexercised options held at the year end, identifying exercisable and unexercisable options separately; and (d) the intrinsic values of in-the-money unexercised options held at the year end, identifying exercisable and unexercisable options separately. Additional information is required where, during the accounting period, the company has re-priced options, that is adjusted the exercise price through amendment, or cancellation and replacement. As well as requiring disclosure of all re-pricings to *any* executive, the compensation committee is required to explain the re-pricing and its basis. This disclosure is intended, according to Quinn (1995), to change company policy on re-pricing.

The SEC also requires disclosure of information about the composition of a company's compensation committee (if any) together with its report on executive compensation. Not only is it necessary to identify the membership of the committee, it is also necessary to provide information on any interlocking and/or insider participation. It is therefore necessary to identify an executive of the company who serves as a director of another company where an executive of that other company serves on the company's compensation committee. The committee's report on executive compensation should include disclosure of the compensation committee's compensation policies applicable to the company's executive officers (including the named executive officers), including the specific relationship of corporate performance to executive compensation, and discussion of the compensation committee's bases for the CEO's compensation reported for the last completed accounting period. This should include the factors and criteria upon which the CEO's compensation was based. The committee should include a specific discussion of the relationship of the company's performance to the CEO's compensation for the last completed accounting period, describing each measure of the company's performance, whether qualitative or quantitative, on which the CEO's compensation was based. Companies are not required to disclose target levels with respect to specific quantitative or qualitative performance-related factors considered by the committee (or board), or any factors or criteria involving confidential commercial or business information, the disclosure of which would have an adverse effect on the company.

Finally, a company is required to provide information showing the company's performance and that of the market and its peers. The disclosure takes the form of a performance graph, a line graph comparing the yearly percentage change in the company's cumulative total shareholder return on its class of common stock for the last 5 years with: (a) the cumulative total return of a broad equity market index; (b) a published industry or line-of-business index; and (c) peer companies selected in good faith either on an industry or line-of-business basis, or else companies with similar market capitalizations if the company does not use a published industry, or line-of-business, index and does not believe it can reasonably identify a peer group. Total shareholder return, the sum of the dividends for the period and change in the market value of the shares between the beginning and end of the period, was chosen because it is used in the reports of most analysts. Companies are, however, free to present other measures in addition to total shareholder return.

United Kingdom

Regulations in the UK on the disclosure of directors' compensation developed over the early 1990s following public concern over the quality of corporate governance and high levels of executive compensation, especially to directors of privatized utility companies. The recommendations of the Cadbury and Greenbury Reports have resulted in changes to the Stock Exchange Listing Agreement and company law, and to the issuance of a recommendation from the ASB. Further changes to the Listing Agreement have been made following the recommendation of the Hampel Committee.

Cadbury Report

The Committee on Financial Aspects of Corporate Governance (the Cadbury Committee), under the chairmanship of Sir Adrian Cadbury, was set up in May 1991 by the Financial Reporting Council, the London Stock Exchange, and the accountancy profession. The Committee was established following concerns, highlighted by a series of corporate failures and financial scandals in the late 1980s, about the quality of financial reporting and audit. Amongst the factors underlying this concern was a perceived lack of board accountability, especially in relation to directors' compensation.

The Committee's approach was to provide a framework for establishing good corporate governance and accountability. This was achieved through a *Code of Best Practice* aimed at listed companies. Two aspects of the Code relating to Executive Directors are of relevance here. First: "There should be full and clear disclosure of directors' total emoluments and those of the chairman and highest-paid UK director, including pension contributions and share options. Separate figures should be given for salary and performance-related elements and the basis on which performance is measured should be explained" (para. 3.2). Second: "Executive directors' pay should be subject to the recommendations of a remuneration committee made up wholly or mainly of non-executive directors" (para. 3.3). A note to the recommendation on compensation committee, which does not itself form part of the code, suggests that the: "(M)embership of the remuneration committee should be set out in the Directors' Report and its chairman should be available to answer questions on remuneration principles and practice at the Annual General Meeting" (note 9).

Urgent Issues Task Force Abstract 10

The Urgent Issues Task Force (UITF) of the Accounting Standards Board (ASB) issued its Abstract Number 10 in May 1994 following growing interest in share options granted to directors subsequent to the publication of the Cadbury Report, and developments in the United States. The Cadbury Report had suggested that there ". . . should be full and clear disclosure of directors' total emoluments and those of the chairman and highest-paid director, including pension contributions and share options." The UITF believed that the grant of share options should be regarded as giving rise to a benefit that should be included in the aggregate directors' compensation. However it concluded that ". . . given the practical difficulties of attributing a meaningful estimated money value to an option at the date of grant, and differing views on whether and if so how to apportion any benefit over time . . . it is not presently practicable to specify an appropriate valuation method for options as a benefit in kind" (para. 9). The UITF drew attention to the complexity of the theoretical models that would be required to value the options, especially those where the rights under the option were contingent on the future performance of the company, or other factors. It also indicated that there was a view that, because of the terms of the options, they were "earned" over the period between grant and exercise and so any value should be attributed in the financial statements over that period.

The UITF recommends disclosure of the main terms of directors' share options in the financial statements[48]. Information to be disclosed for each director relates to the characteristics of the share options and the market price of the underlying shares at the date of any exercise and at the period-end. Specifically, there should be disclosure of the number of shares under options at the beginning and end of the period and of the number granted, exercised and lapsed during the period. In addition, it is necessary to disclose the exercise price of the option, the date from which it may be exercised, its expiry date and a summary of any performance criteria that must be met before the option may be exercised.

The Greenbury Code

The Study Group on Directors' Compensation (the Greenbury Committee), under the chairmanship of Sir Richard Greenbury, was established in January 1995 at the initiative of (but independent from) the Confederation of British Industry (CBI). The Committee's remit, following public concern over both the level and structure of boardroom pay, was to identify good practice in determining directors' compensation and to prepare a Code of such practice for use by UK PLCs.

The Greenbury Committee's report, issued in July 1995, contained a Code of Best Practice with the following main features. A com-

---

[48] The information to be disclosed was already available to shareholders by inspection of the register of directors' interests.

pensation committee, consisting entirely of non-executive directors
with no personal financial interest (other than as shareholders) or
other potential conflicts of interest, should, according to Section A
of the Code, determine the compensation of executive directors.
The members of the committee should be named in their annual
report to shareholders. The compensation committee should, under
Section B of the Code, make an annual report to shareholders. The
report should set out the policies and criteria for determining
directors' pay and provide an analysis of the compensation of each
director by name, together with information on pension entitlements
and share options. The figures should be subject to audit. Companies
should, according to Section C of the Code, pay directors the rate
for the job, but no more. Any performance-related pay should be
based on genuinely demanding criteria. In general there should be
a move away from short-term cash based schemes to longer-term
share based schemes which should be designed to encourage the
holding of shares for the longer term rather than realizing them for
cash. Share-based schemes should aim to measure the company's
performance against that of comparator companies using measures
such as total shareholder return. The consequences of any pay
increases on pension entitlements should be carefully considered
by the compensation committee, and in general annual bonuses
should not be pensionable. Finally, companies should, under Section
D of the Code, generally aim to reduce the notice period of directors'
service contracts to 1 year or less, although in some cases periods of
up to 2 years may be acceptable. Any provision for compensation
payments in the event of early termination should not appear to
reward failure and should have regard to an outgoing director's
obligation to mitigate damages by seeking new employment. The
Code therefore deals with the way that compensation is determined,
transparency, the form of the compensation package, and directors'
service contracts and compensation for loss of office. The Greenbury
recommendations on disclosure are incorporated into the Stock
Exchange Listing Agreement, and into company law.

The London Stock Exchange Listing Requirements

In October 1995 the London Stock Exchange amended the Yellow
Book by adding a non-mandatory annexe Best Practice Provisions:

Directors' Remuneration and some new mandatory disclosures. The new disclosures include: (a) a statement of the company's compensation policy together with a statement that, in framing its this policy, the compensation committee has given full consideration to Section B of the Best Practice Provisions (broadly corresponding to Sections C and D of the Greenbury Code); (b) an analysis of the compensation of each director by name; (c) information on share options presented in accordance with the recommendations contained in UITF Abstract 10; and (d) details of any long-term incentive schemes other than share options, including the interests of each director in the long-term incentive schemes at the start of the year, entitlements and awards made during the year, and showing which crystallize in the same year or in subsequent years. The money value and number of shares, cash payments or other benefits received by each director under such schemes during the period, and the interests of each director in the long-term incentive schemes at the end of the period, should be disclosed. In addition, it is necessary to disclose the unexpired term of the service contract of any director proposed for re-election at the annual general meeting.

These disclosures essentially mirror those proposed in Section B of the Greenbury Code, with the important exception that the Yellow Book does not yet require disclosure of individual directors' pension benefits.

Company Law

In January 1996 the Department of Trade and Industry issued a consultative document on the company law disclosure of directors' emoluments. The proposals were intended to implement specific recommendations of the Greenbury Report, and to align the Companies Act with the new Listing Rules. The new rules were implemented in The Company Accounts (Disclosure of Directors' Emoluments) Regulations 1997.

The Regulations require that listed companies to disclose the ". . . aggregate amount of gains made by directors on the exercise of share options"[49]. The gains made are the difference between the market price of the shares on the date the option was exercised and

---

[49] There is only a requirement to disclose the number of directors who exercised options in the case of a company that is not listed.

the price actually paid for the shares. The figure to be disclosed is unaffected by whether the director immediately sells the shares after exercising the option, or retains them. Because gains made on the exercise of options are likely to vary substantially from year to year, the amounts should be disclosed as a separate figure. This means that the amount reported as the emoluments of a director excludes the value of any options granted to him or her, or the amount of any gains made on the exercise of such options.

Hampel Report and Further Changes to the Listing Rules

The Committee on Corporate Governance (Hampel Committee), under the chairmanship of Sir Ronnie Hampel, was established to review the implementation of the recommendations of the Cadbury and Greenbury Committees. In its review of the recommendations on directors' compensation, the Hampel Report is broadly in agreement with the Greenbury Code. However, the Committee does make comments and recommendations. First, the Committee reiterates the need for a company to have a compensation committee but recommends that the broad framework and cost of executive compensation is a matter for the board on the advice of the compensation committee. The board is also seen as having responsibility for establishing a compensation package for non-executive directors. Second, the Committee expresses concern about the upward pressure on executive compensation that can follow from inter-company comparisons and the full disclosure of total compensation of individual directors. Third, the Committee reiterates the view that the compensation committee should ensure that the compensation package aligns the interests of directors with those of the shareholders. The Committee ". . . urge remuneration committees to use informed judgement in devising schemes appropriate to the specific circum-stances of their company, and to be ready to explain their reasoning to shareholders". Finally, the Committee departs from the view expressed by the Cadbury Committee that the pay of non-executive directors should not be paid in shares or share options. Although it recommends that non-executive directors should not participate in share option schemes, the Hampel Committee suggest that compen-sation in the form of shares may be a useful way of aligning the interests of non-executive directors with those of shareholders.

The Hampel Committee produced a consolidated code (the "Combined Code") setting out principles of good governance and a code of best practice on corporate governance that incorporates its own recommendations with those of the Cadbury and Greenbury Committees. These principles and code of best practice, modified as a result of consultation, has been adopted by the Stock Exchange and the Listing Rules modified so as to achieve consistency with the code. A company is required to indicate in its financial statements whether it has complied with the relevant section of the Combined Code. If it has not complied with all, or part, of the relevant section a company is required to indicate which provisions it has not complied with and to give reasons for any non-compliance.

INCOME MEASUREMENT

The grant of an ESO for less than its fair value results in a reduction in the value of the existing shareholders' claims on the grantor company's net assets. Changes in the value of the ESO during its life from the time of grant also affect the value of the claims of existing shareholders. One way in which this may be reflected in the financial statements of the grantor company is as a dilution to earnings per share (EPS). Both US and UK accounting rules require EPS to be calculated so as to take account of the possible dilution that would arise had the options been exercised during the accounting period.

Another way of viewing the grant of an ESO for less than its fair value is as a compensation expense that is recognized in the grantor company's income statement. Accounting rules have used the *intrinsic* value of an ESO as a measure of the compensation cost. The intrinsic value of many ESOs on the relevant measurement date is nil, and so the compensation cost does not usually result in a reduction of income. An FASB Exposure Draft issued in 1993 proposed that the compensation cost be based upon the *fair value* of the ESO at the time of grant. A significant cost would have been charged against the profits of many, mainly high technology, companies if this proposal had been adopted. This led to an outcry that eventually resulted in a modification to the proposed standard.

Dilution of Earnings Per Share

The grant of an ESO may be viewed as a transaction between a company's existing shareholders and the employee, rather than as one between the company and the employee. The effect of the transaction is to reduce, by the fair value of the option less any amount paid for it, the value of the existing shareholder's claims on the company's net assets. The value of the ESO will change during its life with the passage of time, and with changes in interest rates, the market price and volatility of the company's shares. Such changes will impact on the value of existing shareholders' claims on the company. The only transaction that affects the company is the exercise of the option and this will increase the company's net assets by the amount of the proceeds from the exercise.

Financial statements, as prepared under current generally accepted accounting practice, are predominantly constructed using a proprietary theory of the reporting entity. Under such a theory, a company's net assets are viewed as belonging to the company's owners, and changes in net assets are seen as the owners' income. Transactions with owners, as owners, are excluded from measures of financial performance. The main issue here is whether a future contingent shareholder, such as the holder of an ESO, is an owner or a creditor of the company. The FASB (1990) concludes that under current accounting practice, the obligation of a company to issue its own shares does not have the characteristic of a liability, as defined by *Statement of Financial Accounting Concepts (SFAC) No. 6*, because it does not embody an obligation to transfer the company's assets or to provide services in the future[50]. Contingent shareholders, including the holders of ESOs, are therefore considered as having an equity interest in the company. Although financial statements are constructed from the perspective of current and future contingent shareholders, EPS is a measure attributable to current holders of a company's equity shares[51]. This means that it is necessary to adjust for the interests of preference shareholders and contingent share-

---

[50] The FASB (1999) has recently added an additional requirement that the value of the warrant must be indexed to the fair value of the issuer's equity shares for the warrant to be considered an equity instrument.

[51] Equity shares are the common stock of US companies and the ordinary shares of UK companies.

holders. The adjustment made for future contingent shareholders is based on the concept of dilution.

Dilution is defined by the FASB (1997), in *SFAS No. 128 Earnings per share*, as a: ". . . reduction in earnings per share resulting from the assumption that convertible securities were converted, that options or warrants were exercised, or that other shares were issued upon the satisfaction of certain conditions". Two main components of this definition can be identified. First, the extent of dilution is determined by assuming the equity shares are issued during the accounting period as the result of options being exercised (or convertible securities converted). Second, dilution is viewed as a *reduction* in EPS due to the obligation to issue common stock at some future time.

Diluted EPS for a company that has granted ESOs is computed on the assumption that the ESOs are exercised at the beginning of the accounting period or, if later, the date of grant. Measures of EPS that utilize the concept of dilution differ in the assumptions made about how the company uses the proceeds from the exercise of the ESO. Three assumed uses for the proceeds can be identified: (a) purchase of a company's current common stock; (b) redemption of all, or part of, of the company's debt; and (c) investment by the company in government securities.

The assumption that the proceeds from the issue of shares are used to purchase current shares of the company is referred to as the *treasury stock* method. In calculating diluted EPS, the denominator in the EPS calculation is increased by the number of shares assumed to be issued on the exercise of the option less the number of shares assumed to be repurchased using the exercise proceeds[52]. This method underlies the current UK standard, *FRS 14 Earnings per share*, US standard, *SFAS 128*, and international standard, *IAS 33 Earnings per share*. In all three standards it is assumed that the company will use the proceeds from the exercise of options to purchase its shares at their *average* market price during the accounting period. SFAS 128 replaced *APB Opinion No. 15 Earnings per share*, also based on the treasury stock method, that assumes that the

---

[52] *FASB Interpretation No. 31* (1980) defines the amount of the exercise proceeds as ". . . the sum of the amount the employee must pay, the amount of measurable compensation ascribed to future services (whether or not accrued), and the amount of any 'windfall' tax benefit to be credited to capital" (para. 3).

company will use the exercise proceeds to repurchase shares at the higher of the average market price of the shares and the price at the end of the accounting period.

The alternative assumption is that the proceeds from exercise are used to repurchase the company's debt and/or invest in government securities. Accounting Principles Board (APB) *Opinion No. 15* (1969) required that, under certain circumstances, part of the proceeds be used to repurchase a company's debt or invest in government securities. *SSAP 3 Earnings per share*, which was superseded by *FRS 14*, assumed the proceeds from the exercise were invested in government securities[53].

Accounting for the Cost of Share Option Compensation as an Expense

If the grant of a share option is viewed as a compensation expense, omission of the expense may result in overstatement of income. The amount involved may be considerable. Saldich (1994), for example, reports the results of a study suggesting that the profits of an average US high technology company would be reduced by almost 50% if the fair value of the compensation cost of ESOs was recognized in the income statement. Accounting for the compensation cost of ESOs is however a problem whose complexity may be increased by its economic and political consequences.

Determination of the value of an ESO for accounting purposes is problematic. First, it is necessary to decide the date upon which the value of the option is to be measured. The choice of a measurement date may affect the amount of the compensation expense charged against income. Second, there is an issue in determining what features of an ESO should be measured. In Accounting Research Bulletin (ARB) No. 43, the Committee on Accounting Procedure (1953) note that although there is ". . . a value inherent in a restricted future right to purchase shares at a price at or even above the fair value of shares at the grant date, the committee believes it is impracticable to measure any such value". As a consequence, the opinion of the committee was that the value to be used in financial statements is the excess of the fair value of the shares over the

---

[53] *SSAP 3* assumes that the investment will be in $2\frac{1}{2}$% Consolidated Stock.

exercise price of the option. This means that there is no compensation expense where the exercise price is set at, or above, the fair value of the shares on the measurement date.

Two approaches to the determining the value of an ESO for accounting purposes can be identified. The first, the *intrinsic value* approach follows the opinion expressed in ARB No. 43. This approach is incorporated into Accounting Principles Board (APB) *Opinion No. 25 Accounting for stock issued to employees* and in the Urgent Issues Task Force (UITF) *Abstract 17 Employee share schemes*. The other is the *fair value* approach which underlies Statement of Financial Accounting Standards *SFAS No. 123 Accounting for stock-based compensation*. The proposal to move from intrinsic to fair value measurement resulted in a major political controversy that lead the FASB to modify its position and allow companies to use the intrinsic value approach provided they showed a *pro forma* statement using the fair value method in the notes.

The Intrinsic Value of Share Options

The fair value of an option may be seen as made up of two components: its intrinsic value and its time value. An option's intrinsic value, the difference between the exercise price of the option and the fair value of the underlying share, can readily be determined where the underlying shares are traded in a market. Acceptable models to determine the fair value of traded options were not developed until the early 1970s[54]. Early accounting rules, including APB *Opinion No. 25*, are based upon measures of intrinsic value. Intrinsic value also underlies the more recent UTIF *Abstract 17*. Both APB *Opinion No. 25* and UTIF *Abstract 17* allow certain types of ESO to be exempted from the requirement to account for their intrinsic value, in the former case on the basis that the grant of the option is other than for compensatory purposes.

The principles for accounting for the grant of share options to employees upon which APB *Opinion No. 25 Accounting for Stock Issued to Employees* is based are contained in ARB No. 43. As well as setting out the basis for intrinsic value measurement, the Bulletin

[54] Miller (1994) suggests that when options became widely used in the 1950s accountants turned to academics for guidance in valuing the instruments. Faced with widely varying opinions, accountants decided to do nothing.

distinguishes between non-compensatory and compensatory stock option plans. The former are seen to be designed as a means of raising capital or encouraging wider share ownership, whereas the latter are seen to involve an element of compensation. The view taken in the Bulletin is that, to the extent that share options involve a measurable amount of compensation, they should be accounted for as an expense in computing a company's income.

The distinction between non-compensatory and compensatory stock option plans is retained in APB *Opinion No. 25*, with criteria being defined that have to be met for a plan to be non-compensatory. Four characteristics of non-compensatory plans are identified in the Opinion: (a) substantially all full-time employees meeting limited employment qualifications may participate; (b) stock is offered to eligible employees equally or based on a uniform percentage of wages or salary; (c) the time permitted to exercise the option is limited to a reasonable period; and (d) the discount from the market price of the stock is no greater than would be reasonable in an offer of shares to shareholders or others. In 1999 the FASB issued an exposure draft of the proposed interpretation of *Opinion No. 25* that contains guidance on the application of these criteria. No compensation cost is recognized for options issued through non-compensatory plans.

The compensation cost of ESOs is measured as the difference between the market price of the shares at the measurement date less the amount the employee is required to pay. The measurement date is defined as the first date on which the following are known: (a) the number of shares that an employee is entitled to receive; and (b) the option price. For many ESOs the measurement date is the date of grant. This means that a compensation expense is not recognized where the exercise price of an ESO is set at, or above, the market price of the shares on the date of grant. However, a compensation expense may be recognized for an otherwise similar option that vests only if defined conditions are met. A rise in the share price between the grant and vesting of an option may then result in the recognition of a compensation expense. Eichen (1994) notes that this inconsistency of treatment means that a company that grants conventional ESOs will not generally record a charge against income, whereas one that grants options whose exercise is contingent on the achievement of performance goals may have to make such a charge.

APB *Opinion No. 25* indicates that any compensation expense should be recognized over the period that an employee performs services. It indicates that the grant may specify the period(s) during which the employee performs services, or that the period(s) may be inferred from the terms of the award.

Intrinsic value measurement approach is also adopted by the UITF in *Abstract 17*, issued in 1997[55]. *Abstract 17 Employee share schemes* requires that the intrinsic value of ESOs at the time of grant should, as a minimum, be charged to the profit and loss account. In the case of ESOs that are subject to performance criteria, the UITF requires that initial recognition should be based on "a reasonable expectation of the extent to which performance criteria will be met" (para. 13 (c)). Therefore, unlike APB *Opinion No. 25*, the value of an ESO is always measured at the date of grant. Any uncertainty is dealt with through adjustment to the value of the option. The value of the ESO should generally be charged to the profit and loss account on a straight-line basis over the period to which the performance criteria relate. The amount charged is, where necessary, adjusted to reflect changes in the probability of the performance criteria being met. In other cases, the intrinsic value of the ESO is allocated to accounting periods over the period from grant to the holder becoming unconditionally entitled to the underlying shares.

Employee share schemes that are, or are substantially similar to, Inland Revenue approved SAYE schemes are exempt from the requirement to account for the compensation cost of ESOs[56]. The justification for this is that companies have generally not accounted for options granted under approved SAYE schemes. As the exercise price of options granted under such schemes may be at a discount of up to 20% of the market price of the shares at the date of grant, a compensation cost would have had to be recognized but for the exemption[57].

---

[55] The UITF issued a proposal to revise the Abstract in 1999, but the proposal was subsequently withdrawn.

[56] In its review of *Abstract 17*, the UITF indicates that the majority of its members believe that options granted under SAYE and similar schemes should be accounted for in the same way as options issued under other schemes. However, it has agreed to refer the decision to the ASB who will consider the issue as part of its project on accounting for equity.

[57] In its review of the Abstract, the UITF proposed that where a company takes advantage of this exemption, it should disclose, in the notes for its financial statements, the minimum charge to the profit and loss account that would have been made if it had not taken account of the exemption. This proposal was, however, withdrawn.

The Fair Value of Share Options

In the early 1980s, a number of groups, including the SEC and some of the larger accounting firms, expressed concern about the anomalous results produced by APB *Opinion No. 25*. They also commented on the absence of any conceptual foundation to the Opinion. In response to such expressions of concern, the FASB added a project to reconsider accounting by employers for stock-based compensation plans to its agenda in 1984. At that time the Board issued an "invitation to comment" and in 1987 a "status report". However, work on the project was largely dormant for most of the period up until the early 1990s. Then, in response to political concerns about the size of executive compensation packages, the FASB issued an Exposure draft *Accounting for Stock-based Compensation* in 1993.

Even before the exposure draft was issued, the FASB had received a large number of letters, the majority arguing that it was unnecessary to change the existing rules. Publication of the exposure generated intense opposition to the proposed standard, much of which was mobilized by start-up and high-technology companies, and their advisers. The issues considered were not only ones of how to account for ESOs, but of the economic consequences that would follow from companies being required to charge share option compensation in their income statements. The controversy, which reached Congress, threatened the FASB. As a result the FASB issued a standard that gave companies the option of using intrinsic or fair value measures in determining the charge to the income statement.

The FASB Exposure draft   The FASB Exposure draft examines a number of issues. The Board begins by re-examining the issue as to whether the issuance of ESOs is a compensation expense. If the grant of ESOs is to be treated as a compensation expense then it is necessary to measure their value at the relevant time. Two possible concepts of value are identified by the Board that may be measured: *minimum* value and *fair* value. Whichever method is used to measure the value of ESOs it is necessary to decide the date on which the value is to be measured and the period over which the cost of the ESOs is charged to income. Finally, it is necessary to consider the interaction between treating the ESOs as a compensation cost and dilution to EPS.

The issuance of ESOs is a compensation expense   The FASB's proposed standard would require a company to recognize a compensation cost in respect of the issuance of share options to its employees. The Board's rationale for this is that: (a) the value of share options issued to employees is compensation, (b) compensation is a cost that should be recognized in the financial statements; and (c) an accounting standard that requires non-recognition of costs leads to financial statements that are neither credible nor representationally faithful.

Although the ESO has value at the time of grant, an employee will pay either a nominal amount for the option or nothing. Any difference between the fair value of the option and the amount paid for it is argued to represent the value of services provided by the employee in return for the option. Following this view, an ESO should be viewed as a part of an employee's compensation package. The fact that an ESO has value to the employee however does not necessarily mean that it is an expense to the company. Three arguments against the view that the issuance of share options represents a compensation expense are identified by the FASB. First, attention is drawn to the FASB's Concept Statement No. 6 *Elements of Financial Statements* (FASB, 1985) which indicates that expenses result from outflows, or using up, of assets or incurring liabilities, or both. As the issuance of an ESO is not associated with an outflow, or using up, of assets, nor is it associated with a liability, it is argued that it cannot be treated as an expense. Second, there is the somewhat connected view that the issuance of an ESO is a transaction between the employee and existing shareholders and so should not be included within a company's financial statements. Finally, there are suggestions that the issuance of an ESO is a capital transaction and so has no effect on income.

The FASB attempted to dismiss these arguments. Its position seems to be based upon the view that equity instruments are invariably issued for valuable consideration. Although the consideration is usually in the form of cash, it may be for goods and/or services. The transaction is accounted for as an increase in equity and a corresponding recognition of an asset or an expense. The issuance of an ESO is regarded as being essentially the same as the issue of any other equity instrument; in this case the consideration being given is a service by the employee.

Even if it is considered that ESOs represent a compensation expense, it does not follow that the expense should be recognized in the income statement. In order for any compensation expense associated with ESOs to be recognized it is necessary to be able to measure their value with reasonable accuracy. An alternative to recognition of the compensation expense of ESOs would be to require disclosure of relevant information but not require recognition. It was suggested that time should be allowed in order to assess the effectiveness of the SEC requirements, discussed above, in dealing with excessive compensation. In addition, proposals for expanded disclosure of ESOs had been received by the FASB. However, the FASB reiterated the view that it previously expressed that disclosure is not a substitute for recognition.

Measurement method The decision to recognize the issuance of an ESO as a compensation expense means that it is necessary to measure its value. Two concepts of value are identified by the FASB in the Exposure draft. The first, the *minimum value* of an ESO, represents the least amount that an option writer would demand for issuing the ESO. This is defined as the current price of the shares on the measurement date less the sum of the present value of the exercise price and the present value of the expected dividends on the shares during the life of the option. The proposal in the Exposure draft is that companies whose shares are *not* publicly traded would have been allowed by the FASB to use the minimum value method.

The other concept identified by the FASB is the *fair value* of an ESO, which is defined as the amount at which it would be exchanged between willing parties, other than in a forced liquidation sale. Fair value, the FASB propose, should be measured using an option pricing model such as the Black–Scholes and binomial models. These models, as described in Chapter 4, were developed to value traded options. Also, as discussed in Chapter 4, ESOs differ from traded options in a number of ways. First, as they are written by the company, rather than by a third party, they have the character of warrants rather than options. The main implication of this is that their grant serves to dilute the value of pre-existing shares. Second, the term of ESOs is long (usually 10 years) compared with traded options. This means that some of the assumptions underlying the valuation model become more problematic. For example, assumptions are required about the volatility of the share prices, the risk-free rate of interest, and dividends over the term of the ESOs. Third, ESOs are non-transferable. Unlike traded options, therefore, they cannot be sold to third parties in order to realize value. The only way for a holder to realize their value is to exercise the options and sell the shares. However, if this is done, the holder foregoes the *time value* of the option at the time of exercise. Fourth, a holder of ESOs may forfeit non-vested options by leaving the company before the options vest. Fifth, an employee may be required to either exercise the options he or she holds, or else forfeit them, in the event of leaving employment with the grantor company. The FASB propose that forfeiture of a non-vested ESO, and early exercise or forfeiture of a vested ESO, upon termination of employment with the grantor company, be dealt with by modification of the pricing model. Specifically, the value produced by the option pricing model should be reduced to reflect the risk of the option being forfeited, and that the value should be based on the expected actual life, rather than the maximum term, of the ESO.

Measurement date and attribution period   The value of an ESO, and the corresponding compensation costs, depends upon the date on which it is measured. The FASB identifies a number of possible dates: (a) the date on which employer and employee agree the terms of the compensation award (the *grant* date); (b) the date on which the obligations under the agreement have been fulfilled (the *vesting* date); (c) the date upon which an employee has rendered the services necessary to earn the ESO (the *service* date); (d) the date upon which all service related conditions expire (the *service expiration* date)[58]; and (e) the date on which the ESO is exercised (the *exercise* date). The FASB concluded that the value of ESOs should be measured on the date of grant.

   Although it was proposed to measure the value of an ESO at the date of grant, there remains the question as to the periods over which the value should be recognized as a compensation cost. The grant of an ESO may be viewed as a reward for past services, in which case it seems clear that the compensation cost should be reflected in the financial statements in the period of grant. However,

---

[58] ESOs generally must be exercised, or else forfeited, within a limited period of time after the termination of employment.

it may be argued that at least part of the related employee services are provided in the period after grant. Two periods may be considered: the vesting period and the period between the date of grant and the date upon which all employment conditions have been met. The FASB proposed that, unless there is evidence to the contrary, the compensation cost should be attributed over the vesting period, that is the period over which conditions must be met in order for the option to be exercised.

Another approach identified, but not adopted, by the FASB is to attribute the cost over the period to the time on which all employment conditions have been met. According to the FASB, advocates of this view: ". . . contend that employees have not earned the full benefit to which they are entitled until future service would no longer extend the maximum term of the option. For example, at the vesting date of a 10-year option that vests in 3 years and that must be exercised within 90 days of termination or forfeited, an employee has 'earned' an option with a total term of 3 years plus 90 days and a remaining term of only 90 days. Each additional day of service extends the term of the option by 1 day." The adoption of such a view would spread the compensation cost of the option over the period from grant to the earlier of the time that employment is terminated, or the option matures.

Recognition of a compensation cost and earnings per share   The grant of an ESO may be viewed as a compensation cost which should be recognized in computing earnings, or as discussed previously, as a dilution to earnings. If the grant is to be recognized as a compensation cost then it is necessary to consider how earnings per share should be calculated. In calculating diluted earnings per share, the compensation cost would be recognized in the company's earnings (the numerator) and the dilution to existing shareholder interests would be recognized in the adjustment to the number of shares in issue (the denominator). The FASB received comments that this leads to effective *double counting* of the effect of issuing share options, but disagreed with this view.

In fact there are two issues: one is the grant of the ESO for less than its fair value at the time of issue and the other is change in fair value over the option's life. The dilution adjustment to EPS is an attempt to deal with this second aspect. It does not deal with the grant of the option for less than its fair value. This is dealt with through the recognition of the difference between the fair value of the ESO and the proceeds from its grant, if any, in the income statement.

The Economic Consequences of Treating the Fair Value of ESOs as a Compensation Expense

The proposals contained in the FASB Exposure Draft led to controversy which resulted in the FASB modifying its position. Commenting on the controversy Beresford (1996), then Chairman of the FASB, stated:

> The FASB is in its 23rd year. We have outlived our predecessors. We have achieved a reasonable level of credibility because we have not avoided issues due to potential controversy or political overtones. For the most part, we have been able to strike a reasonable balance among the conceptual, practical and political aspects of our agenda projects. US accounting standards and the process by which they're set are widely recognized as the best in the world.
>
> . . . In its 23 years, the FASB has been involved in only two highly politicized projects—the oil and gas project in the late 1970s and the recent compensation project. Yes there have been lots of threats in other projects . . . But in only the oil and gas and stock compensation cases did political pressure fundamentally alter the outcome of the Board's technical accounting decisions.

Although the pressure on the FASB started shortly after it issued, in 1984, its tentative conclusion that companies should recognize the compensation cost based on the value of options granted to employees, the political pressure intensified with the publication of the Exposure draft in April 1993.

As described in Chapter 1, the concern in the early 1990s was with executive compensation, especially that of CEOs. One measure that followed this concern was the restriction on the tax deductibility of executive compensation to US$1 million[59]. Another was a call by Congress on the SEC and FASB to introduce rules on the disclosure of the value of shares granted to executives. Such measures would provide greater transparency as to the size of executive awards. The

[59] See Chapter 6.

issue of executive compensation was largely resolved by the SEC disclosure rules.

The publication of the FASB exposure draft led to new concerns with the pressure being for the FASB to withdraw its proposals. Concern over the FASB's proposals was expressed in both Houses of Congress, and it was resolved by both houses that: "(1) the accounting standard proposed by the Financial Accounting Standards Board will have grave economic consequences, particularly for businesses in new-growth sectors which rely heavily on entrepreneurship; and (2) the Board should not change the current accounting rules under Accounting Principles Board Decision 25 by requiring that businesses deduct from profits the value of stock options". Before looking at the perceived economic consequences of the FASB's proposals, it is useful to identify the perceived advantages of share options that were identified during debates in Congress.

It is important to note that in the debate there is an implied distinction between share options that are made available to employees generally and those that are restricted to senior executives. The arguments in favour of the use of share options tend to focus on schemes that cover a significant part of the workforce. ESOs are seen to play a crucial role in the growth of high technology companies in the US, and in job creation. This is reflected in such general statements as share options: ". . . have played an invaluable role of the creation of our thriving high technology industry"; and ". . . make it possible to start new companies and create new jobs with significantly less cash than would otherwise be required".

The mechanism through which share option schemes assist in job creation, and in the development of high-technology companies, is identified in the debates as occurring through a number of inter-related factors: (a) share options are used to attract and retain employees; (b) share options provide employees with an incentive to work and to increase the value of the company (and its common stock); (c) share options make it possible for employees to purchase shares in the company, thereby allowing the benefits of employee share ownership to be obtained; (d) share options play a crucial role in creating and sustaining an entrepreneurial culture, encouraging risk taking and spurring technological innovation; and (e) share options allow new companies to conserve cash resources as employees will forego salary and benefits in return for share options.

Senator Lieberman, after indicating concern about stimulating job creation in the US economy, suggested that ". . . it's important not to overlook a powerful job creation engine that is already pumping out thousands of high-quality jobs with a future in this country . . . (T)hat engine is small business, *the fuel is the broad-based employee stock option*" (italics added).

The FASB's proposals were strongly criticized in Congress, mainly on the basis of their economic consequences but also on technical grounds. The main effect of the FASB's proposals would be to reduce the reported earnings of a company that grants share options to its employees. New high-technology companies would be most affected. This is because such companies are more likely to be using share option schemes, and also because of the higher volatility of their share prices means that the values of the options are greater than for otherwise similar options granted by a company with lower share price volatility. It was indicated in Congress that independent analysts had suggested that compliance with the FASB's proposals would result in a reduction in the earnings of high technology companies of between 30 and 50%. The reduction in reported earnings was seen to impact on company value and the ability of companies to raise finance. It was suggested that as a consequence of the FASB's proposals and of their implications for companies' earnings, companies would reduce their use of share option schemes. For example, it was stated that the ". . . FASB's proposal would place companies in the position of choosing between a drastic reduction in reported earnings or simply not using employee stock options". A reduction in the use of ESOs, it was suggested, would make it more difficult to recruit and retain talented employees, and so make it more difficult to start new companies.

The possible restriction in the use of share options was seen to be limited to employees. For example, it was stated by Senator Joseph I. Lieberman introducing the Equity Expansion Act 1993 in the US Senate 29 June 1993 (Congressional Record (103rd Congress) p. 58249): "It's well known that the political pressure on FASB stems in large part from the mistaken belief that stock options only go to a few top executives. It's painfully ironic that FASB's new accounting rule would translate that premise into a self-fulfilling prophesy. Top executives will always be able to bargain for equity compensation, and boards of directors will want them to have it, even if FASB doubles its cost. What will be lost, however, is the tradition of granting stock options to a company's entire work force."

Two technical objections emerged during the debates in congress. The first of these was related to the difficulty in measuring the value of share option compensation. Doubts were expressed on the ability of models to estimate the value of ESOs, and the subjectivity of the estimates. The second was related to the nature of the transaction that is being accounted for: ". . . stock options authorize a future capital transaction between a company's stockholders and employees. The cost of that transaction is borne entirely by the shareholders—not the company—through a dilution in the value of their shares. This cost to shareholders is fully disclosed by current stock option accounting as a reduction in earnings per share."

The resolution of both houses of Congress was that there should be no change to the current accounting rule under APB *Opinion 25.* There are, as indicated, problems with this Opinion. In particular it requires different accounting treatment for fixed and for performance based options. As the exercise price of most options is set at, or above, the market price of the shares at the time of grant, there is usually no charge to income from the grant of fixed options. However, the value of performance options is measured at the time any conditions are met, which is after the time of grant. Therefore, there is likely to be a charge against income in respect of performance option, so creating an incentive to issue fixed options. The proposed Equity Expansion Act of 1993, which was introduced in the summer of 1993, would have required an amendment to Section 14 of the Securities Exchange Act of 1934 as follows:

> The Commission shall not require or permit an issuer to recognize any expense or other charge in financial statements furnished to its securities holders resulting from, or attributable to, either the grant, vesting, or exercise of any option or other right to acquire any equity security of such issuer . . . which is granted to its directors, officers, employees or other persons in connection with the performance of services, where the exercise price of such option or right is not less than the fair market value of the underlying security at the time such option or right is granted.

The effect of such an Act, which would have been to remove the perceived discrimination against performance options, would have been both on the operation of APB *Opinion 25* and the FASB's proposed accounting standard.

The FASB issued *SFAS No. 123* in October 1995. The standard represents a compromise between the original FASB's position, as represented in the exposure draft, and that of its opponents. The reasons for the FASB's change of position are explained in the standard:

> The debate on accounting for stock-based compensation unfortunately became so divisive that it threatened the Board's future working relationship with some of its constituents. Eventually, the nature of the debate threatened the future of accounting standards setting in the public sector.
>
> The Board continue to believe that financial statements would be more relevant and representationally faithful if the estimated fair value of employee stock options was included in determining an entity's net income, just as other forms of compensation are included. To do so would be consistent with accounting for the cost of all other goods and services received as consideration for equity instruments. The Board also believes that financial reporting would be improved if all equity instruments granted to employees, including instruments with variable features such as options with performance criteria for vesting, were accounted for on a consistent basis. However, in December 1994, the Board decided that the extent of improvement in financial reporting that was envisioned when this project was added to its technical agenda and when the Exposure Draft was issued was not attainable because the deliberate, logical consideration of issues that usually leads to improvement in financial reporting was no longer present (SFAS 123 paras. 60–61).

The accounting standard, therefore, does not require companies to follow what the FASB consider to represent *best practice*. However, where companies do not follow best practice, they are required to disclose additional information as footnotes to the accounts.

SFAS 123 provides companies with the choice of accounting for share options in terms of their *intrinsic* or their *fair* values. Accounting for share options in terms of their intrinsic values follows the method in APB *Opinion No. 25.* As indicated above, this generally means that no compensation expense is recognized in respect of the grant of a fixed ESO; whereas a compensation cost may be recognized in respect of a performance-type option. However, where a company chooses to value the option in terms of its intrinsic value, it must: (a) disclose pro forma net income as if the fair value method had been used; and (b) if EPS is presented, this must be based on the fair value method. Therefore, where a company chooses to use intrinsic values, it is required to provide sufficient disclosures of income based on the fair value method.

SUMMARY AND CONCLUSION

The evolution of accounting rules for ESOs has to be set against the background of public interest. Street et al. (1997) examine the reporting of share option compensation in US newspapers and business magazines over the period 1975 to 1993. Commenting on the results of their analysis, they suggest that public opinion about share option compensation changed in the early 1990s when, with the US in recession, there were announcements of "mega-grants and multi-million-dollar payouts" to executives. The new SEC proxy disclosure requirements and the FASB's proposals that share option compensation be treated as an expense are seen as a response to the growing public disquiet. This view is consistent with Quinn (1995). However, Street and her colleagues note a change following the FASB's proposals. They write: "Reacting to the FASB's announce-ment, a new media voice emerged, speaking on behalf of corporate management. This new media theme brought forth reasons and arguments why such action was 'unwise', including concern over measurement problems associated with stock option compensation and the many benefits of such compensation plans to corporate shareholders" (p. 235). The change in climate, which threatened the FASB, eventually led the Board to modify its proposals.

The accounting problems that arise in respect of ESOs, as described in this chapter, basically relate to issues of corporate governance and income measurement. Executive compensation schemes are structured so as to reward executives for their performance, and also align their interests with those of the shareholders. Such schemes are, however, open to abuse. The purpose of accounting in this context is to make executive compensation more transparent with a view to shareholders, and the market, exercising control to restrict excess. Accounting issues of share option compensation also relate to income measurement. The grant of share options to managers and employees is a qualitatively different type of transaction to cash payments as it does not involve a transfer of economic benefit from the grantor company. ESOs are accounted for both as a dilution to earnings per share and as an expense. The developments that have recently occurred in both these areas have taken place against a background of political concern.

There has been a considerable increase in the amount of information disclosed about executive compensation. In both the US and UK it is necessary to disclose information about who determines the compensation of executives and what policies they adopt. Information is also disclosed about incentive schemes. There are two approaches that can be taken to disclosure of information on share options: one is to provide information in order that the user can assess the value of the share options, the other is to indicate the value of the option at the time of grant. The former approach is adopted by the ASB whereas the SEC tends towards the alternative approach. By so doing, the SEC is confronted with the issue of measurement. Companies are allowed either to disclose the profit holders would make, under assumptions about growth in the price of the companies' shares, if they exercised the options at maturity, or their present value as calculated using an option pricing model. Information in this first category could be calculated easily by users of accounts, whereas calculation of the present value of the option is beyond the capability of most users.

Although public concern has been about the perceived abuse of share options granted to executives; the benefits of share option compensation are highlighted in the debate over the FASB's proposals on accounting for share option compensation. The debate that followed the publication of the exposure draft reveals differences as to the way in which certain types of transactions should be accounted for, as well as the potential economic consequences of accounting standards. One view underlying the technical concerns over share option compensation is that the grant of share options is a transaction between shareholders and the recipients of the options and that, apart any payment for the option or amounts received on its exercise, the transaction has no effect on the company itself. An alternative view is that income should be measured after recognizing the grant of the option. If this view is taken then the value of the option should be measured with a reasonable degree of reliability.

The main component of the debate, however, concerned the impact of the potential impact of the proposed accounting standard on the US economy. It is necessary to assess whether accounting standards that affect earnings have any *real* impact on the value of the company. A real effect on the company's value may occur if the accounting standard results in real changes such as the amount of tax payable, the amount of compensation paid under incentive schemes, or potential breaches of debt covenants; or whether the changes are purely cosmetic. If the changes are purely cosmetic then there should be no economic consequences following from a change of accounting rules. However, if the change does have real consequences then there is a real impact on the value of the company. Perhaps the problem lies where managers believe that a cosmetic change will be judged to have a real impact and so change the way in which the company behaves. From the debate it is difficult to assess whether the proposed method of accounting for share option compensation would have been simply cosmetic or whether there was a real impact.

6
Taxation of Share Options

President John F. Kennedy, in his tax message to Congress in 1963, captured one of the main aspects of the tax problem of share options when he said: "Stock options represent compensation for services. Taxpayers are generally required to pay ordinary income tax on their compensation. To the extent that the stock option provisions allow highly-paid executives to pay tax at capital gains rates or to escape all tax on part of their compensation, they are not consonant with accepted principles of tax fairness." It is important, as President Kennedy suggested, for a tax system to be fair. While the principle of fairness is generally accepted, there is less agreement on the method by which fairness can be achieved in the taxation of different forms of executive and employee compensation.

Before deciding how to tax share options it is necessary to determine whether they are, as implied by President Kennedy's remark, a compensation benefit. A decision in the UK courts during the 1930s implies that share options granted to directors and employees are compensation benefits. The US courts came to a similar conclusion in the 1940s, although previously they had drawn a distinction between compensatory and proprietary options, the latter being granted to allow employees, particularly managers, to increase their ownership interest in the company. Once it is decided that share options represent an employment compensation benefit, three problems need to be resolved. These are the occasion of the taxable event, the amount on which tax should be charged, and whether any profit should be subject to income tax, or capital gains tax, or perhaps a mixture of both taxes.

The benefit to employees may be argued variously to arise on the date of the option is granted, the date it is exercised, or the date of disposal of shares acquired on any exercise of the option. In addition, the taxable event for options with vesting provisions and/or performance conditions may be argued to be the date on which all conditions are met. What makes the problem difficult to resolve is that ESOs, unlike traded options, are usually non-transferable. This means their value cannot be realized except by exercising the options and selling the underlying shares. Under both UK and US tax law, the taxable event is usually defined as the date the option is exercised[60]. If the taxable event is when the option is exercised, then the value of the benefit is the difference between the fair value of the underlying shares on the exercise date and the exercise price. Finally, if share options are a compensation benefit, then the benefit should be subject to the same tax as all other forms of compensation, namely income tax[61]. This being the case then, from the perspective of the grantor company, a deduction should be allowed in respect of share option compensation in the same way it is allowed for other forms of compensation. US tax rules follow this logic, but those in the UK do not.

It has been argued that the taxation of share options in the way described above is unfair. The argument is that the compensation benefit that is acquired is the value of the option at the time of grant. After that time employees are in the same position as third parties who invest in options and who may make a *capital* profit on the exercise of the options. Concern over the splitting of the profit in respect of share options would not be present if the rates of capital gains tax and income tax are the same, and if profits as computed under the rules of the two taxes are the same. The problem is that the rates of the two taxes have differed significantly at times over the past half century, with the rate of income tax generally being higher than that on capital gains tax[62]. For example, in the UK capital gains tax was only introduced in 1965 and then at a flat rate of 30%. This contrasts with a combined rate of income tax and the top marginal rate of surtax of up to 83%. When there is such divergence between the rates of income and capital gains tax, and where the option is taxed other than at the time of grant, it is

[60] A House of Lords decision in 1960, however, was that the taxable benefit arises at the time of grant. Legislation was subsequently introduced to make the taxable event the time of exercise.
[61] Although executive and employee compensation may also be subject to social security taxes, the effect of these taxes on share option compensation are not considered in this book.
[62] The Tax Reform Act of 1986 in the US and the Finance Act 1988 in the UK both aligned the rates of tax on capital gains with that on income.

important to determine whether the benefit is charged to income or capital gains tax.

Legislation has been introduced in both the UK and US that provides, subject to conditions, for the benefit of share option compensation to be taxed as a capital gain, rather than as income. In addition, in both countries this legislation generally treats the disposal of shares acquired on the exercise of the options as the taxable event. This means that any tax can be paid from the proceeds of the disposal. Two types of tax-preferred share scheme are to be found in the legislation of both countries. One type of scheme is intended to be of benefit to all the employees of a company, while the other provides benefits to senior managers. A key feature of such all-employee share option schemes is that all eligible employees, i.e. those with sufficient length of service and who work for more than a minimum number of hours per week (or months per year), must be able to participate in the scheme on similar terms. Discretionary share option schemes, on the other hand, provide that options can be granted to selected directors and employees.

The reasons why legislation has been passed to facilitate share option schemes are complex, and probably change over time. Arguments used in parliamentary debates on employee share ownership schemes are explored in Chapter 3. Legislation in respect of discretionary schemes has been supported on grounds of neutrality, the need for companies to attract and retain employees, and on the view that options provide managers with appropriate incentives. The basis of these arguments has been challenged at various times. President Kennedy in his speech to US Congress, for example, suggested that the advantages claimed for executive share options:

> . . . do not appear to be substantiated by experience. Option benefits are haphazardly distributed. The rewards they confer on highly paid executives have been related not so much to their efforts in improving company profits as to changes in investor outlook and stock prices . . . The use of stock options frequently tends to impede rather than to improve executive mobility. The available evidence suggests that options are used almost entirely to reward present management rather than to attract new executives. The conditions of their exercise are usually calculated to tie executives to their present jobs . . .

If President Kennedy, and others holding similar opinions, are correct then it may be that taxation itself is the main reason why companies grant share options to their directors and senior executives. The results of studies by Hite and Long (1982) and Long (1992) give some support for this view.

The concern on both sides of the Atlantic in the early 1990s about excessive executive compensation led to the establishment in the UK of The Study Group on Directors' Remuneration (the Greenbury Committee). When it reported in 1995, the Government immediately announced changes to the legislation on discretionary share option schemes. The US Congress responded somewhat differently to concerns over excessive compensation by introducing legislation designed to restrict the size of payments made to senior executives of US public companies. The rules, which distinguish between performance-related compensation and other compensation, restrict to $1 000 000 the tax deductibility by a company of non-performance-related compensation of certain senior executives. Performance-related compensation, which includes share options, falls outside this restriction on deductibility if it fulfils certain conditions. This legislation, as well as incorporating principles of strong corporate governance, contains provisions to prevent to abuse of certain types of arrangement within share option schemes.

Tax rules on share options are attempting to achieve diverse objectives. On the one hand, the Courts and legislators are attempting to formulate rules that ensure that the taxation of share options is *fair vis-à-vis* other forms of compensation. These rules are applied to *non-approved* share option schemes. On the other hand, legislation has been enacted so as to provide tax incentives to encourage companies to adopt share option schemes. Schemes that receive tax preferences are of two types. One type is the employee share scheme that is open to the majority of employees; the other is the discretionary scheme that is restricted to certain, usually senior, employees and directors. It is concern over the total amounts of compensation paid to directors and senior executives that led to amendments to legislation on discretionary share option schemes in the UK, and the introduction of measures to restrict the deductibility of excessive compensation in the US.

NON-STATUTORY SCHEMES

The tax legislation relating to non-statutory schemes has evolved in a way that attempts to treat share option compensation in the same way as other types of employment income. In order to construct rules that tax share options in the same way as other employment income it is necessary to resolve a number of issues. Not least of these is whether the grant of share options does in fact represent employment income. This is important in determining whether employees should be subject to tax on income profits or capital profits in relation to share options. If share options represent employment income then it is necessary to determine the time when the income is received and the amount of the benefit.

It is possible to identify three dates on which any benefit relating to the grant of share options could be taxed: these are the date of grant, the date of exercise and the date of disposal of any shares acquired on the exercise of the options. If share options are granted as a reward for past effort then the options should be taxed on the grant date. Any subsequent change in the value of the options may be argued to be outside the influence of employees and so cannot be regarded as employment income. In this sense employees are in the same position as outside investors in the company's warrants. Any profit that such investors make in relation to the warrant would usually be treated as a capital profit. The main problem with taxing options at the time of grant is that of determining their value. It is difficult to determine the fair, or market, value of options at the time of grant. As options are frequently granted with an exercise price equal to, or greater than, the market value of the underlying shares at the time of grant, the options are unlikely to have an *intrinsic* value. The problems of valuation are avoided by taxing options at the time of exercise or at the time of disposal of any shares acquired on the exercise of the options. However, any profit arising on these dates relates partly to employment and partly to factors arising after the date of grant that are outside the control of executives and employees. In devising rules to tax share options, it is therefore necessary to achieve a balance between conceptual issues and practical problems of assessing and collecting tax.

UK Tax Law

UK tax law on share options, which is concerned almost exclusively with the tax position of the grantee, developed in two stages. First, case law was developed in the courts and second, when this resulted in a politically unacceptable decision, government introduced legislation. The decisions of the courts were made at a time when income profits were taxable but capital gains were not. Taxpayers were consequently keen to ensure that any profit made in respect of share options was treated as a capital profit. Even with the introduction of capital gains tax in 1965, the rate of capital gains tax was, until 1988, significantly below the marginal rate of income for many taxpayers in receipt of share options. In addition, individual taxpayers have an annual exempt amount for capital gains tax. This, together with the ability to defer capital gains in certain cases, means the effective rate of tax is nil for many taxpayers.

Employment income is charged to tax under the rules of Schedule E. In order to determine whether share option compensation should be subject to income tax it is necessary to determine: (a) whether the recipient of an option granted by the employer should be charged to tax on the benefit under Schedule E; and (b) if it is decided that the receipt the share option does represent a benefit, then when is that income to be assessed to tax. These questions were considered by the Courts. The basis of the decisions of the courts on share options is to be found in the case of *Weight* v. *Salmon* [1935] 19 TC 174. The decision is this case established that where an employee acquires shares at a discount, that discount constitutes a benefit taxable under the general rules of Schedule E. As a share option will only normally be exercised if the market price of the shares is above the exercise price, the exercise of an option usually implies that shares are purchased at a discount.

If option arrangements are to be taxed then it is necessary to determine whether this should be at the time of grant or exercise of the option, or at some other time. This question was first considered in the Scottish case of *Forbes's Executors* v. *CIR* [1958] 38 TC 12. The Court of Sessions decided in this case that the option is taxable at the time it is exercised, rather than at the time of grant. The basis of this decision is that, in order to be chargeable to tax under Schedule E, it is necessary to show that the benefit can be turned into cash. The rights in the option in this case were personal to the holder and could not be transferred. Therefore, at the time of grant the holder could not realize the value of the option. Further, it was noted that in order to exercise the option it was necessary to make a cash payment. As the option is capable of being turned to cash at the time of exercise by selling the shares, it was decided that the option was taxable at that time.

The rule in the Forbes case was subsequently changed by the decision of the House of Lords in *Abbot* v. *Philbin* [1960] 39 TC 82. Here it was decided that the option was a benefit which could be charged to tax in the year of grant. The option was, like that in the Forbes case, not transferable. However, it was considered that there were other ways of turning it to cash than by exercising the option and selling the shares. Lord Reid indicated that ". . . I find nothing to indicate that there would have been much difficulty in finding someone who would have paid a substantial sum for an undertaking by the Appellant to apply for the shares when supplied with the purchase money and called upon to exercise the option, and thereupon to transfer the shares" (p. 120). In deciding that the benefit is taxable at the time of grant, rather than exercise, the court recognized that any increase in the difference between the market price and exercise price between the dates of grant and exercise arises from the rights under the option agreement, rather than from the employment.

The rule in *Abbot* v. *Philbin* was subsequently reversed by legislation. In his 1966 Budget Statement, James Callaghan (Labour), then Chancellor of the Exchequer, proposed that income tax, and surtax, should be charged in respect of the exercise of options on the difference between the value of shares on the exercise date and the exercise price. In announcing this proposal, he stated:

> When a director or employee exercises a share option he is getting something which is worth more than he pays for it, and the difference in value is remuneration which ought to pay Income Tax and Surtax. However, the courts have decided that the tax liability arose when the option was granted, and not when it is exercised, and as a result very little tax can be charged in practice. Hence no doubt the growing popularity of options; and hence my proposal to put their taxation on a proper footing for the future.

The justification for taxing options at exercise is therefore twofold: one is a conceptual argument having to do with what constitutes the benefit; the other has to do with the problem of administering the tax system.

Arguments challenging the conceptual basis of the change were presented during the Committee stage of the Finance Bill. Peter Hordern (Conservative), for example, commented:

> When an option is granted, all that happens is that an employee is invited to engage upon the swings and roundabouts of outrageous fortune in the fortunes of the company. To suggest that the price of the shares increases because of the work of the particular individual and that is the sole reason for the increase in the prices of the shares is a perfectly ludicrous understanding for anyone who knows about the movement of share prices.
>
> Nobody could use the argument that shares have appreciated in value because of the office of the employee or executive. But that is what would have to be argued if this liability to Schedule E were to be incurred. The value of the option, therefore, can only be the consideration given for the option when it is granted. (House of Commons Official Report (Fifth Series), Vol. 730, p. 180)

The problem of administering a tax on the grant of options was indicated by Niall MacDermot (Financial Secretary (Labour)) when he stated that Schedule E tax on the granting of options is ". . . largely ineffective, because usually the options are granted for a nominal sum and it is rarely possible to establish more than a nominal value at that stage" (p. 216).

The legislation contained in the Finance Act 1966 was modified by the Finance Act 1972[63]. This required that, where share options were capable of being exercised more than 7 years (10 years for options granted after 5 April 1998) after it was obtained, income tax would be charged both at the time of grant and at the time of exercise. The amount to be charged at the time of grant is determined as being at least the difference between the market price of the underlying shares and the exercise price. Any tax charged at grant, however, would be deductible from that charged when the option is exercised.

Two types of share option scheme are therefore recognized in legalization. There are schemes where the share options are not capable of being exercised more than 10 years from the time of grant. Here tax is charged at the time of exercise on the difference

---

[63] The legislation is now contained in TA 1988 s 135.

between the market value of the shares at the time of exercise and the exercise price of the option. There are also schemes where the share options are capable of being exercised more than 7 years from the time of grant. Here tax is charged both at the time of grant and exercise, with any tax paid at the time of grant being deducted from that payable at the time of exercise. Since the exercise price of most share options granted under unapproved schemes is at least the market price of the shares at the time of grant, tax is usually not payable at the time of grant.

The grant of a share option to an executive or employee is not treated as an expense of the grantor company. The grant of a share option is, however, a disposal of an asset for capital gains tax purposes. Where an option is granted in consideration for, or recognition of, another's services in employment, then the consideration for the asset is deemed to be its market value[64]. If the option is exercised, the grant of the option and the issue of shares is treated as a single transaction[65] and, as the issue of shares is not a chargeable transaction, the whole transaction is not chargeable. In theory, therefore, a chargeable gain arises on the grant of the option but no tax will be payable if the option is subsequently exercised. In practice it is considered unlikely that tax would be charged on the grant of the option because of the problem of determining the option's market value[66].

US Tax Law

The development of US tax rules on share options is described by Long (1992). Until 1939, the Commissioner of the Internal Revenue ruled that the excess of the market price at the date of exercise over the exercise price is taxable as employment income. A Supreme Court decision in *Palmer* v. *Commissioner* in 1937 that gains from the exercise of warrants are not taxable as income was extended in 1939 to share options that were of a "proprietary" nature. Therefore, share options that were granted by companies so as to allow

[64] Taxation of Chargeable Gains Act 1992 s17(1).
[65] Taxation of Chargeable Gains Act 1992 s144(2).
[66] The possibly of tax being charged on the grant of a share option is recognized in TCGA 1992 s 149A (inserted by FA 1993 s 104) which indicates that, in the case of approved share option schemes, the grantor should be treated as if s 17(1) does not apply.

employees to gain an ownership position were not taxable as income. On the other hand, share options granted as compensation were taxable. No deduction as a business expense of the company was allowed in the case of proprietary options, whereas such a deduction was allowed for options awarded as compensation. The position changed with the Supreme Court decision in *Commissioner* v. *Smith* in 1945. Following this decision, all share options are treated as income at the time of exercise, the taxable amount being the excess of the market price of the shares on the exercise date and the exercise price. A corresponding deduction is allowed by the company. According to Long, this decision forms the basis for taxing non-statutory share options.

The US tax rules on share option schemes are now contained in section 83 of the Internal Revenue Code. The section, which deals with property transferred in connection with the performance of services, has special relevance to employee share options. The general rule in section 83 is that where property is transferred to an employee in connection with the performance of services, the excess of: (a) the fair market value of the property at the first time the rights of the employee in the property are transferable or are not subject to a substantial risk of forfeiture, whichever occurs earlier, over (b) the amount (if any) paid for such property, shall be included in the gross income of the employee in the first taxable year in which the rights of the employee in the property are transferable or are not subject to a substantial risk of forfeiture, whichever is applicable.

In order to determine the amount, and timing, of the taxable income it is therefore necessary to determine the first time that the rights of the employee in the property are transferable or are not subject to a substantial risk of forfeiture. Substantial risk of forfeiture is defined as a restriction that conditions an individual's right to full enjoyment of the property upon the performance of substantial services by the individual; and property is defined as being transferable if the rights are not subject to substantial risk of forfeiture. In theory, therefore, an option that is transferable and not subject to substantial risk of forfeiture would be taxable at the time of grant. However, an option without a readily ascertainable fair market value at the time of grant is not subject to tax at the time of grant.

The taxation of non-qualified share options is considered in detail in regulations to section 83[67]. Two types of share options are distinguished under the regulations; those with a readily ascertainable fair value and those without such a value. The regulations then proceed to define the former. An option has a readily ascertainable market value if the option is actively traded on an established market, or the option is not actively traded on an established market but certain conditions are met. These conditions are: (a) the option is transferable by the optionee; (b) the option is exercisable immediately in full by the optionee; (c) the option or the property subject to the option is not subject to any restriction or condition (other than a lien or other condition to secure the payment of the purchase price) which has a significant effect upon the fair market value of the option; and (d) the fair market value of the option privilege is readily ascertainable. In the case of options that are actively traded in an established market, the fair value is generally the average of the highest and lowest quoted selling prices on the date of grant. In the case of options not actively traded on a market, the valuation must take into account all aspects of the option privilege, and in particular it is necessary to consider whether the value of the property subject to the option can be ascertained, the probability of any ascertainable value of such property increasing or decreasing, and the length of the period during which the option can be exercised.

An employee will recognize, at the time of grant, ordinary income equal to the fair value of the option, less any amount paid, where the option has a readily ascertainable fair market value at that time. There are no further income tax consequences of the option. If the option is exercised and the shares held as a capital asset, any gain is treated as a long-term capital gain. The amount of the gain is measured as the difference between: (a) the selling price; and (b) the amount paid on the exercise of the option together with any amount in respect of the option included in the employee's income at the time of grant. There is no taxable event at the time of grant if the option does not have a readily ascertainable fair market value at that time. The taxable event occurs at the time of exercise when an employee will recognize as ordinary income an amount equal to the fair value of the shares at the time of exercise less the exercise price and any amount paid for the option.

---

[67] Regulation 1.83-7 Taxation of nonqualified share options.

The employer is allowed a deduction equal in amount to that included in the gross income of the employee, and the deduction is allowed in the same period that the employee's income is recognized. Therefore, where the option has a readily ascertainable market value at the time of grant, the employer is allowed a deduction at that time equal to the fair value of the option at that time less any amount paid for it. However, where the option does not have a readily ascertainable market value at the time of grant, the employer is allowed a deduction, at the time of any exercise of the option by the employee, equal to the fair value of the shares at the time of exercise less the exercise price and any amount paid for the option. The tax implications for the employer therefore are symmetrical to the tax treatment of the employee.

Comparison of UK and US Tax Law

A comparison between the tax laws of the UK and US provides useful insights into the problem of taxing share option schemes. In both countries income profits are treated differently from capital profits. This difference underlies much of the debate on the development of tax rules for share options. An employee is assumed in both countries to receive a benefit when granted a share option. If there are no special conditions attached to the option, after grant the employee is in the same position as a third party holding an option on the company's shares and so, like a third party holding an option, any gain on the exercise of the option should be subject to capital gains tax, not income tax. This is basically the position reached in *Abbott* v. *Philbin* and in section 83 of the US tax code. However, there are generally conditions attached to share options granted to employees that make such options different from options that are actively traded in established markets and so it is difficult to determine the value at the time of grant[68]. It is therefore difficult to determine how much tax should be payable at the time of grant.

The intrinsic value of options, unlike their fair value, can be readily determined for companies whose shares are listed. This concept of value has been incorporated into tax rules. UK legislation,

[68] The problem of valuing share options at the time of grant is discussed in detail in Chapter 4. It should be noted that tax law was developed in both countries before the advent of modern option pricing models.

however, is based on the assumption that, since most options do not have an intrinsic value at the time of grant, no tax would be charged. The taxable event is therefore at the time of exercise. However, intrinsic value is important where the options are capable of being exercised on a date more than 10 years after the date of grant. US tax law recognizes the problem of valuation but, unlike UK law, acknowledges the possibility that the value of some options can be determined at the time of grant. Like the UK, most options will be taxable at the time of exercise. UK tax legislation contains specific provisions whereby tax is chargeable at the times of both grant and exercise, with any tax paid at grant being deductible from that payable at exercise. Again, as most options do not have an intrinsic value at the time of grant and because it is difficult to determine the value of the option at that time, tax is unlikely to be payable at the time of grant.

The main difference in the tax laws of the two countries is in the taxation of the employer. There are usually no tax consequences for the employer in connection with non-statutory share option schemes in the UK. Deductions in respect of share options are not allowable but are allowed in respect of most other types of compensation. This may lead to a violation of neutrality between share options and other forms of compensation. US tax rules, on the other hand, maintain a symmetry between the tax treatment of the employee and employer.

DISCRETIONARY SHARE OPTION SCHEMES AND COMPENSATION THAT IS EXCESSIVE

Legislation covering the taxation of share options has been seen to have a discriminatory effect on the use of share option schemes, both for executives and employees generally and for certain groups in particular. It is against this background that legislation on discretionary share option schemes was developed. Participants in discretionary share option schemes are mainly a company's directors and its senior executives. Legislation in both the UK and US offers income tax relief in respect of options granted under approved schemes. Instead of being charged to income tax, holders are liable to capital gains tax on the disposal of shares acquired through exercise of the options. Legislation in both countries also places restrictions on the characteristics of the options, and on the maximum value of shares that can be acquired by exercising the options.

Public concern over boardroom pay in both the UK and the US has resulted in governments introducing, or amending, legislation on the taxation on executive pay, including share options. The US legislation focuses on executive pay that is excessive by restricting the deductibility by the company in respect of an executive's pay to $1million. This restriction, however, only applies to pay that is not performance related. Included in the legislation are measures on share options, some of which are designed to deal with the abuse of share option schemes.

Executive Share Option Schemes

Current UK tax law on executive share option schemes has its origins in legislation contained in the Finance Act 1972. Introducing the proposed legislation, Anthony Barber, then Chancellor in a Conservative Government, expressed concern over the impact of the legislation contained in the Finance Act 1966 on the taxation of share options, and indicated the importance of share option schemes in recruiting, retaining and providing incentives for management. He stated: "I believe it is now recognised on both sides of the House that the 1966 legislation was altogether too drastic and that, contrary to the view which was then put forward by Treasury Ministers, share options have a proper and valuable role to play in stimulating management enterprise and in helping industry to recruit and to keep the management talent that it needs." The Chancellor then went on to describe the main features of the new legislation. In particular, schemes meeting certain conditions would be exempted from the 1966 legislation. He indicated that these ". . . conditions will be broadly similar to those which responsible bodies regard as necessary to safeguard shareholders' interests".

The relief provided by the 1972 legislation was to exempt share options from income tax, but a liability to capital gains tax would arise on the disposal of any shares acquired through the exercise of options. Finance Act 1972 contains a series of conditions that must be met in order for employees to obtain income tax relief. These are that the option was acquired under an *approved* scheme, and that shares are no disposed of until the earlier of: (a) 3 years from the time of grant; (b) cessation of employment by reason of injury, disability or dismissal for redundancy; and (c) death.

A number of conditions must be met for a scheme to be approved. First, the scheme must be adopted by a resolution of shareholders, and shares must not be capable of being acquired under the scheme more than 10 years after its adoption. Second, the shares which may be acquired under the scheme must be shares of the company and be limited to: (a) 10% of ordinary share capital if capital does not exceed £2m; and (b) 5% of ordinary share capital if capital exceeds £2m. Third, the option must not be transferable and must not be capable of being exercised later than 7 years after grant, 6 months after cessation of employment, and 12 months after death. The exercise price, which must not be manifestly less than the market value at the time of grant, must be stated at that time. Finally, all participants must be full-time employees or directors, and the value of shares which may be acquired by a person under the scheme must not exceed four times relevant emoluments.

The legislation contained in Finance Act 1972 was repealed by a subsequent Labour Government in 1974. The then Chancellor, Denis Healey, indicating that: ". . . (A)s we made clear when we were in opposition, we have always regarded the benefits to directors and employees under schemes of this kind as part of the pay for the job, and it follows that such benefits ought to be taxed in the same way as normal remuneration instead of being liable simply at capital gains rates."

The basic provisions of the 1972 legislation were re-introduced in 1984 by a Conservative Government. Introducing the new legislation, the then Chancellor, Nigel Lawson, stated: ". . . I am convinced that we need to do more to attract top calibre company management and to increase the incentives and motivation of existing executives and key personnel by linking their rewards to performance." The reasons stated for introducing the scheme therefore bear close resemblance to those given by Anthony Barber 12 years earlier. The Chancellor then went on to state: ". . . I propose therefore that, subject to certain necessary limits and conditions, share options generally be taken out of income tax altogether, leaving any gain to be charged to capital gains tax on ultimate disposal of the shares". As with the earlier legislation, the approved share option scheme provided income tax relief for options fulfilling the required conditions. The conditions were also broadly in line with the 1972 rules.

Concern over both the level and structure of boardroom compensation resulted in the establishment of The Study Group on Directors' Remuneration (the Greenbury Committee), under the chairmanship of Sir Richard Greenbury, in January 1995[69]. One of the Committee's conclusions was that there is not a good reason why executive share option schemes should receive favourable tax treatment. It therefore recommended that Government should amend tax legislation in order for gains from executive share options to be taxed as income rather than capital gains. On the day the Greenbury Report was published, the then Chancellor, Kenneth Clarke, announced that he proposed to introduce legislation in the next Finance Bill to withdraw the income tax reliefs available to directors and employees participating in executive share option schemes. Announcing his proposals, he commented:

> Tax relief for executive option schemes was introduced in 1984 to help increase the incentive and motivation of executives and key personnel by encouraging the linkage of their rewards to overall company performance. Since then, the use of options and other forms of incentive scheme has grown and, as the Greenbury Report indicates, there is now no case for the tax system to favour one particular form of incentive over another. With this in mind, I believe it is now sensible for the choice of incentive scheme to be left to the private sector to decide in the light of good corporate practice.

The Chancellor's original proposals would have affected holders of options granted prior to the publication of the Greenbury Report. However, in response to representations, he announced later in July that holders of options granted before 17 July 1995 would continue to be entitled to income tax relief.

Later, in his 1995 Budget Statement, the Chancellor announced his proposals for amendments to existing legislation on share option schemes with the introduction of the *company share option plan*. Essentially, the conditions for the new scheme are the same as for the old one, with the exception that the limit is reduced to £20 000 on the holding of options, subsequently raised to £30 000 during the progress of the Finance Bill through Parliament. In announcing the

[69] See Chapter 5.

proposed changes to share option schemes, the Chancellor was keen to emphasize his commitment to employee share ownership. He did so in the following terms:

> All of the old-fashioned distinctions between employee and employer, between capital and labour, are being broken down in our modern enterprise economy. Most employees understand that their rewards depend on the success of the businesses for which they work. Most businesses believe that the best way to motivate staff is to let them share in the rewards of success. The public's willingness to embrace and understand these principles has been a major culture change over the past 16 years.
>
> An important part of this change has been the spread of employee share ownership, which is one of the most attractive features of what has become known as popular capitalism. Holding shares in the company for which they work gives people a stake in the company's future success. Nobody in this House has advocated the cause of performance related rewards and employee share ownership more than I have over the years and I started doing so well before these ideas become fashionable.

In contrast to amendments reducing the attractiveness of discretionary schemes, the Chancellor made proposals to make savings-related share option schemes more attractive.

The rules for *discretionary share option schemes*, renamed *company share option plans* by the Finance Act 1996, allow income tax relief subject to the fulfilment of specified conditions. These are that the option was acquired under an *approved* scheme, and there has not been an exercise of an option granted under the scheme within the 3 years prior to the current exercise. In order for a scheme to be approved it is necessary for it to meet defined conditions. First, the options must be on the ordinary shares of the company and must not be transferable, except on death. The options must not be capable of being exercised within 3 years, and later than 10 years, after grant, or 12 months after death. In addition, the exercise price, which must not be manifestly less than the market value at the time of grant, must be stated at the time of grant[70]. Second, the participants must be full-time directors or qualifying employees, and the value

---

[70] There was an exception before 1996 that, where the company operates an approved savings-related share option scheme and/or a profit-sharing scheme, the exercise price may be 85% of the market price at the time of grant.

of shares which may be acquired by any one person under the scheme must not exceed £30 000. The limit on the value of shares is the main amendment to the scheme. Prior to July 1995, the limit was the greater of £100 000 and four-times relevant remuneration.

Incentive Stock Option Plans

The development of US tax law on executive share option plans is described by Long (1992). He shows that the use of executive share options after the decision in *Commissioner* v. *Smith* in 1945 was infrequent. As a result, large US companies convinced Congress of the need to increase the ownership interest of managers. This resulted in the enactment of legislation, in the Revenue Act of 1950, on restricted stock options. Under the terms of the legislation, a restricted stock option is an option that has an exercise price of at least 85% of the fair market value of the shares, is non-transferable (except on death), and at the time of the option is granted, the individual does not own shares having more than 10% of the voting power of the company. An amendment in 1954 introduced the requirement that the option is not exercisable after 10 years from the date of grant. In order to obtain relief: (a) the option holder must have been an employee of the company at the time of exercise, or until 3 months before the exercise; and (b) the shares acquired must be held for at least the greater of 2 years after grant or 6 months after exercise. The rules on restricted stock options were replaced by ones on qualified stock options in 1963. There are two types of qualified stock options: incentive stock options and employee options.

Incentive stock option plans (ISOs) provide income tax relief[71] subject to the fulfilment of the conditions of the plan. Instead, capital gains tax is charged on the disposal of any shares acquired through the exercise of option. The company cannot treat the option as an expense where income tax relief is given. The rules concerning ISOs relate to both the conditions which must be satisfied in order for the employee to obtain benefit under the scheme, and the nature of the plan under which the option was granted. In order for there

---

[71] The exercise of an incentive stock option has implications for the calculation of the alternative minimum tax (AMT) as the difference between the fair value of the shares on the exercise date and the exercise price of the option is taken as an item of adjustment for AMT purposes.

to be no income arising on the exercise of the option, and no deduction for the company: (a) an employee should not dispose of any shares acquired under the exercise of an option within 2 years from the date of the granting of the option nor within 1 year after the transfer of such share; and (b) at all times during the period beginning on the date of the granting of the option and ending on the day 3 months before the date of such exercise, the individual was an employee of the company granting the option.

An ISO is defined as an option granted to an individual for any reason connected with his or her employment to purchase shares of the company where defined conditions are met. First, the option is granted under a plan which is approved by the shareholders within 12 months before or after the date such a plan is adopted. In particular, the plan should specify (a) the aggregate number of shares which may be issued under options and (b) the employees, or class of employees, eligible to receive options. The option must be granted within 10 years from the earlier of the date the plan is adopted, or the date it is approved by shareholders. Second, the option, which is non-transferable (except in the event of death), must not be capable of being exercised later than 10 years from the date the option is granted. The exercise price of the option should not be less than the fair market value of the shares at the time the option is granted. Third, at the time the option is granted, the employee does not own shares possessing more than 10% of the total combined voting power of all classes of the company's shares. In addition, there is a $100 000 per year limitation which means that, to the extent that the aggregate fair market value of shares with respect to which ISOs are exercisable for the first time by the employee during any calendar year exceeds $100 000, the options are treated as if they are not ISOs.

Comparison of UK and US Tax Law

Legislation has been introduced in both the US and UK to facilitate the use of share option schemes for selected employees, usually directors and senior executives. A comparison of the schemes in the two countries is shown in Table 6.1. The legislation in both countries provides income tax relief subject to compliance with the conditions of the schemes. Instead capital gains tax is charged on the disposal

Table 6.1 Comparison of Discretionary Share Option Schemes

	UK	US
Tax consequences for the employee	Income tax relief—holder charged to capital gains tax on disposal of shares acquired through exercise of options	Income tax relief—holder charged to capital gains tax on disposal of shares acquired through exercise of options
Tax consequences for the company	No chargeable gain arising on the grant of options	No deduction in respect of option allowed in computing taxable profits
Shareholder approval	—	The scheme must be approved by shareholders. The option must be granted within 10 years of the date the plan is adopted or, if earlier, from the date approved by shareholders
Exercise price	Not less than the market value of the shares at the time the option is granted	Not less than the fair market value of the stock at the time the option is granted
Exercise date	Maximum of 10 years from the time of grant	Maximum of 10 years from the time of grant
Transferability	Option must be non-transferable	Option must be non-transferable
Vesting period	Three years from the date of grant	—
Limitation on holdings	£30 000 (Prior to 17 July 1995—the greater of £100 000 and four times relevant remuneration)	The maximum value of stock over which ISOs may be exercisable for the first time in any calendar year is $100 000
Other restrictions on exercise	Income tax relief is not available within 3 years of the date on which an option was last exercised under an approved scheme	—
Death of employee	Option can be exercised by personal representative within 12 months of death	Option may be exercised by personal representatives
Cessation of employment	—	The holder must have been an employee of the company for the period up until at least 3 months before to the exercise of the option
Holding period of shares acquired by exercise of option	—	In order to obtain income tax relief, the employee cannot dispose of shares within 2 years from the date of grant nor 1 year after exercise of the option

of any shares acquired through the exercise of the options. Grantor companies are denied the deduction for options as an expense, available under US rules for non-qualified stock options, in situations where employees obtain income tax relief. In order to obtain income tax relief for options granted under ISOs plans it is necessary for individuals to have been employed by the company at least until 3 months before the option is exercised, and that shares acquired on the exercise of the option be held for a defined period. There is no comparable requirement in UK legislation. However, relief can only be obtained under UK legislation where the exercise of the option takes place 3 years or more after the exercise of other options granted under the scheme.

The main terms of the approved schemes in the two countries are broadly similar. The options, which should be non-transferable (except on death), should have an exercise price that is at least the market price of the underlying shares on the date of grant, and the maximum term of the options should be 10 years. In order to obtain income tax relief, options granted under UK legislation cannot be exercised within 3 years of grant. The main difference between the two countries is in the maximum number of options that can be held. Under UK legislation, the scheme must provide that no individual is granted options over shares with a market value at the time of grant of more than £30 000. On the other hand, holders of ISOs are restricted to options, exercisable for the first time during any calendar year, over shares with a fair value of $100 000.

Executive Compensation that is Excessive

In the Revenue Reconciliation Act of 1993, the US Congress implemented measures designed to curb excessive rewards to some senior executives of US public companies. The provisions, which restrict the tax deductibility by public companies of payments to certain executives, are contained in section 162(m) of the Internal Revenue Code. They are interesting in a number of ways. First, the measures incorporate some of the structure and information from the SEC (1992) disclosure rules on executive compensation[72]. Second,

---

[72] The SEC disclosure rules on executive compensation are discussed in Chapter 5.

a distinction is drawn between compensation and performance related compensation. It is only the deductibility of compensation that is restricted to $1 000 000. Third, for compensation to be performance related, the performance criteria have to be set by a compensation committee composed of outside directors. The compensation committee is also required to certify that the performance criteria have been met in any payments. Fourth, the material terms of performance related pay must be disclosed to shareholders and approved by them. Finally, there are provisions specifically relating to share options.

Section 162(m)

Section 162(m) basically states that a publicly held company[73] is denied a deduction for compensation paid to *covered* employees to the extent that such compensation exceeds $1 000 000. A covered employee is defined as the chief executive officer, or one of the four highest paid officers of the company other than the chief executive officer. Whether or not an individual is the chief executive officer or one of the four highest paid officers is determined by the disclosures made under the SEC rules.

Compensation is basically determined by following the usual rules for calculating deductions. An important exception is the one for *qualified performance-based compensation*. In order to qualify as performance-based compensation, the following criteria must be met: (a) the performance goals are determined by a compensation committee of the board of directors of the company that is comprised solely of two or more outside directors; (b) the material terms under which the compensation is to be paid, including the performance goals, are disclosed to shareholders and approved by a majority vote of shareholders before the payment of such compensation; and (c) before any payment of such compensation, the compensation committee certifies that the performance goals and any other material terms were in fact satisfied. The final regulations issued by the Internal Revenue Service in December 1995 provide further guidance.

---

[73] A publicly held company is defined as one whose common equity is registered under section 12 of the Securities Exchange Act 1934.

Performance-based Compensation

The regulations define the criteria that must be met in order for compensation to be performance based. Before looking at the requirements for share options, it is useful to look at the general rules on the performance goal requirements. These require that there be a pre-established goal, an objective compensation formula, and that only negative discretion may be exercised. The performance goal must be established within 90 days of the start of the period to which the goal relates and at the time the goal is set the outcome is substantially uncertain. Although the rules do not specify the types of goals that may be set, it is essential that the goals are *objective*. This is defined to mean that a third party having knowledge of the relevant facts could determine whether the goal is met or not. Second, there must be a formula for computing the amount that will be paid on achievement of the goal. Again the formula must be objective in the sense that an independent third party having knowledge of the performance goals could compute the amount payable given knowledge of the performance results. Finally, discretion is only allowed to reduce the amount payable on the achievement of the goal.

The treatment of grants of share options is specifically discussed in the regulations. Three basic conditions must be met: (a) the grant is made by the compensation committee; (b) the plan under which the options are granted states the maximum number of shares with respect to which options may be granted during a specified period; and (c) the options have an exercise price that is not less than the fair market value of the shares on the date of grant. The rules deal with two specific situations that may arise where there is a fall in the value of the underlying shares after the grant of options. First, restrictions placed on the number of shares over which options are granted within a period may, in the absence of specific provisions, be circumvented by cancelling options and issuing new ones. However, the rules require that cancelled options should continue to be counted against the maximum number of shares on which options may be granted. Second, where options are repriced by reducing the exercise price, the options are treated as having been cancelled and new options issued.

The Compensation Committee, Outside Directors and Shareholders'
Approval

Performance-based compensation must be awarded by a compensation committee composed of at least two outside directors. In
addition, shareholder approval is required for the performance
plans. The regulations define what is meant by an *outside* director.
Generally an outside director is a director who: (a) is not a current
employee of the company; (b) is not a former employee of the
company who receives benefits, other than retirement benefits,
from the company in respect of prior services; (c) has not been an
officer of the company; and (d) does not receive compensation from
the company other than for director's services. As well as being
responsible for determining the performance goals, the compensation
committee must certify that the performance goals and other material
criteria have in fact been satisfied.

Shareholders must approve all the material terms of the performance goals. This requires that information on the material terms of
the performance plan be disclosed to shareholders. The rules set
out the information that should be disclosed:

- A general description of the class of employees that are eligible
  to receive performance-based compensation.
- A description of the business criteria on which the performance
  goal is based, although there is no requirement to indicate the
  specific targets that must be met. It is sufficient to indicate that
  the bonus plan is based upon earnings per share, for example, if
  the performance goal is that earnings per share increase by 5%.
- The formula used to calculate the amount of compensation that
  could be paid to an executive *or* the maximum amount that
  would be paid to the executive if the performance goal is
  achieved.

Once the terms of the performance goal are disclosed, it is only
necessary to make further disclosures if there the compensation
committee makes material changes to the performance goals[74].

---

[74] If the compensation committee has authority to change the targets under a performance
goal after shareholder approval of the goal then material terms of the goal should be
disclosed to, and re-approved by, shareholders.

Although the concern of the general public seems to be about the large amounts paid to some senior executives of US public companies, the rules in section 162(m) of the Internal Revenue Code reflect the views of institutional shareholders that it is only necessary to penalize compensation that is not related to the performance of the company. In determining the criteria that must be fulfilled for compensation to be treated as qualified performance-based compensation, the legislation and related rules incorporate principles of *good* corporate governance. As well as requiring objectively defined performance goals and formulae for determining performance-based compensation, there are requirements concerning the involvement of a compensation committee composed solely of outside directors, disclosure of information to shareholders and approval of the arrangements by shareholders. The rules on share options are important where options are granted under non-qualified schemes as here employers are allowed deductions. The regulations also deal with potential abuses of by companies, in particular, where options are cancelled or repriced when there is a fall in share price.

EMPLOYEE SHARE OPTION SCHEMES

Schemes have been introduced by governments in both the UK and the US which use share options to facilitate employee share ownership. *Approved savings-related share option schemes* were introduced in the UK and *employee stock purchase plans* in the US. The reasons why governments may wish to promote employee share ownership are explored in Chapter 3. Share options represent one mechanism through which wider employee share ownership may be achieved. It is therefore possible that some of the arguments presented for employee share ownership also underly the option schemes.

The schemes in both countries allow for full or partial exemption from a charge to income tax in respect of the options. Instead, the profit on the disposal of any shares acquired on the exercise of options is charged to capital gains tax. Unlike discretionary share option schemes, employee share option schemes in both countries allow options to be issued at a discount. In order to ensure that the schemes provide benefits to *all* employees, both schemes contain rules to ensure that all employees fulfilling closely defined criteria are eligible to participate on equal terms.

Approved Savings-related Share Options

The origins of the approved savings-related share options scheme are to be found in the *share savings scheme* introduced by a Conservative government in 1973. One main reason for introducing the legislation was to achieve fairness as the tax benefits of the share option scheme introduced the previous year had mainly been confined to directors and senior executives. Anthony Barber, the then Chancellor, commented that existing share schemes had been directed to senior staff, and in any event, were unattractive to other employees. He indicated that ". . . (W)hat is wanted is a wider share-ownership scheme which will encourage companies to make it possible and practicable for each and every one of its employees who wants to, to acquire a real stake in the company for which he works". The share savings scheme, which provided for income tax relief, combined share purchase with a Save-As-You-Earn (SAYE) scheme and gave employees the option not to acquire the shares at a future date.

The rationale for introducing a scheme to encourage wider share ownership was indicated in the Committee Stage of the Finance Bill by the then Chief Secretary, Patrick Jenkin. He stated that: "Over the years there has been a great demand from all sides of the political fence to try to break down the barriers that exist between those who work for companies and those who own them. One of the ways . . . in which that can be achieved is to aim for a closer community of interest by making it possible for employees to become owners of and participators in the company in which they work". Employee share ownership is therefore being seen as a way of improving human relations. The legislation underlying the scheme was repealed following a change of government in 1974.

The savings-related share option scheme was proposed by a Conservative government in 1980. The then Chancellor, Sir Geoffrey Howe, introduced the scheme as a part of proposals to encourage personal investment. In his budget statement he indicated:

> I turn now to an area where the tax system can be used to involve the individual more closely in the workings of the economy. I refer to proposals which will encourage direct personal investment in stocks and shares of British industry. In the last 20 years, the proportion of

the equity of British companies, held in direct individual ownership, has almost halved. This is a trend I should like to reverse.

It is generally agreed that share ownership and profit sharing can help employees' understanding of, and commitment to, business and industry. I believe that ownership can also spread wider understanding of the role of risk-taking and initiative in the economic system.

After outlining his proposals for a savings-related share option scheme, similar to the 1973 scheme, the Chancellor stated that the measures ". . . will help to fulfil our promise to encourage employee share ownership and provide the incentive to save and build up capital". The scheme itself, like the 1973 scheme, combines savings with the possibility of share ownership.

Under the savings-related share option scheme, introduced in the Finance Act 1980, there is no income tax on the grant of the option, nor on its exercise. There is, however, a charge to capital gains tax on the disposal of any shares acquired through the exercise of the option. The chargeable gain is calculated using the amount paid for the shares. In addition, the bonus given in lieu of interest on the savings contract is free of tax. A number of conditions must be met in order for a savings-related share option scheme to receive approval from the Inland Revenue. First, there are rules about eligibility to participate in the scheme. The scheme must permit participation by every person who is an employee or a full-time director of the company[75], and who has been such during a qualifying period[76]. The qualifying period cannot exceed 5 years. The legislation requires that all participants who satisfy the conditions must participate on similar terms. This means that the exercise price and the circumstances under which the option may be exercised must be the same for all participants. However, the number of shares that may be acquired through the exercise of options may vary with such factors as level of compensation or length of service.

Second, the scheme provides for the grant of options, which must not be transferable (except if the participant dies), to acquire shares using the repayments, including the bonus, from a contractual savings scheme[77]. The contributions to the savings scheme must be

---

[75] Options may also be granted under a group scheme.

[76] A person must not be allowed to obtain or exercise rights under a scheme if he or she has a material interest in the grantor company, and that company is a close company.

[77] The amount may include, or exclude, the bonus payable under the savings scheme.

sufficient to pay for any shares to be acquired under the exercise of the option, but they must not exceed £250 per month. The time at which repayments are due, the bonus date, is taken to be the earliest date on which the bonus is payable (3 or 5 years) or, in the case of a 5-year savings contract, the earliest date on which the maximum bonus is payable (7 years).

Third, there are conditions relating to the exercise of options. The options must not be capable of being exercised before a bonus date, nor more than 6 months after such a date. If the option holder ceases to be employed by the company then: (a) the rights must lapse if the person has held them for less than 3 years; or (b) the rules may allow the person to exercise the option, within 6 months of cessation, if he has held it for more than 3 years. However, if the person ceases employment for reason of injury, disability, redundancy, or retirement, then the scheme must provide that the options may be exercised within 6 months of leaving employment. The scheme must also provide that in the event of the death of the option holder, the shares may be exercised within 12 months of death (or within 12 months following a bonus date when the holder dies within the 6-month period following a bonus date).

Fourth, there are conditions relating to the price at which shares may be acquired. The exercise price must be stated at the time of grant and must not be less than 80% of the market value of the shares at that time. The exercise price may be adjusted to take account of any variation in the share capital of the company.

Finally, the shares which may be acquired under the scheme must form part of the ordinary share capital of the company. The shares must be quoted on a recognized stock exchange, or be shares in a company that is not controlled by another company, or be shares in a company that is controlled by another company that is quoted on a recognized stock exchange. In addition, the shares must be fully paid up, not redeemable and not subject to any restrictions other than restrictions that apply to all shares of the same class. The only exception is that the employee may be required to dispose of the shares if he or she leaves the company.

The contractual savings scheme used by the company may be a Department of National Savings SAYE issue or a SAYE Sharesave scheme operated by a building society, bank or an authorized European savings institution. The employee agrees to pay an amount between £5 and £250 per month under such a scheme, with the savings normally being deducted from pay. A bonus is payable at the end of 3 or 5 years, but if repayment is not claimed for a further 2 years on a 5-year contract, a larger bonus is payable. Any bonus or interest payable under the scheme is free of UK income tax.

Employee Stock Purchase Plans

Employee stock purchase plans provide a company with a mechanism for allowing employees to acquire its shares. As with approved savings-related share schemes in the UK, the plans are designed to allow participation by all the employees of a company. Their advantage is that an employee is not taxed on the option granted under the plan at the time of grant, nor at the time of exercise. Instead the employee is taxed when he or she sells the shares acquired on the exercise of the option. The profit recognized at the time of sale is usually treated as a capital gain instead of income. Where this is the case, the company is unable to make a deduction in respect of the options.

The rules concerning employee stock purchase plans, like those for ISOs, relate to both: (a) the nature of the plan under which the option was granted and (b) the conditions which must be satisfied in order for the employee to obtain benefit under the scheme. An employee stock purchase plan must have the following conditions incorporated into its terms. The plan itself must be approved by the company's shareholders within 12 months before or after the date such plan is adopted. Only employees of the company, or its parent or subsidiary company, may participate in the plan, and under the terms of the plan all the company's employees are to be granted options. There are, however, two exceptions. First, no employee can be granted an option under the terms of the plan if he or she immediately after the option is granted, would own shares carrying 5% or more of the total combined voting power of the company. Second, certain employees *may* be excluded. These are: (a) employees who have been employed less than 2 years; (b) employees whose customary employment is 20 hours or less per week; (c) employees whose customary employment is for not more than 5 months in any calendar year; and (d) highly compensated employees. A highly compensated employee is essentially one who during the current, or the preceding, year: (i) is at any time a 5% owner; or (ii) receives compensation from the company in excess of $75 000; or (iii) receives compensation from the employer in excess of $50 000 and was in the top-paid group of employees for the year. In addition, no employee may be granted an option which permits his or her rights to purchase shares under all such plans of the company to accrue at a rate which exceeds $25 000 of fair market value of the shares (determined at the time such options are granted) for each calendar year in which the options are outstanding.

Options granted under the terms of employee stock purchase plans should have an exercise price that is not less than the lower of: (a) an amount equal to 85% of the fair market value of the shares at the time the option is granted, or (b) an amount which under the terms of the option may not be less than 85% of the fair market value of the shares at the time the option is exercised. The terms under which the options are granted should ensure that they cannot be exercised after: (i) 5 years from the date the options are granted if, under the terms of such plan, the option price is to be not less than 85% of the fair market value of such shares at the time of the exercise of the option; otherwise (ii) 27 months from the date the option is granted. Options granted under the plan should not be transferable except in the event of death. Finally, all employees granted options under the terms of the plan should have the same rights and privileges. The number of shares which may be purchased by any employee, however, may bear a uniform relationship to the total compensation, or to the basic or regular rate of compensation, of the employee. A maximum number of shares that may be purchased by an employee may nevertheless be fixed under the plan.

Employees are not taxed on options acquired under the plan until they sell any shares acquired on the exercise of the options. At that time employees generally treat any profits on disposal as a capital gain. The company in such cases is not allowed a deduction as a trade or business expense in respect of the options. There are three situations in which employees are subject to ordinary income tax and where the company is allowed a deduction. The first is where the employee makes a *disqualifying disposition*. This is where there is a disposal of shares within 2 years of the date of grant or 1 year after exercise. The second is where the person making the disposal was not an employee of the company during the period beginning with the date of grant and ending 3 months before the exercise of the option. In the cases where there is a disqualifying disposition and where the option is exercised by an individual who does not meet the employment condition, the company can make a deduction in respect of the option. Finally, there are special rules where the exercise price is between 85 and 100% of the fair value of the shares. In this case, an employee has income in the year in which there is a disposal of any share acquired as a result of the exercise of the option. The amount of the income is equal to the lesser of: (a) the excess of the fair market value of the shares at the time of disposal over the exercise price of the option, or (b) the excess of the fair market value of the shares at the time the option was granted over the exercise price. The profit on the disposal is therefore split into two components: one component, representing the difference between the exercise price and the lower of the fair value of the shares at the times of grant and disposal, is liable to income tax: and the other component, representing the remaining profit on the disposal of the shares, is liable to capital gains tax. In this case the company can make a deduction equal to the amount the employee is charged to income tax.

Comparison of US and UK Schemes

Both US and UK tax law contains provisions to encourage wider employee share ownership through the use of share option schemes. A comparison of the schemes in the two countries is shown in Table 6.2. The basic way in which options are taxed is the same under the legislation of both countries. This is that the employee receives income tax relief and is charged to capital gains tax on the disposal of shares acquired through the exercise of the options. However, under US legislation, there are two components to the taxation of discount options. Income tax is charged on the difference between the exercise price of the option and fair value of the shares at the time of grant, or at the time of exercise, whichever difference is the lower. Capital gains tax is charged on the remainder of the profit. In order to qualify for relief under US legislation, the shares must not be sold before the latter of 2 years after grant and 1 year after exercise, and the holder must have been employed by the company at least until 3 months before the option was exercised. There are no such requirements under UK legislation.

In both countries there are requirements to allow all employees meeting certain conditions to participate. There are differences, however, between the tax laws of the two countries as to who can be excluded from participation. UK legislation permits the exclusion of individuals who have not been employees for a qualifying period, whereas a more complex set of exclusions is allowed under US legislation. Included in this set are highly compensated employees. Under the legislation of both countries, the terms of the options must be the same for all employees although the number of shares over which options are granted may differ. There are small differences, however, in the way in which the number of shares is determined.

Options can be issued at a discount under the schemes in both countries, although there are differences in the size of the discount, and in the way in which the permissible discount is determined. The maximum lives of the options are defined in the laws of both countries. In UK legislation the exercise date is defined in terms of the bonus dates on the savings plans that provide funds for the purchase of shares. On the other hand, the maximum life of a US option is determined by the relationship between the fair value of the shares and the exercise price. The value of shares to be acquired is limited in both countries. In the UK it is limited by the maximum monthly contribution that can be made to a SAYE plan; in the US by a fixed value amount and by a percentage of the total shares that can be held. Finally, options granted under the schemes must not be transferable except in the event of the death of the holder.

The main differences between UK and US legislation are in the way in which the purchase of shares is funded and in the holding requirements for the shares. Approved savings-related share option schemes combine a share option with a savings scheme. Employees can therefore fund the purchase of shares using the proceeds from the SAYE scheme. There is no savings element in the US scheme. In order to gain income tax relief, employees in US schemes are required to hold the shares acquired on the exercise of options for a period by the legislation. Further, in order to obtain income tax relief, individuals must have been employed by the grantor company within a period of 3 months prior to exercise. There are no equivalent requirements in UK legislation.

Table 6.2   Comparison of Employee Share Option Schemes

	UK	US
Tax consequences for the employee	Income tax relief. An employee is charged to capital gains tax on the disposal of shares acquired through the exercise of options	Income tax relief. An employee is charged to capital gains tax on the disposal of shares acquired through the exercise of options. An exception is for discount options. Here there is a charge to both income and capital gains tax
Tax consequences for the company	No chargeable gain arising on the grant of options	No deduction is generally given in respect of the option as an expense. An exception is for a discount option where a deduction equal to the amount on which the employee is charged to income tax is allowed
Shareholder approval	—	Shareholder approval within 12 months before of after the plan is adopted
Savings plan	Employees contribute to a SAYE plan in order to have funds to meet the exercise price of the option. Bonuses received from the plan are free of tax	—
Exercise price	The exercise price must not be less than 80% of the fair value of the shares at the time of grant	The exercise price must not be less than 85% of the fair value of the shares at the time of grant or at the time the option is exercised
Exercise date	The exercise date must not be before the earliest date on which a bonus is payable, and not more than 6 months after a bonus date (3, 5 or 7 years from grant)	The exercise date must be not more than 5 years from the date of grant where the exercise price of the option is not less than 85% of the fair value of stock at the time of exercise; or where the option is determined in any other manner, 27 months from the date of grant

Table 6.2   (*cont.*)

	UK	US
Option terms	The option terms must be the same for all employees. The number of shares to be acquired under the option may vary according to such factors as level of remuneration or length of service	The option terms must be the same for all employees. The number of shares to be acquired under the option may bear a direct relationship to total compensation or regular rate of compensation
Transferability	Options must be non-transferable except in the event of death	Options must be non-transferable except in the event of death
Limitation on holdings	The maximum contribution to a SAYE plan, which must be sufficient to pay for any shares acquired under the scheme, is £250 per month	No employee can accrue rights which accrue at a rate that exceeds $25 000 of the fair value of the stock for each calendar year in which the option is outstanding; and no employee can hold more than 5% of the stock
Eligible employees	Employees and full-time directors	Employees and directors
Permitted exclusions from participation in the scheme	Individuals who have not been employees for a qualifying period. The qualifying period cannot exceed 5 years	Employees: (a) who have been employed for less than 2 years; (b) whose customary employment is less than 20 hours per week; (c) whose customary employment is 5 months or less in any calendar year; and (d) who are highly compensated
Death of employee	Option can be exercised by personal representatives within 12 months of death (or within 12 months of a bonus date if the employee dies within the 6-month period following a bonus date)	Option may be exercised by personal representatives
Cessation of employment	—	In order to obtain income tax relief the option must be exercised within 3 months of cessation
Holding period of shares acquired on the exercise of options	—	The shares must be held for until the latter of 2 years after the grant and 1 year after the exercise of the option

SUMMARY AND CONCLUSION

The aim of the courts and legislators has to been to achieve fairness
by taxing share options in the same way that other employment
benefits are taxed. There are, however, a number of factors that
make the taxation of share option compensation difficult. Not least
of these is determining why companies grant share options to their
employees and senior managers. Share options may be seen as a
reward for past employment services, or as an incentive to future
performance, or as a combination of both. They may also be seen as
serving some other purpose, for example, broadening employee
share ownership. ESOs differ from traded options in that they
usually non-transferable, cannot be exercised for a period of years
after grant and may be forfeited if the holder leaves employment
with the grantor company. It may also be necessary for performance
conditions to be met before they can be exercised. If the grant of
share options is regarded as an employment benefit, the differing
reasons for the issue of ESOs, together with the structure of the
instruments, make it difficult to determine the timing of the taxable
event. If it is a reward for past services then the date of grant is the
most obvious candidate for the time of the taxable event. In this
case, the holder may be seen to be in the same position of a third
party investor in the company's warrants. This means that any
profit made subsequent to the grant of the option would be treated
as a capital gain. However, if share options are an incentive to
future performance then the taxable event arises throughout the
period when work is performed. The timing of the taxable event
would not be so important were it not for large differentials, over
much of the post-War period, between the rates of income and
capital gains taxes. Although the time of grant would seem the most
appropriate time to charge income tax on the share option benefit,
there are problems in determining the value of the benefit. For this
reason share option compensation is generally charged to income
tax under the laws of the UK and US at the time the option is exercised.

The taxation of share options at the time of exercise has been seen
as unfair and as inhibiting the use of share option schemes. As a
consequence, both UK and US tax law contains provisions to tax the
employment benefit of share options as a capital gain, usually
determined at the point any shares acquired through the exercise of

the options are sold. Two types of schemes are to be found in both countries: one covering *all* employees and the other allowing restrictions to certain groups of employees and directors. Tax rules in relation to the all-employee schemes are largely designed to ensure that all employees are allowed to participate on equal terms in the schemes. Those employees that may be excluded from the schemes are therefore clearly defined in both UK and US legislation. There are also provisions to ensure that employees are treated equally under the scheme, although differences in the number of shares underlying the options may be related to employees' level of compensation and/or length of service. The rules of the two countries allow share options granted under all-employee schemes to be issued at a discount, although for US schemes this means that employees are subject to both income and capital gains taxes in respect of the options. A major difference between the UK savings-related share option scheme and its US counterpart is that it incorporates a tax-preferred savings plan to provide employees with funds to exercise their options.

Discretionary share option schemes are usually intended for directors and senior employees. Unlike all-employee schemes, options cannot be granted at a discount and there is no requirement that all employees are treated equally. However, the value of the underlying shares over which options may be granted is greater for discretionary schemes than is permitted in all-employee schemes. Many of the other characteristics of the schemes represented "good" corporate governance practice at the time the legislation was introduced, intended to limit self-dealing by directors. Current ideas of corporate governance are reflected in the US legislation designed to curb excessive pay to company directors. This legislation also incorporates provisions to restrict abuse by re-pricing share options.

Two types of schemes are therefore recognized under the tax laws of both the UK and US: non-statutory and statutory schemes. The laws relating to non-statutory schemes are constructed from the point of view of ensuring that share option compensation is taxed fairly *vis-à-vis* other types of employee benefit, whereas the laws relating to statutory schemes are either removing disincentives associated with the non-statutory schemes or providing incentives for companies to use share option schemes. The benefits of statutory schemes largely come about through taxing the share option benefits as a capital gain rather than as income[78]. This means that the value of these schemes depends on the difference between employees' marginal rates of income and capital gains tax. Where this difference is large then the tax advantages to employees may more than compensate for the non-deductibility of the benefit for the employer company. However, where the difference is small, or eliminated completely, the advantages of statutory schemes may disappear. The progressive reduction of the top rates of income tax in the UK throughout the 1980s, followed by provisions in the Finance Act 1988 treating capital gains as if they were the top slice of income and taxing at that rate, make approved share option schemes unattractive. One exception is where employees are able to utilize their annual tax-exempt amount for capital gains tax for any profits on the disposal of shares acquired on the exercise of option, so making their effective rate of tax 0% on share option compensation. The relationship between the rates of capital gain and income taxes followed a similar pattern in the US. Paradoxically, because of deductibility of share option compensation under non-statutory schemes, non-statutory schemes became more attractive than statutory ones. Matsunaga et al. (1992) present evidence that it is optimal for some companies to encourage disqualifying dispositions of ISOs.

[78] In addition there is the possibility of deferring tax from the exercise date until the shares are sold.

7
Conclusion

The debate in the US Congress at the beginning of the 1990s reveals two sets of views about share option compensation. On the one hand, share option compensation is seen as an integral part of the perceived abuses by senior executives that were highlighted in the hostile debates about excessive executive compensation. In the UK too there has been concern about "fat-cat" compensation schemes and, as in the US, much of the interest has been directed towards executive share option schemes. On the other hand, company-wide share option compensation schemes are viewed positively. Indeed, reading the Congressional debates gives the impression that such schemes were critical to the regeneration of the US economy during the early 1990s.

Share option schemes for senior executives are seen as one solution to the problems stemming from the separation of the ownership and control of the modern public corporation. It is often assumed, in both the academic literature and more generally, that share option schemes are a means of aligning the interests of a company's managers with those of its shareholders. However, as a component of executive compensation, it is necessary to ensure that the overall package is fair but not excessive. The last decade or so has seen, on both sides of the Atlantic, the development of corporate governance mechanisms to control excessive executive compensation. In particular, determination of senior executive compensation is increasingly the responsibility of a compensation committee of the board of directors whose membership is restricted to *independent* non-executive directors. Shareholder involvement, especially by institutional investors, is also seen to be important. This has led to the increased disclosure requirements on executive compensation and, in the US, to revised proxy rules. Institutional investors, either individually or collectively through their industry groups, may have corporate governance policies, including guidelines on executive compensation in general and share option compensation in particular, that influence voting. Share option compensation is therefore perceived as both a mechanism of corporate governance that ensures alignment between the interests of managers and those of the shareholders, and a component of executive compensation that needs to be constrained in order to ensure that the total compensation package is not excessive.

The rationale for all-employee share option schemes is less clear than that for executive schemes. One advantage highlighted in the Congressional debate is that employees are willing to forego cash wages in exchange for share options. This allows companies, and particularly high technology companies, to conserve scarce cash resources. The reasons why governments promote, and companies adopt, all-employee share option schemes may be subsumed within the justification for employee share ownership generally. Employee share ownership is sometimes seen as a method of improving company performance. The effect of employee share ownership on company performance may be assumed to be either through share ownership providing a financial incentive to employees to improve their own productivity and to monitor the performance of other employees, or through improvement in the attitudes of employees that follows from share ownership. In practice, the relationship between employee share ownership and company performance seems to depend on the company adopting other methods of employee participation. Others view employee share ownership as a means of achieving wider social goals. These range from the "New Capitalism" of the early part of the twentieth century in the US, to concepts of "stakeholder capitalism" and "participatory capitalism" at the end of the century. No assumption is usually made by those who see employee share ownership as a method of achieving wider social goals that share ownership has any effect on company performance.

The adoption of share option schemes is seen by many as being at least partly determined by the perception that they are preferentially taxed[79]. Taxation may also affect the characteristics of share option compensation. Two distinct types of schemes for the taxation

---

[79] Social security taxes may also contribute to determining the attractiveness, or otherwise, of share option compensation.

of share option compensation are provided by legislation on both sides of the Atlantic. These are *non-statutory* schemes that cover the taxation of share option compensation generally, and *statutory* schemes designed to encourage companies to adopt schemes with particular characteristics. The rationale underlying the taxation of share options granted under non-statutory schemes is to ensure that share option compensation is taxed in the same way as other types of compensation. The tax system should therefore be both *fair* in that the same level of tax should be borne on all types of compensation, and *neutral* in that the tax system should not provide incentives, or disincentives, to adopt a particular type of compensation policy. Statutory schemes, on the other hand, provide tax incentives, through income tax relief, for companies to adopt particular types of executive and all-employee share option schemes. One of the reasons for the introduction of statutory schemes is to counter disincentives that were perceived to exist within non-statutory schemes. In order to prevent abuse of the income tax relief provided by these schemes, the scheme rules incorporate some of the principles of corporate governance from a quarter of a century ago. On the other hand, one of the reasons for their introduction all-employee share option schemes is to promote wider employee share ownership. The rules governing these schemes therefore contain provisions to ensure that substantially all of a company's employees are eligible to participate in the company's all-employee scheme on equal terms. Whether or not income tax relief provides an incentive for a company to a adopt statutory scheme(s) depends on the relative marginal rates of income and capital gains taxes of potential scheme members, and on the relative rates of individual and corporate taxes.

The accounting aspects of share option compensation fall into two distinct categories. First, there is disclosure of the share option compensation received by executive directors. Disclosure of such information is seen as critical to shareholder involvement in compensation issues. For example, the Greenbury Committee suggests that companies and their compensation committees should adopt a philosophy of full transparency so that shareholders have access to *all* information that could reasonably be required in order for them to assess a company's policies on executive compensation. Appropriate disclosure of information on executive compensation is seen as enabling shareholders, and the market generally, to control excessive executive compensation. The problem is in deciding what information to disclose and in respect of which individuals should disclosure be made. To be consistent with other forms of compensation, a company should disclose the fair value of the options. It is, however, difficult to measure the fair value of share option compensation at the relevant time(s). This has led to disclosure requirements that relate more to the characteristics of the options than their value[80]. The problem of measurement also underlies the second category problem relating to share option compensation. This is one of accounting for the cost of share option compensation to the company. An argument, that has wide support, is that share option compensation should be accounted for in the same way as other types of compensation. Because of measurement problems, the accounting practice in both the US and UK is for companies to charge the *intrinsic* value of share options[81]. Many options do not have an intrinsic value at the time of grant because the exercise price is set at, or above, the market price of the underlying shares at that time. The FASB's proposed accounting standard would have required public companies to treat the *fair* value of share option compensation as expense in the income statement. The reaction to this proposal would suggest that the absence of a requirement to charge the fair value of share option compensation against income is one of the main reasons why companies adopt share option schemes.

The issues of share option compensation extend far beyond the characteristics of the instruments that form the basis of this form of compensation. Issues of corporate governance underlie much of the debate on executive share option compensation. Although share option compensation is seen as a way of aligning the interests of managers with those of a company's shareholders, like other forms of managerial compensation it is potentially subject to abuses which may be limited by other corporate governance mechanisms. All-employee share option schemes are seen variously as providing incentives to improved employee performance and/or attitudes, and as a method of achieving wider social goals. Finally, underlying all types of share option compensation is the concern that companies reward managers and employees in this way because of the way it

[80] The SEC does require a measure of the value of the options to be disclosed.
[81] Exceptions to this are where the options are granted under approved SAYE schemes in the UK and, in the US, under non-compensatory schemes.

is treated in the financial statements of grantor companies and the way it is taxed. The accounting and tax treatments of share option compensation arise partly from difficulties both in determining when the compensation is earned, and in measuring its value at the time(s) it is earned.

The remainder of the chapter takes up some of these issues by looking first at the relationship between share option compensation and company performance. The incorporation of relative performance evaluation into executive share option schemes in an attempt to improve their effectiveness is then examined. This is followed by an examination of the interaction between executive share option compensation, excessive compensation and corporate governance. Finally, the influence of tax and accounting rules on share option schemes is considered.

SHARE OPTION COMPENSATION AND COMPANY PERFORMANCE

It is frequently suggested that share options are granted to managers, and to a lesser extent to employees, with a view to improving company performance, and hence shareholder wealth. In the case of managers, the suggested purpose is to align the interests of managers with those of the company's shareholders. Managers are often viewed, especially in the economic literature, as being risk and effort averse, and as having a propensity to derive non-pecuniary benefits from the company. Share option compensation is assumed to provide managers with financial incentives to encourage them to act so as to maximize shareholder wealth. The impact on company performance, and shareholder wealth, of managerial actions comes through the strategic, financial and operating decisions that they make. This link between individual action and company performance is less easily identified for ordinary employees. All-employee share option schemes have the problem that it is difficult for each employee to see the effect of his or her efforts on the performance of the company's shares, and free-riding may be encouraged by the scheme. Free-riding is likely to occur in a situation in which it is difficult for management to monitor each individual employee's performance and where each individual's reward depends on the efforts of everyone else.

When considering share option compensation, it is necessary to distinguish between the grant of the options, and the period between the time of grant and the time the options are exercised, or allowed to lapse. Although share options have a value at the time of grant and that value must be regarded as compensation for past and/or future services, the main incentive effects come about through holding the options, and any underlying shares acquired on the exercise of the options. It is during the period after the time of grant that the value of share options is sensitive to changes in the value of the underlying shares and so any incentive effect of share option compensation is likely to be in this period. In order for there to be an incentive effect, however, managers must understand how the value of the options changes with movement in the price of the underlying shares. Hall (1998) provides evidence that many managers do not understand this relationship and so, for them, the incentive component of share option compensation may not be very strong. If managers do understand the determinants of the value of options, and if they are self interested and acting to maximize the value of the options, then the incentives provided by share options may not always be to the benefit of shareholders.

Managerial decisions may affect the value of any options they hold in a number of ways. First, the value of share options may be increased through managerial decisions that affect company performance and its share price. In this case, share options serve to align the interests of managers with those of the shareholders. There is some evidence that the adoption of long-term incentive performance (LTIP) plans, which may include share option schemes, is viewed positively by the market. So there is at least some support for the view that market participants believe that there is a link between share option compensation and future company performance. Second, the value of share options is increased with expectations that dividends will be less than previously forecast. Share option compensation therefore provides managers with incentives to reduce company dividends. Lambert et al. (1989) provide evidence that there is a reduction in the level of dividends with the initial adoption of an executive share option scheme followed by a downward drift, compared with forecasted levels, in the level of dividends. As reduction in the level of dividends may not be in the interests of shareholders, share option compensation is here acting as an adverse incentive. Third, the value of options increases with a rise in the volatility of the market price of the underlying share. Share option compensation therefore provides managers with incentives to increase the volatility of the company's share price. This involves increasing the volatility of the company's earnings stream by, for example, selecting higher risk new investment projects, and/or by increasing the company's level of gearing[82]. The results of a study by DeFusco et al. (1990) indicate that volatility does in fact increase following the announcement of the adoption of a share option scheme. In addition, the findings of a study by Agrawal and Mandelker (1987) would suggest that both acquisition and divestment decisions, and capital structure decisions are influenced by managerial holdings of share options in a way that increases the volatility of a company's share price. If managers are risk averse then the incentive provided by share option compensation for managers to increase the volatility of a company's shares is in the interests of shareholders as it is a correction to managerial risk aversion.

The incentives provided by share option compensation are therefore complex. Not only does it provide an incentive to increase company performance, but also an incentive to reduce dividends and to make decisions which increase the volatility of the company's shares. Share option compensation may have other effects on company performance. The political case for share option compensation is partly founded on the view that a company needs to offer share options to managers in order to attract them to join the company, and to retain them. Following this argument, share option compensation enables companies to attract, and to retain, high quality managers whose strategic, operating and financial decisions will increase company performance and hence shareholder wealth. In this case, the cost to the company, and its shareholders, of share options at the time of grant is a cost in acquiring managerial labour.

Although it is sometimes suggested that all-employee share option schemes provide incentives to improved productivity and company

---

[82] There is an alternative argument which is that share option compensation provides managers with an incentive to make decisions which *reduce* share price volatility. This argument is based on the risk averseness of managers who are unable to hedge option risk and who have a significant part of their wealth, including human capital, invested in the company.

performance, it is somewhat difficult to comprehend the mechanism through which this result is expected to be achieved. The financial incentives offered to holders of share options depend on the activities of individual employees affecting the company's share price. However, it is difficult for each employee to see the effect of his or her efforts on the performance of the company's shares. There is also a free-rider problem that arises where managers do not monitor individual performance, and where individual rewards depend on collective efforts. As the number of employees sharing benefits under the scheme increases, the greater the tendency of each employee to rely on the efforts of others while withholding his or her own effort. Weitzman and Kruse (1990) and Levine and Tyson (1990) suggest that it may be possible to resolve the free-rider problem by the company creating a corporate culture than promotes group cooperation. Following this, all-employee share option schemes on their own are unlikely to be effective in improving employee productivity and company performance unless the company creates an appropriate corporate culture.

The other approach to linking employee share ownership to company performance is through the effect that ownership has on the attitudes of employees, especially their attitudes to the company. The findings in the research literature suggest that share ownership without participation in company decision making is unlikely to have a significant effect on employee attitudes and company performance. There are different methods of employee participation and the problem for a company is one of identifying the combination of type of employee share scheme and method of employee participation that is most effective in improving employee productivity and company performance. McNabb and Whitfield (1998), for example, find that employee share ownership is only positively associated with company performance in those companies with downward communication, such as team briefings, as a method of employee participation. Although it is frequently assumed that different forms of employee share schemes, including share option schemes, are equally effective, this may not be the case. For example, Pierce et al. define three components of *formal* ownership: (a) equity possession—the claim on the company's net assets and its profits; (b) influence/control—the right to exercise some influence or control over the company; and (c) information sharing—the right to be informed about the company. These are essentially the legal rights attached to the *shares* of a company. Holders of share options, however, only acquire these rights through the acquisition of shares on the exercise of their options. It may be that the sense of *ownership* of the company associated with share ownership is, at least partially, absent in the case of share options. In this case, share options may have even less an impact on employee attitudes and company performance than share schemes.

SHARE OPTION COMPENSATION AND RELATIVE PERFORMANCE EVALUATION

It is often assumed that the rewards from managerial incentive contracts should depend only on factors within the control of managers. The Greenbury Report, for example, suggests that: "(D)irectors should not be rewarded for increases in share prices or other indicators which reflect general price inflation, general movements in the stock market, movements in a particular sector of the market or the development of regulatory regimes." The value of executive share options at maturity, or when the option is exercised, depends on the market price of the underlying shares at that time. Holders are rewarded if the market price of the shares is higher than the exercise price (usually the market price of the shares at the time of grant), and are not rewarded if the market price of the shares is below the exercise price. The market value of the underlying shares at maturity depends on industry- and market-wide factors as well as on factors specific to a company. Share option schemes, therefore, can deliver rewards to company managements even when the company's performance is judged to have been poor.

Efficient incentive contracts should, it is frequently suggested, link managerial rewards to those aspects of company performance over which managers have control. In the case of share compensation schemes, this means that it is necessary to filter out industry- and economy-wide factors. For example, the Association of British Insurers (ABI) (1999), in *Share Incentive Schemes—A Statement of Principles*, recommends that: "Challenging performance conditions should govern the vesting of awards or the exercise of options under any form of long-term share-based incentive scheme . . .

Performance conditions should be measured *relative* to an appropriate defined peer group or other relevant benchmark" (italics added). The problem is one of devising a method that incorporates relative performance criteria into share option schemes. Two approaches have been suggested: one requiring that performance criteria are met before the options vest, and the other is to adjust the options' exercise price for movement in the price of a market index or the price of shares in peer group companies.

Both the ABI and the National Association of Pension Funds (NAPF) recommend that performance criteria be incorporated into share option schemes. Specifically, they recommend that performance criteria be met before share options vest. The ABI guidelines (ABI, 1991) originally required that share options only vest when there has been a real growth in earnings per share (EPS) over a 3-year period. However, the NAPF argued that EPS was not a good measure because it is open to manipulation by management, and indicated its preference for a measure based on relative performance in share prices over a 3-year period. Subsequently, joint ABI/NAPF guidelines (ABI/NAPF, 1993) recommend that it is for the compensation committee of the grantor company to determine appropriate performance criteria. A survey by the accounting firm KPMG (1994) indicates that companies in its survey used a variety of performance criteria. These include: (a) earnings per share with a base of the retail prices index (RPI) or RPI plus 2%; (b) share price with a base of the FTSE All Share Index, or FTSE 100 Index; and (c) total shareholder return[83] with a base of the RPI, the FTSE All Share Index, or the FTSE 100 Index.

Although it is necessary for performance criteria to be met before the options vest, the amount of any reward depends on factors outside the control of a company's management. For example, the performance criterion could be that the total shareholder return of the company is in the top quartile of total shareholder returns of FTSE 100 companies. Once this criterion is met, the value of the reward depends on the market price of the company's shares and this, at least in part, depends on industry- and market-wide factors. It is therefore conceivable that vested options are allowed to lapse because of a general fall in share prices when, although the company

---

[83] Total shareholder return incorporates the dividends paid by the grantor company and the change in its share price over a period of time.

has done well relatively, the market price of its shares has generally fallen since the options were granted and the options are "out-of-the-money" when they expire. On the other hand, the management of a company that has just met the performance conditions may be highly rewarded because of a general rise in the stock market. Share options which only vest when performance criteria are met, therefore, do not meet the Greenbury principle that managers ". . . should not be rewarded for increases in share prices or other indicators which reflect general price inflation, general movements in the stock market".

The alternative to performance based vesting provisions is to link the options' exercise price to an index external to the grantor company. This indexed option method is developed by Nalbantian (1993) and Angel and McCabe (1996). Although the concept of index options is relatively simple, the application of the concept to practice is far from straightforward. Nalbantian suggests that it is necessary to have a pricing formula that automatically adjusts the exercise price in response to industry, or market, wide changes. He proposes a three-stage process: (1) construction of a peer group index; (2) estimation of a share price equation; and (3) development of a price adjustment mechanism. If, as would seem most appropriate, the option is indexed against a peer group, it is necessary to create an index. This means identifying those companies that are in the peer group and attaching a weight to each company within the index. The index can then be used to develop a share price equation. Here, the parameter values of the model, which may include market-wide as well as peer group indices, may be estimated using historic data. Finally, the share price equation is incorporated into a formula to adjust the exercise price.

Indexed share options have the advantage of filtering out industry and market-wide factors, thereby linking rewards to company specific factors. They also offer a solution to re-pricing share options following a fall in the market price of the underlying shares. This practice is often criticized. For example, in its statement of principles, the ABI states that the ". . . (R)epricing of 'underwater' options in the event that the share price has fallen below the exercise price is not considered appropriate". Saley (1994), however, suggests that re-pricing may be appropriate to maintain the incentive properties of share options when there is a significant downturn in the market.

Indexed share options ensure that the options are appropriately re-priced when there is a decline in the industry sector or the market.

Although indexed options would appear to have significant advantages over ordinary share options, and options with performance criteria incorporated into their vesting provisions, companies rarely use indexed options. Angel and McCabe (1996) identify four possible explanations for this. First, there is the problem of implementing the indexed share option schemes. As described above, implementation of such schemes requires the development of a price adjustment mechanism reflecting industry-, and market-wide, factors. Second, companies may use share option compensation as a hidden salary for their senior executives. Options granted to senior managers often have a life of 10 years, and it would be expected at the time of grant that stock market prices would be higher when the option expires than at the time of grant. Therefore, senior managers are given options as reward at the time of grant that is related to the expected increase in market prices over the life of the option. Third, indexed options may not qualify for income tax relief under the company share option plan in the UK or the incentive stock option plan in the US. This is because there is a requirement under both schemes that the exercise price is not less than the market value of the shares at the time the option is granted. However, the limit on the value of shares over which options may be granted under company share option plans may mean that the loss of income tax relief is not important for options granted to senior managers. Angel and McCabe also conclude that, in the US it is unlikely that tax considerations have been a significant factor in companies' decisions not to issue indexed options. Finally, companies may be discouraged by the accounting treatment of indexed options. The problem arises from the accounting rules contained within APB *Opinion No. 25*. There is no charge against profits under APB *Opinion No. 25* where the exercise price of the option is fixed at the time of grant, and where this exercise price is at least the fair value of the shares at that time. Different rules, however, apply in the case of *variable* options (options where the exercise price is not known at the time of grant). In this case there is a charge against income during the service period of the option; the charge being the difference between the current exercise price of the option and the fair value of the shares. The accounting treatment of indexed options would be that for variable options. Angel and McCabe suggest that the accounting treatment of indexed options is the most likely reason why companies do not adopt them.

CORPORATE GOVERNANCE, SHARE OPTION COMPENSATION AND EXCESSIVE COMPENSATION

Increasingly high levels of executive compensation, together with widening of the gap between the highest and lowest paid individuals within a company, underlie much of the public and political debates on executive pay. While the populist response is one of outrage, with calls for measures to constrain "fat-cat" compensation, the responses of governments and institutional shareholders have been to restrict excessive compensation. Compensation is seen as being excessive when it is more than can be justified by the services rendered. This is seen by Elson (1995) to arise because the board of directors finds itself more aligned with the interests of managers than the company's shareholders in negotiations over pay. Although high levels of executive compensation may be acceptable, there is a perceived need to constrain compensation that is excessive.

A number of governance mechanisms have evolved over the past decade or so in an attempt to constrain executive pay. One is to ensure that compensation schemes link pay with company performance. Governments and institutional investors have acted to ensure that an increasing proportion of senior management's total compensation is performance related. The US Congress, for example, implemented the Revenue Reconciliation Act of 1993 which distinguishes performance-related from other compensation, and restricts tax deductibility by the company of the latter to $1 million. In the UK, the Stock Exchange Combined Code states that "(T)he performance-related elements of the total remuneration should form a significant proportion of the total remuneration package of executive directors and should be designed to align their interests with those of shareholders and to give these directors keen incentives to perform at the highest level" (B.1.4).

Share option compensation provides one method of relating reward with company performance. As with other forms of compensation, however, it needs to be constrained, in terms of both its design and the value of shares over which options are granted. This is provided through other corporate governance mechanisms. In particular, it is frequently assumed that compensation committees, made up of independent non-executive directors, and shareholder action are effective in constraining excessive compensation. For shareholder action to be effective it is necessary to ensure that there is sufficient and appropriate disclosure on executive compensation and related matters. This combination of mechanisms is reflected in the conditions that must be met in order for compensation to qualify as performance-based compensation under s162(m) of the Internal Revenue Code. These conditions are: (a) the performance criteria are determined by a compensation committee of the board of directors comprised solely of two or more outside directors; (b) the material terms under which the compensation is to be paid is disclosed to shareholders and approved by a majority vote of shareholders before any payment of such compensation; and (c) the compensation committee must certify that the performance criteria and any other material terms were in fact met before any payment of such compensation. A similar combination of mechanisms is to be found in the consultation document Directors' Remuneration published by the UK Government in 1999. Here, the Government recommends that "(A)ll quoted companies should be required to set up a remuneration committee of independent non-executive directors". There is also recognition of the need for shareholder involvement in compensation issues. Here the Government suggests that ". . . (T)he main justification for increasing shareholder power over directors' remuneration would be that, despite the setting up of remuneration committees of non-executive directors, directors still face a conflict of interest". Alternative mechanisms are identified in the document for involving shareholders. Finally, the Government expresses the view that "(P)roper reporting to shareholders is of fundamental importance to strengthening accountability and en-couraging enhanced performance".

Although it seems to be generally accepted that the three inter-linked components of corporate governance (compensation com-mittees of independent non-executive directors, increased trans-parency of executive compensation, and shareholder involvement in compensation issues) are the solution to the problem of excessive executive compensation, there is less agreement as to precise characteristics of the mechanisms. There is also a problem that the evidence to support this assumption is not strong. First, non-executive, and especially independent non-executive, directors are increasingly being seen as having a critical role in the governance of companies. One problem is in defining an independent director. This problem is recognized by policy makers. For example, the UK Government in its consultative document expresses a concern that potential conflicts of interest exist is setting executive compensation. The Government note that there are ''. . . many instances where the company's non-executive chairman is a member of the remuneration committee in circumstances where it is far from clear whether the person is (to quote from the Combined Code) 'independent of management and free from any business or other relationship which could materially interfere with the exercise of their independent judgement'''. Another problem is in the assumed role of the independent non-executive director. Non-executive directors potentially have a number of roles to play within a company's governance structure. These include advising the board on matters such as company strategy and monitoring the performance of executive directors. Non-executive directors also have a role in specific situations where there is a conflict between the interests of senior executives and shareholders. Such situations include the response to takeover offers and senior executive compensation. The empirical literature generally does not present a picture consistent with the enthusiasm of policy makers for non-executive directors. This general picture is also reflected in the empirical research on the role of independent directors in linking compensation to company performance. While Mehran (1995) finds that the compensation of executives of companies whose boards are dominated by non-executive directors is more likely to be sensitive to company performance, this finding is not confirmed by Core et al. (1999).

Although shareholder involvement in compensation issues is seen to be important, it is less clear as to what this involvement should be. For example, the UK Government in its consultative paper identifies five feasible options: (a) creating special procedures under which shareholders could move a resolution on compensation at the annual meeting; (b) requiring quoted companies to ask shareholders to vote on the board's compensation report every year; (c) requiring quoted companies to have a compensation policy and to seek shareholder agreement to that policy every year; (d) requiring directors of quoted companies to stand for (re-)election every year; and (e) requiring quoted companies to ask shareholders to (re-)elect the chairman of the compensation committee every year. As with US companies until the early 1992, it is difficult for shareholders in UK companies to move resolutions on compensation issues[84]. Therefore if this approach were to be adopted, it would be necessary to amend company law. The other options provide for voting on specified matters.

Shareholders have weak incentives to monitor and vote on matters affecting the companies in which they invest where they only hold a small fraction of the companies' shares. As it is rational for such investors to free-ride, the concern of policy makers has turned to institutional investors. This is expressed in a speech by Stephen Byers[85], Secretary of State for Trade and Industry: "One of the key roles of investors is their direct role as shareholders. There was, for many years, a tradition of institutional investors not using their voting powers in a particularly active way. Many institutions preferred to sell their holdings if a company's performance deteriorated rather than engage in positive dialogue. This is changing. Indeed we are seeing the beginning of the shareholder activism that exists in the USA". Although institutional investors often hold valuable stakes in companies, they rarely hold more than a small fraction of a company's share capital. Therefore, like individual investors in these companies, institutional investors have weak incentives to monitor and to intervene in a company's affairs where necessary. This may be resolved in one or other of two ways. First, some institutional investors may choose to allocate a larger weight of their total investments to certain companies. In this situation it may be rational to monitor and intervene in the affairs of those companies in which the weighting of the investment in the fund is high relative to the weighting of the investment in the funds of

---

[84] Under UK company law the problem is that notice must be given at least 6 weeks prior to the annual meeting either by a single shareholder holding 5% or more of the voting rights, or by 100 or more shareholders each holding an average of at least £100 of nominal value of the company's capital. As companies are only obliged to send the annual report to shareholders at least 21 days before the annual meeting, shareholders may not have sufficient information six weeks ahead of the meeting to move a resolution.

[85] Speech of 19 July 1999 on *Directors' Remuneration* at a seminar organized by the Association of British Insurers and the National Association of Pension Funds.

other institutional investors. Such a strategy has been adopted in the UK by Hermes Investment Management. In 1998, Hermes and Lens Investment Management, the US corporate governance investment group, set up Hermes Lens Asset Management to manage the Hermes UK Focus Fund. This is a fund that invests in large UK public companies whose share performance has been poor and/or whose corporate governance structures are questionable. It is reported that at any one time, the fund is likely to own up to 10% of the shares of approximately 10 companies[86]. Hermes has also issued a statement[87] on its voting policy that includes its views on executive compensation. The following is included in the statement of general principle: "A remuneration committee of independent NEDs (non-executive directors) is best placed to decide executive remuneration on behalf of the board. Actual and potential awards should not be excessive and should be directly related to the success of the company and aligned over time to the returns achieved by shareholders" (para. 1.4). The statement also contains the qualities that a non-executive director must have in order to be considered by Hermes as being independent, and its views on share option compensation.

The second way of dealing with the weak incentives that institutional investors have in monitoring and intervening in the companies in which they invest is through industry groups and investor services. Industry groups and investor services, from time to time, formulate guidelines on corporate governance issues and/or monitor individual companies. The ABI and NAPF in the UK have developed guidelines on corporate governance issues in general, and on executive compensation in particular. Their guidelines provide a major constraint on share options granted by UK companies. The guidelines on share schemes issued by the ABI[88] deal first with the proportion of a company's share capital that can be set aside for share, and share option, schemes. In order to restrict the potential dilution arising from such schemes, no more than 10% of the issued ordinary share capital should be set aside for all the company's schemes in any rolling 10-year period, and no more than 5% of the issued ordinary

---

[86] *Financial Times*, 16 March 1998.
[87] Hermes Investment Management Limited *Statement on Corporate Governance and Voting Policy* (1998).
[88] ABI *Share Option and Profit-sharing Incentive Schemes* (1995).

share capital in any rolling 10-year period should be used for executive schemes. Any options granted in excess of this 5% should be super-options; these are options where the minimum period before exercise is not less than 5 years and where the exercise of the options is subject to demanding performance targets. Second, all executive schemes should require the satisfaction of performance targets as a condition of the exercise of options. The performance criteria, which should be set and explained by the compensation committee, should be based on sustained and significant improve-ment in the underlying financial performance of the company. The Joint Statement by the ABI and NAPF in July 1993, *Share Scheme Guidance*, sets out the principles which a company's compensation committee may consider in determining performance targets. Here a distinction is drawn between absolute and comparative targets. An absolute target may be 2% per annum growth, in excess of inflation, over a 3-year period[89]. Where comparative targets are used, there should be out-performance of an index, or of the median or weighted average of a predefined peer group, in the case of basic options, or the achievement of top quartile performance in the case of super-options. The comparative performance targets that are identified in the *Guidance* are: (a) normalized earnings per share; (b) net asset value per share; (c) total shareholder return; and (d) share price. Third, there should be full disclosure of the details of the performance criteria when the scheme is first adopted and then annually in the company's financial statements, and shareholders must have the opportunity to vote on schemes at least every 10 years. Fourth, the total market value of shares over which all options are granted to any individual under an executive scheme of shares should not exceed four times the individual's total annual compensation. Share options on shares with a market value of up to a further four times an individual's compensation may be granted in the form of super-options. Fifth, options should not be exercisable within 3 years from the date of grant (5 years in the case of super-options), nor later than 10 years after grant. The exercise price of the options may not be at a discount to the market price of

---

[89] In its document *Share Incentive Schemes—A Statement of Principles* (1999) the ABI suggests that new schemes should move away from the practice of *retesting*, this means that the performance criteria must be met for, say, *any* 3-year period in 10 years, towards using a single pre-determined performance measurement period.

the shares at the time of grant, and the rules of a scheme provide that options should normally be granted only within a period of 42 days following the date of publication of the results of the company. Finally, the guidelines deal with the situations in which replacement options may be granted. These are basically where the grantor company is taken over. The guidance provided by the ABI therefore defines the main characteristics of the options—vesting period, expiry date, exercise price and performance criteria—as well as the maximum value of shares over which options can be granted and the proportion of a company's share capital that may be subject to share incentive compensation. In addition there are requirements for disclosure of information about, and shareholder approval for, the scheme.

The other aspect of institutional shareholder involvement in corporate governance is guidance on voting provided by institutional investor services such as the Council of Institutional Investors (CII) in the US, Pensions & Investment Research Consultants Limited (PIRC), the NAPF Voting Issue Service and Institutional Voting Information Service (IVIS) in the UK. PIRC, the NAPF Voting Issue Services and IVIS review company Reports and Accounts, and Notices of meeting, report on compliance with ABI guidelines, The Combined Code, and other relevant recommendations and guide-lines, and provide recommendations on voting. The combination of industry guidelines and monitoring by institutional investor services may reduce the disincentives of institutional investors to vote on corporate governance matters. It may not, however, lead to respon-sible voting. In their joint statement[90], the ABI and NAPF state that responsible voting is not achieved by a simple "box-ticking" approach to corporate governance. It is recommended that "(W)here an institutional investor would judge it appropriate to vote against a proposal which it considers undesirable, it is important that, wherever possible, representations are made in time for the problem to be considered and for consultation to take place with a view to achieving a satisfactory solution" (para. 4.4).

Corporate governance mechanisms, in particular independent non-executive directors and institutional investors, are perceived to have an important role in containing excessive compensation. The

[90] *Responsible Voting—A Joint ABI–NAPF Statement* (1999).

use of these mechanisms, alongside improved transparency, is supported by legislation such as s162(m) of the US Internal Revenue Code, and institutional guidelines such as those of the ABI and NAPF in the UK. The effectiveness of these mechanisms in containing excessive compensation remains largely untested. One problem in considering the effectiveness of independent non-executive directors is the definition of "independent". Independent is defined differently in the various guidelines and legislation where the term is used. Institutional investors, particularly through their industry bodies, have had an important role to play in the structure of executive share option schemes. In the UK, the guidelines of the both ABI and the NAPF, individually and jointly, have shaped the structure and amount of share option compensation.

TAXATION, ACCOUNTING AND SHARE OPTION SCHEMES

The debate on share option compensation in the US congress centred on issues of excessive executive compensation and in the way such compensation is accounted for in the financial statements of the grantor company. Among the measures intended to restrain excessive executive compensation in the Corporate Pay Responsibility Act introduced in the US Senate by Senator Carl Levin is the specification of the method for calculating the present value of share option compensation and the requirement that this cost be reflected in corporate earnings statements. A proposal, by the FASB, for an accounting standard on share option compensation that was broadly consistent with this measure of the Corporate Responsibility Act, had a hostile reception. The main problem seems to have been the effect that implementation of the proposed standard would have on the reported earnings of US companies, and particularly high-technology companies. There were suggestions that the total expense that would be recognized if the proposed standard was implemented under the new rule would be in the region of $15 billion. The debate over share option compensation also extends into tax legislation. Section 162(m) of the Internal Revenue Code is an attempt to deal with the problem of excessive executive compensation by restricting the tax deductibility by the company of compensation paid to certain individuals, other than performance related compensation, to $1 million. In the UK, on the publication of the Greenbury Report, the government announced measures to reduce the attractiveness of statutory executive share option schemes.

Taxation and accounting rules may affect share option compensation in two ways. First, they may provide incentives, or disincentives, for companies to adopt share option schemes. Low rates of capital gains tax, compared with tax rates on income, may make share option compensation more tax efficient than alternative ways of rewarding executives and employees. Accounting rules which allow companies not to charge the fair value of share option compensation may also explain the adoption of share option schemes. The response of many companies and industry groups to the FASB's proposed standard on share option compensation suggests that the accounting treatment is an important factor in the decision to implement share option schemes. In an ideal world, however, taxation and/or accounting rules should not influence the way in which individuals are rewarded for the employment services they provide to companies. Accounting and tax rules should be neutral with respect to decisions about the structure of compensation packages. The nature of share option compensation, however, makes it difficult to formulate such rules. One problem lies in determining when the compensation benefit of share options is received by executives and employees. Another is in measuring the value of the benefit at the time it arises. In their decisions on the way that share option compensation should be taxed, the courts have determined the time when the compensation benefit is received. If, as the courts conclude, the compensation benefit is received at the time the options are granted, there is a problem in measuring the value of the benefit at that time. If the intrinsic value of the options is used then, as most options do have an intrinsic value, little or no tax would be charged[91]. Accounting rules based on the intrinsic value of options at the time of grant also mean that the cost of share option compensation is not usually charged against income. Although ideally both tax and accounting rules should be based on the fair value of share option, estimation of the fair value of most ESOs is

[91] This position, which followed from the rule in *Abbot* v. *Philbin*, led James Callaghan to introduce legislation in his 1966 Budget Statement to tax share option compensation at the time the option is exercised (see Chapter 6).

complex. Further, it may be thought that the measurement is not sufficiently reliable for regulatory purposes.

Second, tax and accounting rules may shape the structure of share option schemes. The rules of statutory share option schemes in both the US and UK restrict the structure of options granted under the provisions of the schemes. For example, the options must be non-transferable, must be exercised with a defined time from the time of grant, and may not be exercised during the early years of the options' lives. The rules may also place limits on the value of the companies' shares over which options may be granted under the scheme. These features were in the minds of legislators when they introduced the relevant legislation. Regulations may, however, have unintended consequences. For example, although *indexed* share options would seem to have advantages over those with performance-based vesting conditions, taxation and accounting rules may be providing disincentives for their adoption by companies.

Share option compensation is controversial because it is thought that the share options granted to the senior executives of public companies have considerable monetary value. Unlike cash compensation, the real value of share option compensation is difficult to measure with any reasonable degree of accuracy. This has led to tax and accounting rules that are often thought to favour share option compensation over other forms of payment for employment services[92]. Accounting rules have, until recently, also hidden the cost of share option compensation from shareholders.

---

[92] Whether or not share option compensation in fact receives preferential treatment depends on the relative rates of income, capital gains and corporate taxes. Share option compensation was tax preferred at times when the marginal rates of income tax for many executives were considerably higher than capital gains tax rates. It is less clear now whether share option compensation is, or is not, tax preferred.

References

Abdel-Khalik, A.R., Chi, C. and Ghicas, D. (1987) Rationality of executive compensation schemes and real accounting changes. *Contemporary Accounting Research*, 4, 32–60.

Accounting Principles Board (1969) *Opinion No. 15 Earnings per Share.* New York: AICPA.

Accounting Principles Board (1972) *Opinion No. 25 Accounting for Stock Issued to Employees.* New York: AICPA.

Accounting Standards Board (1992) *SSAP 3 (amended) Earnings per Share.* London: ASB.

Accounting Standards Board (1998) *FRS 14 Earnings per Share.* London: ASB.

Agrawal, A. and Mandelker, G.N. (1987) Managerial incentives and corporate investment and financing decisions. *The Journal of Finance*, 42, 823–837.

Aggarwal, R.K. and Samwick, A.A. (1998) Executive compensation, strategic competition, and relative performance evaluation: theory and evidence. Working paper: Dartmouth College.

Aggarwal, R.K. and Samwick, A.A. (1999) The other side of the tradeoff: the impact of risk on executive compensation. *Journal of Political Economy*, 107, 65–105.

Angel, J.J. and McCabe, D.M. (1996) Market-adjusted options for executive compensation. Working Paper: Georgetown University, Washington DC.

Association of British Insurers (1991) *Share Incentive Scheme Guidelines (Amended).* London: ABI.

Association of British Insurers (1995) *Share Option and Profit Sharing Incentive Schemes.* London: ABI.

Association of British Insurers (1999) *Share Incentive Schemes—a Statement of Principles.* London: ABI.

Association of British Insurers & National Association of Pension Funds (1993) *Share Scheme Guidance: a Joint Statement from the Investment Committees of the ABI and NAPF.* London: ABI.

Association of British Insurers & National Association of Pension Funds (1999) *Responsible Voting—a Joint ABI–NAPF Statement.* London: ABI.

Bachelier, L. (1900) *Théorie de la Spéculation.* Paris: Gauthier-Villars. Translated by A.J. Boness in P. Cooner (ed.) *The Random Character of Stock Market Prices.* Cambridge, MA: MIT Press.

Baddon, L., Hunter, L., Hyman, J., Leopold, J. and Ramsay, H. (1989) *People's Capitalism: a Critical Analysis of Profit-sharing and Employee Share Ownership.* London: Routledge.

Baliga, B.R., Moyer, R.C. and Rao, R.S. (1996) CEO duality and firm performance: What's the fuss? *Strategic Management Journal,* 17, 41–53.

Baysinger, B.D. and Butler, H.N. (1985) Corporate governance and the board of directors: performance effects of changes in board composition. *Journal of Law, Economics and Organization,* 1, 101–124.

Ben-Ner, A. and Jones, D.C. (1995) Employee participation, ownership, and productivity: a theoretical framework. *Industrial Relations,* 34, 532–554.

Beresford, D.R. (1996) What did we learn from the stock compensation project? *Accounting Horizons,* 10, 125–130.

Berle, A.A. and Means, G.C. (1932) *The Modern Corporation and Private Property.* New York: Macmillan.

Bhagat, S. and Black, B. (1998) The uncertain relationship between board composition and firm performance. In: K. Hopt and H. Kanda (eds) *Corporate Governance: the State of the Art and Emerging Research.* Oxford: Clarendon Press.

Black, B.S. (1990) Shareholder passivity reexamined. *Michigan Law Review,* 89, 520–608.

Black, B.S. (1998) Shareholder activism and corporate governance in the United States. In: P. Newman (ed.) *The New Palgrave Dictionary of Economics and the Law.* London: Macmillan.

Black, B.S. and Coffee, J.C. (1994) Hail Britannia?: institutional investor behavior under limited regulation. *Michigan Law Review,* 92, 1997–2087.

Black, F. and Scholes, M. (1973) The pricing of options and corporate liabilities. *Journal of Political Economy,* 81, 637–654.

Blasi, J.R. (1987) *Employee Ownership Through ESOPs: Implication for the Public Corporation.* New York: Pergamon.

Boness, A.J. (1964) Elements of a theory of stock option values. *Journal of Political Economy,* 72, 163–175.

Brickley, J.A., Coles, J.L. and Jarrell, G.A. (1994) Outside directors and the adoption of poison pills. *Journal of Financial Economics,* 35, 371–390.

Brickley, J.A., Coles, J.L. and Jarrell, G. (1997) Leadership structure: separating the CEO and chairman of the board. *Journal of Corporate Finance*, 3, 189–220.

Brookings, R. (1929) *Economic Democracy: America's Answer to Socialism and Communism*. New York: Macmillan.

Buchko, A.A. (1993) The effects of employee ownership on employee attitudes: an integrated causal model and path analysis. *Journal of Management Studies*, 30, 633–657.

Byrd, J.W. and Hickman, K.A. (1992) Do outside directors monitor managers? Evidence from tender offer bids. *Journal of Financial Economics*, 32, 195–221.

Carpenter, J.N. (1998) The exercise and valuation of executive stock options. *Journal of Financial Economics*, 48, 127–158.

Clinch, G. and Magliolo, J. (1993) CEO compensation and components of earnings in bank holding companies. *Journal of Accounting and Economics*, 16, 241–272.

Coffee, J.C. (1991) Liquidity versus control: the institutional investor as corporate monitor. *Columbia Law Review*, 91, 1277–1368.

Committee on Accounting Procedure (1953) Accounting Research Bulletin No. 43, Chapter 13B. New York: AIA.

Committee on Corporate Governance (Hampel) (1998) *Committee on Corporate Governance: Final Report*. London: Gee.

Committee on the Financial Aspects of Corporate Governance (Cadbury) (1992) *Report of the Committee on the Financial Aspects of Corporate Governance*. London: Gee.

Core, J.E., Holthausen, R.W. and Larcker, D.F. (1999) Corporate governance, chief executive officer compensation, and firm performance. *Journal of Financial Economics*, 51, 371–406.

Cotter, J.F., Shiivdasani, A. and Zenner, M. (1997) Do independent directors enhance target shareholder wealth during tender offers? *Journal of Financial Economics*, 43, 195–218.

Coughlan, A.T. and Schmidt, R.M. (1985) Executive compensation, management turnover, and firm performance: an empirical investigation. *Journal of Accounting and Economics*, 7, 43–66.

Cox, J.C., Ross, S.A. and Rubenstein, M. (1979) Option pricing: a simplified approach. *Journal of Financial Economics*, 7, 229–263.

Cuny, C.J. and Jorion, P. (1995) Valuing executive stock options with endogenous departure. *Journal of Accounting and Economics*, 20, 193–205.

Defeo, V.J., Lambert, R.A. and Larcker, D.F. (1989) The executive compensation effects of equity-for-debt swaps. *Accounting Review*, 64, 201–227.

DeFusco, R.A., Johnson, R.R. and Zorn, T.S. (1990) The effect of executive stock option plans on stockholders and bondholders. *The Journal of Finance*, 45, 617–627.

Del Guercio, D. and Hawkins, J. (1999) The motivation and impact of pension fund activism. *Journal of Financial Economics*, 52, 293–340.

Department of Trade and Industry (1999) *Directors' Remuneration: a Consultative Document*. London: DTI.

Dhillon, U.S. and Ramírez, G.G. (1994) Employee stock ownership and corporate control: an empirical study. *Journal of Banking and Finance*, 18, 9–26.

Dodd, P. (1986) The market for corporate control: a review of the evidence. In: J.M. Stern and D.H. Chew (eds) *The Revolution in Corporate Finance*. Oxford: Blackwell.

Eichen, S.P. (1994) Taking account of stock options. *Harvard Business Review*, January–February, 28–32.

Elson, C.M. (1995) The duty of care, compensation, and stock ownership. *University of Cincinnati Law Review*, 63, 649–711.

European Commission (1996) *PEPPER II: Promotion of participation by employed persons in profits and enterprise results (including equity participation) in the Member States*. (COM(96)697).

Financial Accounting Standards Board (1980) *FASB Interpretation No. 31: Treatment of stock compensation plans in EPS compurations*. Stamford, CT: FASB.

Financial Accounting Standards Board (1985) *Statement of Financial Accounting Concepts No. 6, Elements of financial statements*. Stamford, CT: FASB.

Financial Accounting Standards Board (1990) *Discussion Memorandum: Distinguishing between liability and equity instruments and accounting for instruments with characteristics of both*. Norwal, CT: FASB.

Financial Accounting Standards Board (1993) *Accounting for stock-based compensation. Exposure draft No. 127-C*. Norwalk, CT: FASB.

Financial Accounting Standards Board (1995) *SFAS No. 123: Accounting for stock-based compensation*. Norwal, CT: FASB.

Financial Accounting Standards Board (1996) *Exposure Draft: Earnings per share and disclosure of information about capital structure*. Norwal, CT: FASB.

Financial Accounting Standards Board (1997) *SFAS No. 128: Earnings per share*. Norwalk, CT: FASB.

Financial Accounting Standards Board (1999) *Proposed interpretation: accounting for certain transactions involving stock options—an interpretation of APB Opinion No. 25*. Norwalk, CT: FASB.

Foster, T.W., Koogler, P.R. and Vickrey, D. (1993) Valuation of executive stock options and the FASB proposal: an extension. *The Accounting Review*, 68, 184–189.

Franks, J. and Mayer, C. (1990) Capital markets and corporate control: a study of France, Germany and the UK. *Economic Policy*, 5, 191–231.

Franks, J. and Mayer, C. (1996) Hostile takeovers and the correction of managerial failure. *Journal of Financial Economics*, 40, 163–181.

French, J.L. (1987) Employee perspectives on stock ownership: financial investment or mechanism of control? *Academy of Management Review*, 12, 427–435.

Gates, J.R. (1998) *The Ownership Solution: Toward a Shared Capitalism for the Twenty-first Century*. Reading, MA: Addison-Wesley.

Gaver, J.J., Gaver, K.M. and Austin, J. (1993) *Additional evidence on the association between income management and earnings-based bonus plans*. Working paper: University of Georgia.

Georgen, M. and Renneboog, L. (1999) *Strong managers and passive institutional investors in the UK*. Working paper: European Corporate Governance Network.

HM Treasury (1998) *Consultation on Employee Share Ownership*. London: HM Treasury.

Hall, B.J. (1998) *The pay to performance incentives of executive stock options*. Working Paper: Harvard Business School, Harvard MA.

Hall, B.J. and Liebman, J.B. (1998) Are CEOs really paid like bureaucrats? *The Quarterly Journal of Economics*, 113, 653–691.

Hanford, T.J. and Grasso, P.G. (1991) Participation and corporate performance in ESOP firms. In: R. Russell and V. Rus (eds) *International Handbook of Participation in Organizations. Volume II: Ownership and Participation*. Oxford: Oxford University Press.

Healy, P.M. (1985) The effect of bonus schemes on accounting decisions. *Journal of Accounting and Economics*, 7, 85–107.

Hemmer, T., Matsunaga, S. and Shevlin, T. (1996) The influence of risk diversification on the early exercise of employee stock options by executive officers. *Journal of Accounting and Economics*, 21, 45–68.

Hermalin, B.E. and Weisbach, M.S. (1988) Endogenously chosen boards of directors and their monitoring of the CEO. *The American Economic Review*, 88, 96–118.

Hermes (1998) *Statement on Corporate Governance and Voting Policy*. London: Hermes Investment Management.

Higson, C. and Elliott, J. (1998) Post-takeover returns: the UK evidence. *Journal of Empirical Finance*, 5, 27–46.

Hite, G.L. and Long, M.S. (1982) Taxes and executive stock options. *Journal of Accounting and Economics*, 4, 3–14.

HM Treasury (1986) Profit-related pay: a consultative document (Cmnd. 9835). London: HMSO.

Holmström, B. (1982) Moral hazard in teams. *Bell Journal of Economics*, 13, 324–340.

Holthausen, R.W., Larcker, D.F. and Sloan, R.G. (1995) Annual bonus schemes and the manipulation of earnings. *Journal of Accounting and Economics*, 19, 29–74.

Huddart, S. (1994) Employee stock options. *Journal of Accounting and Economics*, 18, 207–231.

Huddart, S. and Lang, M. (1996) Employee stock option exercises: an empirical study. *Journal of Accounting and Economics*, 21, 5–43.

Hutton, W. (1997) An overview of stakeholding. In G. Kelly, D. Kelly and A. Gamble (eds) *Stakeholding Capitalism*. Basingstoke: Macmillan.

Institutional Shareholders' Committee (1991) *The Responsibilities of Institutional Shareholders in the UK*. London: ISC.

International Accounting Standards Committee (1997) *IAS 33 Earning per share*. London: ISAC.

Jennergren, L.P. and Näslund, B. (1993) A comment on "valuation of executive stock options and the FASB proposal". *The Accounting Review*, 68, 179–183.

Jensen, M.C. (1993) The modern industrial revolution, exit, and the failure of internal control systems. *The Journal of Finance*, 48, 831–880.

Jensen, M.C. and Meckling, W.H. (1976) Theory of the firm: managerial behavior, agency costs and ownership structure. *Journal of Financial Economics*, 3, 305–360.

Jensen, M.C. and Murphy, K.J. (1990) Performance pay and top-management incentives. *Journal of Political Economy*, 98, 225–264.

Jensen, M.C. and Ruback, R.S. (1983) The market for corporate control: the scientific evidence. *Journal of Financial Economics*, 11, 5–50.

Jones, D.C. and Pliskin, J. (1991) The effects of worker participation, employee ownership, and profit-sharing on economic performance: a partial review. In: R. Russell and V. Rus (eds) *International Handbook of Participation in Organizations. Volume II: Ownership and Participation*. Oxford: Oxford University Press.

KPMG (1994) *Executive Share Options and Performance Targets*. London: KPMG.

Keef, S.P. (1998) The causal association between employee share ownership and attitudes: a study based on the Long framework. *British Journal of Industrial Relations*, 36, 73–82.

Kelly, G., Kelly, D. and Gamble, A. (1997) Stakeholder capitalism. In G. Kelly, D. Kelly and A. Gamble (eds) *Stakeholder Capitalism*. Basingstoke: Macmillan.

Kelso, L.O. and Adler, M.J. (1958) *The Capital Manifesto*. New York: Random House.

Klein, A. (1998) Firm performance and board committee structure. *Journal of Law and Economics*, 41, 275–303.

Klein, K.J. (1987) Employee stock ownership and employee attitudes: a test of three models. *Journal of Applied Psychology*, 72, 319–332.

Kruse, D.L. (1993) *Profit Sharing: Does it Make a Difference?* Kalamazoo, MI: W.E. Upjohn Institute.

Kullatilaka, N. and Marcus, A.J. (1994) Valuing employee stock options. *Financial Analysts Journal*, 50, November–December, 46–56.

Lambert, R.A., Lanen, W.N. and Larcker, D.F. (1989) Executive stock option plans and corporate dividend policy. *Journal of Financial and Quantitative Analysis*, 24, 409–425.

Lambert, R.A., Larcker, D.F. and Verrecchia, R.E. (1991) Portfolio considerations in valuing executive compensation. *Journal of Accounting Research*, 29, 129–149.

Levine, D.I. and Tyson, L.D. (1990) Participation, productivity and the firm's environment. In: A.S. Blinder (ed.) *Paying for Productivity: a Look at the Evidence*. Washington, D.C.: The Brookings Institution.

Long, R.J. (1978a) The effects of employee ownership on organizational identification, employee job attitudes, and organizational performance: a tentative framework and empirical findings. *Human Relations*, 31, 29–48.

Long, R.J. (1978b) The relative effects of share ownership vs. control on job attitudes in an employee owned company. *Human Relations*, 31, 753–763.

Long, M.S. (1992) The incentives behind the adoption of executive stock option plans in U.S. corporations. *Financial Management*, 21, 12–21.

Loughran, T. and Vigh, A.M. (1997) Do long-term shareholders benefit from corporate acquisitions? *The Journal of Finance*, 52, 1765–1790.

McNabb, R. and Whitfield, K. (1998) The impact of financial participation and employee involvement on financial performance. *Scottish Journal of Political Economy*, 45, 171–187.

McNichols, M. and Wilson, G.P. (1988) Evidence of earnings management from the provision for bad debts. *Journal of Accounting Research*, 26 (Supplement), 1–40.

MacDuffie, J.P. (1995) Human resource bundles and manufacturing performance: organizational logic and flexible production systems in the world auto industry. *Industrial and Labor Relations Review*, 48, 197–221.

Mallette, P. and Fowler, K.L. (1992) Effects of board composition and stock ownership on the adoption of poison pills. *Academy of Management Journal*, 35, 1010–1035.

Manne, H.G. (1965) Mergers and the market for corporate control. *Journal of Political Economy*, 73, 110–120.

Marsh, T.A. and Merton, R.C. (1987) Dividend behavior for the aggregate stock-market. *Journal of Business*, 60, 1–40.

Martin, K.J. and McConnell, J.J. (1991) Corporate performance, corporate takeovers, and management turnover. *The Journal of Finance*, 46, 671–687.

Matsunaga, S., Shevlin, T. and Shores, D. (1992) Disqualifying dispositions of incentive stock options: tax benefits versus financial reporting costs. *Journal of Accounting Research*, 30 (Supplement), 37–68.

Maug, E. (1998) Large shareholders as monitors: is there a trade-off between liquidity and control. *The Journal of Finance*, 53, 65–98.

Mehran, H. (1995) Executive compensation structure, ownership, and firm performance. *Journal of Financial Economics*, 38, 163–184.

Merton, R.C. (1974) On the pricing of corporate debt: the risk structure of interest rates. *The Journal of Finance*, 29, 449–470. (See Agrawal and Mandelker (1987) p. 828.)

Miller, M.H. (1994) The case for expensing stock options against earnings. *Journal of Applied Corporate Finance*, 7, 88–90.

Mørck, R., Shleifer, A. and Vishny, R.W. (1988) Characteristics of targets of hostile and friendly takeovers. In: A.J. Auerbach (ed.) *Corporate Takeovers: Causes and Consequences*. Chicago: University of Chicago Press.

Mozes, H.A. (1995) An upper bound for the firm's cost of employee stock options. *Financial Management*, 24, 66–77.

Myers, S.C. and Majluf, N.S. (1984) Corporate financing and investment decisions when firms have information that investors do not have. *Journal of Financial Economics*, 13, 187–221.

Murphy, K.J. (1995) Politics, economics, and executive compensation. *University of Cincinnati Law Review*, 63, 713–748.

Nalbantian, H.R. (1993) Performance indexing in stock option and other incentive compensation programs. *Compensation & Benefits Review*, 25, 25–40.

Nesbitt, S.L. (1994) Long-term rewards from shareholder activism: a study of the "CalPERS effect". *Journal of Applied Corporate Finance*, 6, 75–80.

Noreen, E. and Wolfson, M. (1981) Equilibrium warrant pricing models and accounting for executive stock options. *Journal of Accounting Research*, 19, 384–398.

Opler, T.C. and Sokobin, J. (1997) *Does coordinated institutional shareholder activism work?* Working paper: Ohio State University.

Park, S. and Song, M.H. (1995) Employee stock ownership plans, firm performance, and monitoring by outside blockholders. *Financial Management*, 24, 52–65.

Paul, J.M. (1992) On the efficiency of stock-based compensation. *The Review of Financial Studies*, 5, 471–502.

Pavlik, E.L., Scott, T.W. and Tiessen, P. (1993) Executive compensation: issues and research. *Journal of Accounting Literature*, 12, 131–189.

Pendleton, A. (1997) Stakeholders as shareholders: The role of employee share ownership. In: G. Kelly, D. Kelly and A. Gamble (eds) *Stakeholder Capitalism*. Basingstoke: Macmillan.

Pendleton, A., Wilson, N. and Wright, M. (1998) The perception and effects of share ownership: Empirical evidence from employee buy-outs. *British Journal of Industrial Relations*, 36, 99–123.

Pierce, J.L., Rubenfeld, S.A. and Morgan, S. (1991) Employee ownership: a conceptual model of process and effects. *Academy of Management Review*, 16, 121–144.

Quinn, L.C. (1995) Executive compensation under the new SEC disclosure requirements. *University of Cincinnati Law Review*, 63, 769–782.

Rechner, P.L. and Dalton, D.R. (1991) CEO duality and organizational performance: a longitudinal analysis. *Strategic Management Journal*, 12, 155–160.

Romano, R. (1992) A guide to takeovers: Theory, evidence, and regulation. *The Yale Journal on Regulation*, 9, 119–180.

Rosen, C. (1991) Employee ownership: Performance, prospects, and promises. In: C. Rosen and K.M. Young (eds) *Understanding Employee Share Ownership*. Ithaca, NY: ILR Press.

Rosen, C., Klein, A. and Young, K. (1986) *Employee Ownership in America: the Equity Solution*. Lexington, MA: Lexington Books.

Rosenstein, S. and Wyatt, J.G. (1990) Outside directors, board independence and shareholder wealth. *Journal of Financial Economics*, 26, 175–191.

Saldich, R.J. (1994) Taxing account of stock options. *Harvard Business Review*, January–February, 32–33.

Saley, P.J. (1994) Repricing executive stock options in a down market. *Journal of Accounting and Economics*, 18, 325–356.

Samuelson, P.A. (1965) Rational theory of warrant pricing. *Industrial Management Review*, 6, 13–32.

Schizer, D.M. (1999) Executive stock options and derivatives: the irony of accident. Working paper: Columbia Law School, Columbia OH.

Scholes, M.S. and Wolfson, M.A. (1992) *Taxes and Business Strategy: a Planning Approach*. Englewood Cliffs, NJ: Prentice Hall.

Schwert, G.W. (1997) *Hostility in takeovers: In the eyes of the beholder?* Working paper: University of Rochester, Rochester NY.

Servaes, H. (1991) Tobin's Q and the gains from takeovers. *The Journal of Finance*, 46, 409–419.

Shivdasani, A. and Yermack, D. (1999) CEO involvement in the selection of new board members: an empirical analysis. *The Journal of Finance*, 54.

Shleifer, A. and Vishney, R.W. (1997) A survey of corporate governance. *The Journal of Finance*, 52, 737–783.

Smith, M.P. (1996) Shareholder activism by institutional investors: evidence from CalPERS. *The Journal of Finance*, 51, 227–252.

Sprenkle, C.M. (1961) Warrant prices as indicators of expectations. *Yale Economics Essays*, 1, 178–231.

Steel, D. (1986) *Sharing Profits.* Hebden Bridge: Unservile State Group.

Street, D.L., Fordham, D.R. and Wayland, A. (1997) Stock options as a form of compensation for American executives: impact on accounting rules of themes and arguments reported in newspapers and business magazines, 1975–1993. *Critical Perspectives on Accounting*, 8, 211–242.

Study Group chaired by Sir Richard Greenbury (1995) *Directors' Remuneration: Report of the Study Group Chaired by Sir Richard Greenbury.* London: Gee.

Sundaramurthy, C., Mahoney, J.M. and Mahoney, J.T. (1997) Board structure, antitakeover provisions, and stockholder wealth. *Strategic Management Journal*, 18, 231–245.

Thompson, J.K. (1993) Promotion of employee ownership through public policy: the British example. *Journal of Economic Issues*, 27, 825–847.

Urgent Issues Task Force (1994) *UITF abstract 10: Disclosure of directors' share options.* London: ASB.

Urgent Issues Task Force (1997) *UITF abstract 17: Employee share schemes.* London: ASB.

Uvalic, M. (1991) *The PEPPER report: promotion of employee participation in profits and enterprise results in the Member States of the European Community,* revised edition. *Social Europe* Supplement no. 3. Luxembourg: Office for the Official Publications of the European Communities.

Wahal, S., Wiles, K.W. and Zenner, M. (1995) Who opts out of state antitakeover protection—the case of Pennsylvania Sb-1310. *Financial Management*, 24, 22–39.

Warner, J.B., Watts, R.L. and Wruck, K.H. (1988) Stock prices and top management changes. *Journal of Financial Economics*, 20, 461–492.

Watts, R.L. and Zimmerman, J.L. (1986) *Positive Accounting Theory.* Englewood Cliffs, NJ: Prentice-Hall.

Weisbach, M.S. (1988) Outside directors and CEO turnover. *Journal of Financial Economics*, 20, 431–460.

Weitzman, M.L. (1987) *The Case for Profit-Sharing.* London: Employment Institute.

Weitzman, M.L. and Kruse, D.L. (1990) Profit sharing and productivity. In: A.S. Blinder (ed.) *Paying for Productivity: a Look at the Evidence.* Washington, DC: The Brookings Institution.

Index